T0247792

Dawn's Early Light

Dawn's Early Light

Taking Back Washington to Save America

Kevin Roberts, Ph.D.

Foreword by J.D. Vance

BROADSIDE BOOKS

HarperCollins books may be purchased for educational, business, or sales promotional use. For information, please email the Special Markets Department at SPsales@harpercollins.com.

Broadside Books™ and the Broadside logo are trademarks of HarperCollins Publishers.

FIRST EDITION

Designed by Michele Cameron

Library of Congress Cataloging-in-Publication Data

Names: Roberts, Kevin, 1974– author.
Title: Dawn's early light: taking back Washington to save America / Kevin Roberts.
Description: First edition. | New York: Broadside, 2024. | Includes bibliographical references and index.
Identifiers: LCCN 2024016677 (print) | LCCN 2024016678 (ebook) |
    ISBN 9780063353503 (hardcover) | ISBN 9780063353510 (ebook)
Subjects: LCSH: Conservatism—United States. | Political culture—United States. |
    Politics, Practical—United States. | United States—Politics and government—21st century.
Classification: LCC JC573.2.U6 R627 2024 (print) | LCC JC573.2.U6 (ebook) |
    DDC 320.520973—dc23/eng/20240517
LC record available at https://lccn.loc.gov/2024016677
LC ebook record available at https://lccn.loc.gov/2024016678

24 25 26 27 28 LBC 7 6 5 4 3

For my two greatest heroes,
my grandparents Mark & Betty Pitre,
for their faith, love, and patriotism

CONTENTS

FOREWORD

In the classic American film *Pulp Fiction*, John Travolta's character, recently returned from Amsterdam, observes that Europe has the same consumer goods as America, but there it's just a "little different." That's how I feel about Kevin Roberts's life. He grew up in a poor family in a corner of the country largely ignored by America's elites—but his corner was in Louisiana and mine in Ohio and Kentucky. Like me, he's a Catholic, but unlike me, he was born into it. His grandparents played an outsized role in his life, just as mine did. And now he works far from where he grew up, just a few steps from my office, in Washington, DC: he is the president of one of Washington's most influential think tanks, and I'm a US senator.

Now he has written the book you hold in your hands, which explores many of the themes I've focused on in my own work. Yet he does so profoundly, with a readable style that makes accessible its real intellectual rigor.

Never before has a figure with Roberts's depth and stature within the American Right tried to articulate a genuinely new future for conservatism. The Heritage Foundation isn't some random outpost on Capitol Hill; it is and has been the most influential engine of ideas for Republicans from Ronald Reagan to Donald Trump. Yet it is Heritage's power and influence that makes it easy to avoid risks. Roberts could collect a nice salary, write decent books, and tell donors what they want to hear. But Roberts believes doing the same old thing could lead to the ruin of our nation.

If you've read a lot of conservative books or think you have a good sense of the conservative movement, I suspect the pages that follow will be surprising—even jarring. Roberts understands economics and supports basic free market principles, but he doesn't make an idol out of decades old theories. He argues persuasively that the modern financial corporation was almost entirely foreign to the founders of our nation. The closest eighteenth-century analogue to the modern Apple or Google is the British East India company, a monstrous hybrid of public and private power that would have made its subjects completely unable to access an American sense of liberty. The idea that our founders meant to make their citizens subjects to this kind of hybrid power is ahistorical and preposterous, yet too many modern "conservatives" make such an idol out of the market that they ignore this. A private company that can censor speech, influence elections, and work seamlessly with intelligence services and other federal bureaucrats deserves the scrutiny of the Right, not its support. Roberts not only gets this at an instinctive level; he can articulate a political vision to engage in that scrutiny effectively.

Roberts sees a conservatism that is focused on the family. In this, he borrows from the old American Right that recognized—correctly, in my view—that cultural norms and attitudes matter. We should encourage our kids to get married and have kids. We should teach them that marriage isn't just a contract, but a sacred—and to the extent possible, lifelong—union. We should discourage them from behaviors that threaten the stability of their families. But we should also do something else: create the material circumstances such that having a family isn't only for the privileged. That means better jobs at all levels of the income ladder. That means protecting American industries—even if it leads to higher consumer prices in the short term. That means listening to our young people who are telling us they can't afford to buy a home or start a family, not just criticizing them for a lack of virtue. Roberts is articulating a fundamentally Christian view of culture and economics: recognizing that virtue and material progress go hand in hand.

My childhood was not, by any objective measure, easy. Neither was that of Kevin Roberts. Both of us were negatively impacted by family instability, and both of us were saved by the resilience of the thick network of family—grandparents, aunts, uncles—that is often the first and most effective component of our social safety net. Both of us saw how a factory leaving a town could destroy the economic stability that provided the foundation for those families. And both of us learned to love the country that gave both of us and our families second chances, despite some bumps along the way. In these pages, Kevin is trying to figure out how we preserve as much of what worked in his own life, while correcting what didn't. To do that, we need more than a politics that simply removes the bad policies of the past. We need to rebuild. We need an offensive conservatism, not merely one that tries to prevent the left from doing things we don't like.

Here's an analogy I sometimes use to articulate what the previous generation of conservatives got right and wrong. Imagine a well-maintained garden in a patch of sunlight. It has some imperfections of course, and many weeds. The very thing that makes it attractive for the things we try to cultivate makes it attractive for the things we don't. In an effort to eliminate the bad, a well-meaning gardener treats the garden with a chemical solution. This kills many of the weeds, but it also kills many of the good things. Undeterred, the gardener keeps adding the solution. Eventually, the soil is inhospitable.

In this analogy, modern liberalism is the gardener, the garden is our country, and the voices discouraging the gardener were conservatives. We were right, of course: in an effort to correct problems—some real, some imagined—we made a lot of mistakes as a country in the 1960s and 1970s.

But to bring the garden back to health, it is not enough to undo the mistakes of the past. The garden needs not just to stop adding a terrible solution, though it does need that. It needs to be recultivated. The old conservative movement argued if you just got government out of the way, natural forces would resolve problems—we are no longer in this situation and must take a different approach. As Kevin Roberts writes, "It's fine to take a laissez-faire approach when you are in the safety of the sunshine. But when the twilight descends and you hear the wolves, you've got to circle the wagons and load the muskets."

We are now all realizing that it's time to circle the wagons and load the muskets. In the fights that lay ahead, these ideas are an essential weapon.

—J.D. Vance

Dawn's Early Light

CHAPTER 1

The Conspiracy Against Nature

My spirit kindles to fire, and rises in wrath to avenge my dying land.
—Aeneas, in *The Aeneid* of Virgil

I n 2020, our country went up in flames. Some of those conflagrations were intentional arson, such as the "mostly peaceful" protests that caused more than a billion dollars in damage in some of America's greatest cities. Others were more unintentional, such as the record-setting California wildfires that torched more than 4 million acres of our most beautiful forests.

In fact, all those fires were connected. They spring from a conspiracy against nature—against ordered, civilized societies, against common sense and normal people—orchestrated by a network of political, corporate, and cultural elites who share a set of interests quite apart from those of ordinary Americans. Spanning across the partisan aisle, they are known as the Uniparty.

Most people in the Uniparty hardly ever set foot outside the coastal corridors of power, but their influence can be felt in almost every corner of our country. Be it Black Lives Matter (BLM) in the cities or the

Bureau of Land Management (BLM) in the countryside, the Uniparty's playbook is the same: destroy the embodied institutions that define the American way of life and replace them with ideological commitments and bureaucratic imperatives.

It is time to fight fire with fire.

For too long, the American Right has made extinguishing fires its sole purpose. And as a conservative, I understand. Fire has the potential to destroy, and we must prudently protect what we have. But the heart of tradition, as Gustav Mahler said, is "the preservation of fire, not the worship of ashes"—the kind of fire that can warm a home, restore a forest, and light the way ahead in darkness.

To escape our current darkness, restore America's civic life, and take back our country for good, conservatives can't merely continue putting out fires; we must be brave enough to go on the offense, strike the match, and start a long, controlled burn.

There's plenty of fuel. Like deadwood in a forest, many of America's institutions have been completely hollowed out—fully captured by the Uniparty. Decadent and rootless, these institutions serve only as shelter for our corrupt elite. Meanwhile, they block out the light and suck up the nutrients necessary for new American institutions to grow. For America to flourish again, they don't need to be reformed; *they need to be burned*. A nice start would include:

Every Ivy League college, the FBI, the *New York Times*, the National Institute of Allergy and Infectious Diseases, the Department of Education, 80 percent of "Catholic" higher education, BlackRock, the Loudoun County Public School System, the Boy Scouts of America, the Bill and Melinda Gates Foundation, the World Economic Forum, the Chinese Communist Party, and the National Endowment for Democracy.

Of course, starting a forest fire doesn't seem like something Smokey Bear would approve of. It doesn't seem *nice*. It doesn't *seem* as though it would be good for the environment. Yet any good conservationist can tell you that fire is an intrinsic part of the cycle of life. Indeed, without regular controlled burns, a conflagration eventually occurs that wrecks the forest rather than renews it, that chars the earth instead of laying the ground for new life.

That was what happened in 2020. And it will be even worse in 2024 if nothing changes. Americans know this. That's why overwhelming numbers of them report feeling that our country is headed in the wrong direction. What they don't know, however, is what they can do about it. Slowly but surely, a deep despair and paralysis has set in.

The aim of this book is to confront our present situation, to inspire the New Conservative Movement to rekindle the fire of the American tradition, and to empower real Americans to take back our country. This is going to be a radical book in the original Latin sense of *radix*, the roots. We're going to go beyond the ideological battles of our current political debate—the buzzwords and clichés and partisan sound bites—to get to the institutional root causes of America's decline.

At the heart of many of America's problems is a trillion-dollar conspiracy against nature. The most important cleavage in Western politics today is not liberals versus conservatives or the people versus the elite; it is the struggle between the Party of Creation—those who defend the God-given natural order that is capable of generating flourishing and new life if we learn to live within it—and the Party of Destruction—those who seek to abolish the existing order in the name of emancipation, freedom, and progress.

The association of politics and conspiracy is deeply attested in history. The word *conspiracy* comes from the Latin *conspirare*, literally "to breathe together." Most political conspiracies aren't cloak-and-dagger affairs involving intelligence agencies or secret societies; they're just the kinds of handshake deals and in-group ideas that are made by people who breathe the same air, who socialize in the same circles. In Latin, *conspirare* was used to mean both "to conspire" or "to plot" and "to sing in unison."

In modern Europe, thinkers and revolutionaries emerged who wanted to overthrow *all* traditional societies, in the same way they believed modern science to have overthrown the ancient understanding of the cosmos. Just as modern science had unlocked new material prosperity through technology, they believed that a new science of man would unleash social and spiritual prosperity, a heaven on Earth. They formed networks, societies, and political organizations under many names, all offshoots of an overarching Party of Destruction.

The Party of Destruction viewed the existing order of human life as a prison. Religion, it averred, didn't provide human beings with meaning, it entangled people in superstition. Old-fashioned craft or guild businesses didn't cultivate excellence and skill, they trapped people in traditional work. Culture, law, and strong family ties didn't provide life-giving civic life, they repressed people by forcing them into traditional villages and traditional gender roles. A lack of education trapped people in a folk mindset. Traditional institutions trapped people in hierarchy, superstitious religion, and old ways of doing things. Rather than negotiating trade-offs between different underlying traditional values, the Party of Destruction sought the revolutionary reestablishment of all human relationships.

What did it want instead? It almost can't help but sound appealing, if only we can forget what it really means. The Party of Destruction wants liberation, emancipation, *Befreiung* in the words of the Frankfurt School theorists. What connects the "liberation" of liberalism, the World Revolution of communism, and the "critical" of Critical Theory is a vision in which tradition is the enemy of human potential, in which the individual must be freed from everything that stands in the way of his self-expression (whether he wishes to be freed or not—perhaps *especially* if he wishes to retain a traditional way of life). The Party of Destruction is the enemy of the existing human order as such, the enemy of *all* human orders.

At least the Communists didn't mince words, saying in *The Communist Manifesto* that "Communists everywhere support every revolutionary movement against the existing social and political order of things." But none of the other factions of the Party of Destruction has made much of an attempt to conceal their program. In fact, they're proud of it!

But here's the most uncomfortable truth of all: the parasites that have taken over so much of our country—pantsuited girlboss advertising executives, Skittle-haired they/them activists, soy-faced pajama-clad work-from-home HR apparatchiks, Adderall-addicted dog mom diversity consultants, nasally voiced Ivy League regulatory lawyers, obese George Soros–funded police abolitionist district attorneys, hipster trust fund socialists—are some of the least impressive people in the history of the world. The Uniparty would never have achieved what it has in this country without a great degree of rottenness, of decadence, of torpor, of complacency already afflicting us. The first enemy we must face in our crusade to take back our country is within ourselves.

I believe that our best days are in front of us. There are no shortcuts or silver bullets. America's restoration is a task that will require generational sacrifice and toil. The seeds of its renewal, however, are numerous, and many are already in the ground. To see them sprout and watch them grow, we need only to strike the match and burn away the deadwood.

American Malaise

I know this because it has happened before. It's how Ronald Reagan engineered the great turnaround from the darkness of the 1970s to the dawn of the '80s.

At the time of the 1980 presidential contest between Jimmy Carter and Ronald Reagan, the United States had experienced a decade of painful economic disruption and stagnant growth, punctuated by fiscal insolvency and a massive energy crisis.

Everyday Americans were suffering as inflation spiraled upward, wages didn't keep up, and rising interest rates put owning a home further and further out of reach. Energy prices crept steadily higher; supply failed to keep up with demand. A recession loomed. Violent crime raged on city streets, and once flourishing urban centers were emptying out. In the wake of violent killings and riots, racial tensions had never been worse.

Beneath the turmoil lay something deeper. President Carter put his finger on the problem in a July 15, 1979, prime-time address on Americans' "crisis of confidence." What America was facing, he claimed, was not really an energy crisis but a spiritual one: "The erosion of our confidence in the future is threatening to destroy the social and the political fabric of America." In the face of serious problems such as energy shortages, high inflation, stagnant growth, and exploding crime, Americans found nothing but gridlock, stasis, and decline.

Americans were losing faith not just in their government but in the idea of self-government, their ability to unite and overcome the challenges their communities and the nation were facing, the way they always had. The American people were losing hope. The flame in every institution was flickering.

Of course, Carter's speech is usually remembered today as the "malaise" speech, thanks to a bit of clever branding from Ronald Reagan. Why'd it stick? Because despite putting his finger on the problem, Carter himself was stuck. His vision of the future fell woefully short, amounting to resignation to decline and defeat. Americans overwhelmingly agreed with President Carter that the roots of America's challenges went much deeper than an energy crisis; they concluded that he was part of the problem and voted him out of office.

Instead of retreating from America's challenges and accepting new limits on growth, prosperity, and ambition, Reagan set out to make America great again, by calling her back to her greatest traditions: "I believe we can embark on a new age of reform in this country and an era of national renewal." He symbolized his commitment to focusing on America's future in his inauguration ceremony at the Capitol, which faced not eastward, toward the Old World and the past, but (for the first time) westward, toward expansion, the frontier, the future.

A mere four years later, in one of the greatest turnarounds in American history, the fog of American malaise had evaporated. In 1984, Reagan won reelection in a landslide, winning every state except Minnesota. What accounted for this newfound American confidence?

The American people evidently agreed with the Reagan presidential campaign's countervailing vision. It was stated succinctly in one of the most successful electoral ads in history, which proclaimed that it was once again "Morning in America," ticking off accomplishment after accomplishment. The Reagan campaign made its case: "Now that our country is turning around, why would we ever turn back?" Why indeed?

Getting to the Roots

America has gone through cycles of decay and renewal many times. But today, America is even more stuck than it was in the Reagan era. In the face of some of the evils Americans today endure with seeming equanimity—fentanyl overdoses, childhood gender mutilation, dead-end jobs, racial quotas, online censorship, grocery-shelf shortages, open borders, religious persecution, violent carjackings, chronic shoplifting—we have to ask ourselves: What happened to our country? And what will it take to see morning in America again?

It's not enough to identify this or that policy choice. Something deeper has gone terribly wrong. And spiritual problems require spiritual solutions.

To say that America's problems are spiritual requires no religious faith. It is an empirical statement. We've been trained to accept a flat materialist worldview that says that the only things that are real are those we can hold in our hands, or, better yet, measure with a contraption. As a result, we have adopted a form of politics and policy making that ignores problems that are difficult to measure or bureaucratize. It's one of the ways we got into this mess.

Going back to at least Aristotle, we have understood there to be an essence, a form or structure or energy, that pervades and animates the material body. This soul or animating principle or *psyche* (to use Aristotle's word) is as real and substantial as the difference between a living body and a dead one.

A spiritual attack may leave no physical marks, but it damages your confidence, your hope, your aspirations, your self-certainty. How can you tell whether someone or something is in the midst of a spiritual crisis or, worse, has already succumbed? "By their fruits you shall know them," the Good Book says. Spiritual reality has to do with an inner substance, which cannot necessarily be seen on the surface but which with equal necessity will show itself over time until the outer appearance matches the inner reality. (I've often found truth in George Orwell's quip that "At fifty, everyone has the face he deserves.")

Think back to that 1980 contest between Carter and Reagan. They both agreed that America's crisis was not merely about this or that policy but reflected a deeper spiritual affliction. But even as, after Reagan's victory, the country adopted successful policies to fight some of the symptoms of its underlying crisis, it failed to address the spiritual roots of the problem. In the 1980s and '90s, conservatives won the policy fight but lost the spiritual war.

You can see the problem in Reagan's "Morning in America" ad. What the narrator talks about is jobs, interest rates, homebuyers, number of marriages—things that can readily be measured and that a bureaucracy can understand. In retrospect, many conservatives assumed that numbers-focused narration was the "real" appeal of Reagan's vision.

But the context the video provides, what the images show, is so much richer: a beautiful young couple getting married (a man and a woman, it does not need to be specified) in a church surrounded by a loving community, with a look of pride and wonder; a group of children, reverently watching Old Glory being raised up a flagpole. Today, the ad looks like a lost dispatch from a foreign country.

What pulled the heartstrings of TV viewers in the 1980s, what drew Reagan to a landslide victory in the 1984 election, was that *vision* of America, of restored pride, confidence, and hope for the future; an America of strong families, strong communities, and a strong economy, proud of its history, sure of its identity, building a more prosperous future for its children. No number of policy victories can make up for the country's loss of a shared vision and the institutions of civil society that nurtured it. The weakness of the "Morning in America" ad was that it assumed that none of those things was under threat; it took them for granted. Forty years later, we know that isn't the case.

The only way to revive our country, to breathe life into the bones of

America's great institutions now haggard with age, decay, and bloat, is to burn away the rot and restore a shared vision of a glorious future.

We Must Go a Different Way

This will require many on the right to reconsider some of their unquestioned maxims. There's a scene in the Cormac McCarthy novel *No Country for Old Men* in which hit man Anton Chigurh has taken a fellow hired gun captive. Holding him at gunpoint and asking about his life's philosophy, Chigurh asks him, "If the rule you followed brought you to this, of what use was the rule?"

It is a question we must ask ourselves. After all, if what the old conservative coalition understood to be its foundational principles led us to this—the total domination of the Uniparty, the demise of the American working class, and the erosion of the institutions that defined American life—of what use are those principles?

The old conservative movement held that if you just got government out of the way, the free market, civil society, individual liberty, the nuclear family, and more would take care of themselves. Forty years ago, it might have had the right idea. But in today's America, a conservative movement that limits itself to this stale program is cosigning the Uniparty's euthanasia of the American nation.

When you reach a dead end, no matter how far you have traveled to get there, no matter how historic and well trod the path has been, no matter the strength of the arguments that led in that direction, there is no point debating the matter anymore. You must pick yourself up and go in a different direction.

My young conservative friends often say of the wax-museum conservatives who refuse to recognize that we're in a dead end that they "don't know what time it is." What they mean is that the old conservative principles presume that a healthy American society exists. It did once. But the tough truth is that many young people today have never experienced that society. They know better than anyone that the conservative movement can no longer merely conserve certain principles; rather, it must be in the business of *regenerating a tradition.*

Maybe the ultimate example of not knowing what time it is comes from one of the oldest stories in the West, the great Latin epic *The Aeneid.* Aeneas, an exile from Troy, recounts how the city was sacked. The great heroes of Troy had been fighting the besieging Greeks for many years, their feats recorded for all of time in the Homeric *Iliad.* After a decade of exhausting war and the death of the great hero Achilles, the Greeks seemingly pack up and head home, leaving as a parting gift and sacrifice to the goddess Athena a giant wooden horse.

The fathers of the city have an argument about the horse. Some argue that the statue is Greek perfidy and they should burn it. They are ignored. From the standpoint of a city that has withstood Greek assaults of all kinds, it's hard to see how a wooden horse might be a threat. King Priam and the other Trojan leaders believe that they stand at the hour of their victory, and they celebrate accordingly. But they don't know what time it is. It's Trojan horse time.

We all know what happened next. Their whole civilization burned to the ground.

The years after the Reagan Revolution have turned out in a similar way. Like the feckless Trojans, we sat around toasting our victories, telling stories about our founders and heroes, proud that our enemies had given up, had even surrendered a trophy to the magnificence of our victory! (President Bill Clinton passed NAFTA and welfare reform! The Democrats even support free trade now! We've balanced the budget! We accomplished deregulation and tax cuts!) We ignored Cassandras such as Pat Buchanan, Robert Lighthizer, Family Research Council's Tony Perkins, and even one Donald J. Trump. We became complacent. We ignored the growing despair of our countrymen and the decadence of our elites. We ignored the lurking threat inside the city walls.

Today there are still wax-museum conservatives who sit around in their cushy DC sinecures, toasting the Reagan Revolution and failing to face today's threats. They don't know what time it is, that twilight, fire, and ruin are upon us.

We can't kid ourselves about where we stand. The sun is going down, and there are wolves in the dark. If you just keep trundling along whistling "Yankee Doodle Dandy," ignorant of the rising danger, you're going to make a tasty dinner.

It's fine to take a laissez-faire approach when you are in the safety of the sunshine. But when the twilight descends and you hear the wolves, you've got to circle the wagons and load the muskets.

"If the rule you followed brought you to this, of what use was the rule?"

A Certain Hope

I didn't set out to write this book because of all the doom and gloom in America today. Quite the opposite. It's true that, in Washington, things look dire. But traveling around the country, talking to everyday Americans and community leaders all over, has led me to a profound and hopeful conviction: we are going to win.

And it's not going to be close. It's going to be a glorious restoration of the country.

We're going to win because we're on the side of natural law, of reality, of deep-seated human instincts, which ideology and technology can defer for only so long. Because hard times, when they come, exorcise soft living and comfortable beliefs.

We're going to win because, in the long run, excellence beats mediocrity, fecundity beats sterility, courage beats cowardice, justice beats false equality, truth beats lies, virtue beats vice, faith beats cynicism, and hope beats despair.

We're going to win because the Uniparty's vision for America's future is at odds with reality and it can only leech off of what better men built before. And because the Uniparty is increasingly hostile to meritocracy and talent, it is driving the best men and women America has to our side, on account of their skin color or their creed.

We're going to win because we seek to honor God and be sure we are on His side. And if He is with us, who can be against us?

So the question is not whether God-fearing, liberty-loving Americans will once again rule from sea to shining sea; it is rather how much damage will we allow to be done to our great land and home before we take it back? What will remain of our constitutional system, our republic, our traditions of self-government and liberty? How much real human damage will there be prior to the restoration, how many broken lives, how many mutilated children? How much of our inheritance will have been squandered forever?

If we are going to rescue our great American institutions, we need a radical plan—we need to get back to our roots. We need to rediscover the meaning of self-government, constitutionalism, and federalism in a twenty-first-century context. And we need to do it not to reclaim some wonderful past but to take back our *future*, to preserve the American inheritance for our children.

This is not a book about what we have lost. Sappy nostalgia is a symptom of giving up, but we have not yet begun to fight. This is a book about the future and the conviction that we will not surrender the future to a sterile, vampiric Left that hates the future even more than it does the past, hates fruitfulness and growth even more than our heritage and history. We will not pass gently into the night.

We are going to reclaim the promise of our patrimony in order to secure a vibrant future for our posterity. We will remember who we are in order to manifest a bright American tomorrow, one full of children, prosperity, community, growth, faith, virtue, and liberty.

CHAPTER 2

Fighting Fire with Fire

Tradition is the preservation of fire, not the worship of ashes.

—Gustav Mahler

I n 1992, Patrick Buchanan ran a primary campaign against President George H. W. Bush for the Republican nomination for president. It was an audacious move by someone who had, up until then, loyally served within the GOP's halls of power, including in the Richard Nixon, Gerald Ford, and Ronald Reagan White Houses. But he felt that the George H. W. Bush administration had forgotten the needs and values of ordinary Americans. His message resonated with me as a young man, so much so that I helped organize a rally for him in Lafayette, Louisiana, which ended up being one of his best attended in the whole country.

The heart of Buchanan's message was that in the Washington establishment's eagerness to institute technocratic solutions to the problems of the post–Cold War world, the ordinary people of this country and their values and traditions were being forgotten, tossed into the garbage bin at the end of history. Buchanan recognized that the root of the problem was not geopolitical, economic, or legal but spiritual, a war for the soul of America.

In this struggle for the soul of America, it was her people who were the key battleground. They were natural allies. They might not "read Adam Smith or Edmund Burke," Buchanan belted out, "but they come from the same schoolyards and the same playgrounds and towns as we come from. They share our beliefs and convictions, our hopes and our dreams. They are the conservatives of the heart."

What he was actually recognizing was the distinction between the Party of Creation and the Party of Destruction. He correctly perceived that the Party of Destruction, aka the Uniparty (which Buchanan identified with "Clinton and Clinton"—the husband-wife package deal on the 1992 ballot), aimed to instantiate a radical cultural revolution in America. And the hapless Republicans, out of touch with or even privately scornful of everyday Americans, were going along with policies of economic, political, and cultural globalization that had destroyed much of the social solidarity and deep roots of our people and installed in power, for the first time in our history, a singular ruling class made up of coastal elites.

As a conservative, I believe that politics and economics are usually downstream of culture. But in a hurricane, the bayou whose waters normally flow out to the gulf will reverse course and flow inland. The colossal, politically orchestrated changes to our institutional and economic life of the past thirty years washed over many corners of American society like a cultural Hurricane Katrina. The conservative movement, reasoning that politics are downstream of culture, didn't make any plans for a hurricane.

Vast, uncontrollable forces such as water and fire don't always behave the way we predict. At its best, the free market functions in a similar way, providing a creative destruction that generates new growth and prosperity—but it still uproots traditions in ways that a just political order would work to counterbalance. At its worst, left to the devices of a callous globalist elite, it just provides destruction—a strip mining of human talent and local culture that leaves our communities and home places barren of jobs and dignity, breeding grounds for opioid addiction.

That was what I experienced growing up in Louisiana. All of the traditions and institutions that supported a rich Cajun culture, including good local jobs, a family orientation, public schools that celebrated our heritage, and so much more had deteriorated by the end of the 1990s—not due to wokeness, not due to immigration, but due to the birth of what President George H. W. Bush announced in his 1991 State of the Union address as the "New World Order." Ushering in that order sacrificed the permanent things (such as family stability) on the altar of the measurable things (such as the S&P 500). We are still reckoning with the consequences.

Conservatives today must reimagine what is required to support ordinary Americans and restore the American way of life. We can't just wait for it to happen.

How can we reconcile the need to wield political power to rebuild civic society with our skepticism of government intervention? How can we recreate an economy that serves the family and not the other way around? How can we reintroduce a generation to traditions that were never handed on to them? How can we rekindle a fire that has almost gone out?

That's what this book is about.

The Party of Creation Runs on Gratitude

Man's taming of fire is the cornerstone of human culture.

That's the funny thing about fire. It is so fleeting, a flame flickering from moment to moment, yet in its evanescence, it is eternal. Of all the elements, fire is most associated with transformation, renewal, and change. You can't have a blaze without some kind of sacrificial transformation of fuel into fire. Yet precisely for this reason, fire demands an attention to continuity. Unlike any of the other elements, fire *dies*. You can set down a bucket of water or a pile of earth, and when you return it will be right where you left it. But a fire must be continually tended.

Tradition is not the worship of ashes but the preservation of fire, Mahler said. It's a deep metaphor. The connections among tending to a tradition, a nation, and a sacred fire were already ancient to the Greeks and Romans. They believed that the spirits of their city, their household, and their ancestors lived in the sacred hearth fire found in every home. The gravest act of neglect was to let the fire be extinguished.

The sense of what we owe to others on account of what we have been given, of *gratitude* for what we have inherited, is at the heart of a conservative life. Conservatives acknowledge that our lives depend on what we have been given: by God, by our country, by our forebears, by our communities and home places. In gratitude, our hearts move us to defend, improve, and pass on what we have inherited. We experience our gratitude as a glad calling to duty.

The Romans called this notion piety (*pietas*), and it was for them the chief of virtues, the one from which all others flowed, and the foundation of their republic. The great Renaissance scholar and classicist James Hankins explained:

> In uncorrupt societies, children grow up with a sense of gratitude for the unearned benefits they have received. If we have normal moral responses, we feel grateful for all the things we have been given that we have done nothing to deserve: the love and nurture of parents and family; the kindness of friends and benefactors; the benefits of a well-ordered society. . . . We have to admit, if we are honest, that we have done little to deserve what we have been given. We have, indeed, done many things that would justify our being stripped of what we have been given. If we have any decency—if we know what is *decens*, what is fitting—our only response can be gratitude and love for family, country, and God. We have obligations we can never repay, and that fact imposes on us an obligation of loyalty to the sources of those benefits. The proper human response to all the unearned blessings we have received is *pietas*.

In a normal and healthy society, formative institutions help open the eyes of their charges to the magnitude of what they have inherited, instituting practices such as Founder's Days and putting portraits of forerunners in a place of honor. It is evidence of deep moral inversion that the leaders of institutions such as the University of Pennsylvania and Yale so readily slander their founders and forebears, tear down their statues, and take down their portraits. The involuntary twisting knot in our stomach we feel when we see activists tear down a statue of George Washington is a sense of *indecency*, that this is a kind of ingratitude that is gross and destructive, that betrays a narcissistic entitlement with no understanding of the sacrifices others made to tend the fire on their behalf.

In the classical tradition, one figure above all others stands out for his piety. "Pious Aeneas," Virgil called him twenty times in *The Aeneid*. Time and again, Aeneas suffers in order to do his duty to his gods, his family, and his people.

Aeneas's piety is embodied by the hearth-gods (*penates*) he brings with him out of Troy. He flees with his household, carrying his elderly father (*penates* in arms) on his shoulders and leading his son by the hand. He risks his life to preserve the sacred hearth fire, and he keeps the flame alive through the years of wandering the Mediterranean that follow.

When the Greeks poured into Troy, they pillaged it and set it ablaze, a fire of destruction meant to extinguish the hearth of Trojan civilization forever. But Aeneas carried the real fire of Troy with him and constantly renewed it, carrying it at last to Latinate Italy, where the Trojans carved out a new home. Rome's sacred fire of Vesta, an eternal flame for an eternal city, was none other than the fire of Troy that Aeneas had safeguarded. Thanks to his faithfulness, it burned a thousand years more and sparked a civilization that conquered the known world.

The image of a pious statesman carrying the flame of civilization over the waters was a precious one to our classically educated Founding Fathers, so much so that the motto on the back of the Great Seal of the United States comes from Virgil: *Novus ordo seclorum*. That translates to "a new order of the ages," but to the Founders it evoked not "the birthday of a new world" (in Thomas Paine's words) but the renewal of civilization in the natural order of things. Later Christians believed that stanza from Virgil's *Eclogues* to prophesy the founding of a Christian civilization on top of the Roman order, carrying forward the flame of the West as Aeneas had.

That attitude of carrying the fire of the inherited order made the American Revolution different from the French Revolution, Edmund Burke believed, though both were fought for the sake of freedom and democracy, at least on the surface. But the French Revolution was premised on a system of abstract principles inspired by *philosophes* such as Jean-Jacques Rousseau and Voltaire. It dictated a program of social transformation that led to the guillotine and Napoleon.

We Americans fought not to establish a new constitution but to preserve and restore one we already had. The American Revolution was a controlled burn, fought to keep an existing tradition of liberty and self-government alive, as George Washington eloquently expressed in the first presidential inaugural address. Preserving the "sacred fire of liberty" demanded the destruction of an increasingly tyrannical British colonial regime. The French Revolution denied the existence of what Washington called "the eternal rules of order and right, which Heaven itself has ordained." The American Revolution was founded upon them.

The Permanent Things

What, then, are "the eternal rules of order and right" that Washington saw as being beyond a matter of opinion? They're what Russell Kirk called "the permanent things."

Today, the assault on the American way of life is aimed not just at our Constitution and political traditions but more insidiously at the foundations of civilization, which is to say, the permanent things. There is no point in preserving certain political forms if the society they were meant to protect has died.

The Party of Creation needs to get over the old conservatism's reluctance to "impose" its "values" on others. There is no way to avoid taking a stance on the practices that sustain the human race. We can say with certainty what the "permanent things," the vital tasks of any culture, are. The aegis of every civilization protected them; the best of all that has been thought and said from each distinctive human culture has pointed to them.

Family: Men and women should marry (and do so younger than most do today). They should marry for life and should bring children into the world (more than most do today). Parents have the right and responsibility to raise their children, to educate them, to pass on their traditions, and to make important family decisions (including rejecting experimental medical treatments) in line with their conscience and values. Children owe their parents a measure of obedience and gratitude, and family members should take care of one another. The nuclear family is the foundation of the human order, but it should reach beyond itself to form the fabric of an extended family, community, and local place.

Faith: Mankind is made to worship, and our republic depends on the moral strength and habits of heart brought about by piety. We have in this country a glorious tradition of religious freedom, but it is not freedom *from* religion but freedom *for* religion. A man's religious tradition is a matter of his conscience, but *that* we have a faithful people is a matter of public concern. Accordingly, the state must not discriminate against religious organizations in government programs, and freedom of religion should take precedence over the enforcement of other rights. Policies that encourage religious observance, such as Sabbath laws and voucher programs that include religious schools, should be encouraged. American society is rooted in the Christian faith—certainly public institutions should not establish anything offensive to Christian morals under the guise of "religious freedom" or "diversity, equity, and inclusion."

Community: Americans' pride has always been in their communities, the "little platoons" where citizens freely associate with one another and practice self-government. In communities, people from different backgrounds and walks of life orient themselves around the common good in its most concrete and practical form. Communities are places where we lift up one another's burdens and practice the art of neighborliness, but also where we celebrate the holy days and feast together. If they are well ordered, our communities permit a feeling of comfort and safety at any hour of the day.

Work: Man is *Homo faber*, the animal that makes. By his labors, man provides for himself and his family. There is deep dignity in work, in the ownership one has of a job well done, that cannot be replaced by simply giving someone something they have not worked for or earned. Moreover, we know that the material prosperity that makes many of the other elements of the human order possible comes from productive human labor and the habits of discipline, skill, and care that undergird that productivity. At the same time, there is an appropriate time to rest from our labors together with our families and communities. The division of labor has also held political significance throughout human history. In the Western tradition, a republican government befitted only men who were masters of themselves, who were economically self-sufficient.

Nation: Man's gratitude toward all the "little platoons" of human order culminate in his devotion to his broader nation and homeland. In a republic, this is experienced as a duty to safeguard the *res publica*, literally "the public thing" but better translated as "the common good." The nation is cemented by a shared national origin story, according to which all citizens are "brothers, and children of the self-same earth" (literally or figuratively). Our deepest traditions about the purposes of government are reflected in the ancient ceremony for crowning England's kings, when the archbishop of Canterbury hands to his sovereign the Sword of State with these words: "With this sword do justice, stop the growth of iniquity, protect the holy Church of God and all people of goodwill, help and defend widows and orphans, restore the things that are gone to decay, maintain the things that are restored, punish and reform what is amiss, and confirm what is in good order."

The ideas outlined above constitute the enduring record of human flourishing stretching back into the mists of history. They constitute the *minimum* of what any well-ordered human society needs to have.

While our patrimonies may dictate particular traditions to sustain the order of the permanent things (the Catholic faith, Acadian notions of family, Texan ideas about nationhood, American beliefs about work, and so on), that such an order exists is something like a human universal, what Christians would understand to be the natural law. One of the beautiful things about America is that we have the freedoms and the space for true pluralism, people and their communities living out quite different self-understandings and practices of the permanent things. Without suggesting that every tradition is equally good or equally true, we can say that no conservatism is possible that does not attend to the basic practices and institutions that support human flourishing, which we know by the unanimous testimony of nature, history, revelation, and tradition.

Controlled Burn

What does it mean to fight fire with fire?

The notion of fighting fire with fire isn't some metaphor: it's an essential task of forest management.

The idea of fighting fire with fire comes from a practice called backburning, in which fire crews set a small fire in the path of a larger one, thus consuming the fuel that would have allowed the larger fire to rampage on.

But fighting fire with fire isn't limited to damage control. Forests, especially in North America, need fire to flourish. Fire transforms rot and deadwood into new soil, clears the ground for new life to take root, lets sunlight into the forest floor, and renews the forest ecology. Some species even depend on fire.

There are no more awe-inspiring flora in the American forest than the giant sequoias, the biggest specimens of which are hundreds of feet tall and some of the oldest creatures on Earth. And giant sequoias love forest fires. Their cones open to spread their seeds only in the heat of a big fire, which thins out competitor trees but leaves the sequoias unharmed and creates rich new soil for the seedlings to thrive in.

Like our great American forests, our country's life requires periodic renewal. America isn't an idea but an ecosystem—a vast forest—and our institutions are the trees that serve as "essential pillars of our moral lives," in the words of Yuval Levin. They hold the country together, give it structure, and make it beautiful.

And like America's great western forests, our institutional life is being woefully mismanaged by our incompetent Uniparty. The problem isn't too much fire but too little. Deadwood is piling up unnaturally, creating the conditions for a cataclysmic fire that could destroy everything.

Wise forest management works with the natural cycle of decay and renewal. As deadwood and other fuel accumulate in the forest, the woodsman will conduct a controlled burn, setting a fire that lowers the fuel load and renews the forest responsibly. Controlled burns are also used to combat invasive species and fight particular kinds of decay or disease.

These include diseases such as Dutch elm disease, a fungus from Asia that threatens the American elm. From the East Coast to the Rocky Mountains, these "great leafy high arching cathedrals" (in the words of Phil McCombs) once dominated the American wilderness and dotted our city parks and thoroughfares. That was until the 1930s, when the disease began devastating tree after tree, killing 75 percent of American elms by 1989.

In recent decades, these towering trees have been slowly making a comeback, aided by the efforts of conservationists across the country. Their work has revealed that saving the American elm requires three steps, according to the Elm Institute: First, conservationists treat the trees they can. If the disease is caught early enough, sometimes cutting off the infected branches or severing root connections to nearby trees will do the trick. Second, planting new trees can help. Biologists have identified strains that are more tolerant of the fungus, and thousands of saplings have been planted across the United States. The third step, however, is the most crucial: *Infected trees that cannot be saved must be condemned, cut down, and promptly burned.* Otherwise, the disease will spread further, negating any work done in the first two steps.

America's institutional ecosystem is today threatened by a pathology far worse than Dutch elm disease. It goes by many names—critical race theory, cultural Marxism, DEI (diversity, equity, and inclusion), progressivism, gender theory—but most just call it "wokeness." Ultimately, it amounts to a new and alien principle of government intended to displace our constitutional order of liberty. Woke ideology is a parasite; it doesn't build any new institutions, it merely takes over existing institutions, sucks out their substance, and zombifies them. They live on, but unmoored from their traditional missions or the health of the country. Without drastic action our institutions won't recover.

Conservatives should attempt to save the institutions that can be saved. Think, for example, of the conservative resurgence in the Southern Baptist Convention (SBC), the largest Protestant denomination in the United States. During the 1960s, the SBC's leadership had been infected by liberalism and theological modernism, though most people in the pews remained conservative. Rather than abandoning their denomination, throughout the 1980s conservative Baptists systematically took control of every level of the organization, reformed their seminaries, and slowly turned churches toward more orthodox positions on theological and social issues. Conservatives today can do the same by taking back their local school boards, reinvigorating their churches, and cleaning up their neighborhoods.

Likewise, conservatives must plant new trees—that is, found new institutions. Christendom College, which my son attends, is an excellent example of a new conservative institution that is thriving. Founded in 1977 on the banks of the beautiful Shenandoah River, Christendom is a coed Catholic college that exists "to restore all things in Christ, by forming men and women to contribute to the Christian renovation of the temporal order."

These new institutions have begun to form their own flourishing ecosystem. You can see this in Moscow, Idaho, where worshippers at Christ

Church began to attract like-minded builders, establishing New Saint Andrews College, Canon Press, and now a growing orchard of start-ups, small businesses, flourishing families, and more. Preserving our way of life isn't just about fighting for past glories. Attending to America's future often means starting families, planting churches, and founding communities of our own, just like in Moscow.

None of this will matter, however, if conservatives remain unwilling to take the crucial third step: to destroy the institutions that can't be saved. Just as with Dutch elm disease, if conservatives take the first two steps but fail to do this, the institutions we take back and the new ones we found will eventually be infected and taken over by Uniparty elites and woke ideology.

In 2020, covid-19—like Dutch elm disease, an import from East Asia—made this abundantly clear. As Anthony Fauci's National Institute of Allergy and Infectious Diseases (NIAID) locked the country down, the churches that conservatives faithfully attended were helpless as federal bureaucrats locked their doors. Millions of parents were likewise at the mercy of Randi Weingarten and the American Federation of Teachers, not to mention all her friends in the Department of Education, who pushed tirelessly for schools to shut down or go remote.

It should have been clear that some of our most important institutions were rotten to the core well before the pandemic. The last decade has been full of grim Inspector General reports of weaponized law enforcement at the senior levels of the FBI, of obscene waste and fraud in the United States' wars in Afghanistan, of corruption and incompetence in our surface navy, not to mention cover-ups of sexual abuse in the Catholic Church, the Boy Scouts, and (with the Jeffrey Epstein scandal) the upper reaches of the ruling elites.

Those truly shocking revelations have numbed us to the steady drumbeat of incompetence, deceit, misconduct, and self-dealing that seem endemic to many parts of American life: public school test scores getting worse (even before the pandemic), new Boeing planes falling out of the sky, Harvard's and Stanford's presidents caught faking their research, real wages stagnating amid record profits, the imposition of rolling blackouts while politicians brag about renewable energy.

There is no one-size-fits-all solution, of course. Politics—as always—requires prudence. But the simple truth is, there is no fixing Harvard or reforming the FBI. The same goes for the NIAID and the Department of Education. These institutions cannot be saved. And so they must be defanged, defunded, and destroyed for the good of the overall ecosystem.

What is stopping us from burning down rotten institutions?

Part of the reason is a delusional belief by many instinctual conservatives that these institutions might yet be saved or that burning them down is not "realistic," that we need to take an incremental and compromising approach. These "moderates" prefer to talk about pluralism and reform, not plans for battle and reconquest. But you can't reform a cancer cell, and you'd fire an oncologist who made the kinds of strategic suggestions "moderates" do.

What is unrealistic and extreme is expecting our problems to go away if we're only nice enough. I've never heard anyone present a serious plan for wresting control of the Harvard Corporation or the Ford Foundation from the burrowed-in progressive class that has controlled them for decades. It is hard to see any plan that requires getting them to act in good faith as anything but a fantasy. The day after a Supreme Court decision overturning affirmative action, for instance, Ivy League colleges were proudly touting their workarounds.

The fact is, institutions that are not accountable to anyone cannot be reformed, and patterns of behavior and culture, once established, are unbelievably sticky. Many of our great institutions of civic life have traditionally been accountable to their members and, through them, to the American people. It's what makes reforming Congress or the Southern Baptist Convention plausible. But where institutions are captured by Uniparty networks and removed from real accountability—through administrative procedures, closed board governance, pseudo credentialism, loyalty hires, and more—they are beyond saving.

In contrast, where the idea of reforming these institutions seems like reckless and delusional optimism, I can easily imagine the steps required to destroy them, to strip them of wealth and status, and otherwise to totally marginalize them from power in America.

The Conspiracy Against Nature

Conservatives' instinctual aversion to fire has led them to support the Uniparty's disastrous mismanagement of the American forests.

The famed American naturalist and Sierra Club founder John Muir said of the sequoias that "Through all the wonderful, eventful centuries since Christ's time—and long before that—God has cared for these trees, saved them from drought, disease, avalanches, and a thousand straining, leveling tempests and floods; but he cannot save them from fools." It's supremely ironic that by far the most dangerous predators the giant sequoia has faced in its history are California environmentalists.

Since 2015, up to 20 percent of all giant sequoias have been killed by forest fires, with over half of them dying in the 2020 Castle Fire alone. Many of those destroyed were centuries-old titans that had survived dozens of fires before. In a few decades, environmental activism and technocratic forestry managed to accomplish what no other force of nature ever had: generating forest fires big enough and hot enough to destroy thousand-year-old fire-loving giant sequoias.

You see, before modern forestry "discovered" controlled burns (after having dismissed Native American forestry traditions as primitive and unscientific), state and federal forest officials suppressed every fire that came along, allowing fuel loads to reach unsustainable levels. But while foresters now recognize the need for controlled burns, state and federal environmental regulation has made forest management impossible. Activists use lawsuits to stop planned burns and prevent commercial uses of forest land that serve to lower fuel loads, such as cutting timber. And environmental rules stymie public and private forest managers alike. A controlled burn counts as carbon emissions in ESG scores, while letting a forest burn down in a superfire does not.

According to the sociologist Philip Rieff, the Party of Destruction undermines human cultures, not to replace them with something different but to replace them with a vacuum, an "anti-culture," that attempts to produce a "culture that persists independent of all sacred orders" that is "unprecedented in human history." This is one of the ironies we will explore in the book: that the Party of Destruction, which presents its goal as "progress," tries to use speed, violence, and enthusiasm to avoid answering the question "Progress toward what?"—and to avoid the oxymoron buried at the heart of a "continually progressive" politics.

For this is the dirty secret stalking supposed progressives: theirs has become an ideology of despair and decay. John Senior long ago grasped the problem: "The strongest reactionary force impeding progress is the cult of progress itself, which, cutting us off from our roots, makes growth impossible and choice unnecessary."

The prophets of progress don't even buy what they're selling anymore. When was the last time you met an optimistic progressive? A hopeful one? One with a large family? One with a smile on his or her face instead of a scowl?

The Party of Destruction is stuck in a loop. All it can advocate is more "liberation" and, at the same time, more governmental control to fill in where their destruction of the human order has left a vacuum. As the Canadian conservative George Grant pointed out, that's the irony of embarking on a course of revolution: the word itself means something that goes around "again and again and again."

The conspiracy against nature is doomed to fail, because in its desire for control and the destruction of limits it counteracts the forces that bring renewal. But the conservatism of the bucket brigade protects only a senile rot, zombified leadership, and decay that has run its course. It's time for a conservatism of fire, to burn it down and steward once again the natural order of the world, the Western order of civilization, and the American order of government.

Rather than join the fight, however, many self-styled conservatives prefer to sit on the sidelines and look down their noses at those of us who are working to save our country. They use words such as *divisive* and *populist* to delegitimize their opponents as radical revolutionaries. Many will even describe this book that way.

And, in a certain sense, they're correct to do so.

This book *is* divisive (of the wheat from the chaff). And it is also unapologetically populist. Populism is not the enemy of America's institutions but just another word for the fire that keeps the American forest healthy. It can get out of control sometimes, sure, but it also kills off the deadwood—those morally corrupt institutions that are no longer serving the American people—enriching the soil and making room for new trees to grow in their place. America's institutions are not unlike California's sequoias, releasing their seeds only upon feeling the heat of a flame. So let them label us "populist." The American forest is overdue for a fire, and the job of the Party of Creation is to ensure a long, controlled burn.

The Faith of My Fathers

Why is there so much disregard for the permanent things now? It's hard to have gratitude for something you've never experienced. I did not first learn to love tradition from a history book. I learned what it means to keep faith with God and my forefathers, to pass on the fire, from my own personal Aeneas.

My grandfather Mark "Pete" Pitre was a man of deep devotion to God, country, and family. Born in Opelousas in St. Landry Parish, Louisiana, in 1919, he grew up dirt poor, dropping out of school to work at a local mechanic's shop. After Pearl Harbor, he answered his country's call, volunteering to serve as a US Marine in World War II.

With his outstanding mechanical ability, he was trained as an airplane mechanic and assigned to a base in southern California, where he met my grandmother Betty French in the engine well of an airplane they were working on. Not even five feet tall, she had found her niche installing radar and other systems in the nose of aircraft. She could easily maneuver where the burly marine mechanics would be unable to go.

Their romance blossomed, and they married days after Victory in Europe Day in May 1945. They quickly got pregnant, and my mom was born the next year. Upon their discharge from the marines, PaPa Pete persuaded my grandmother to move the family back home to Opelousas.

The Pitre clan were Cajuns, descendants of some of the earliest French Catholic settlers of the New World colony of Acadia, in the area surrounding present-day Nova Scotia. Jean Pitre had settled in Acadia in the 1650s, married a fellow colonist, and settled on the banks of the Rivière Dauphin (today the Annapolis River), where he sired eleven children.

When French Acadia was conquered by the British during Queen Anne's War in 1710, *Les Acadiens* were put into a difficult position. Unwilling to abandon their Catholic faith or take an unconditional oath to the British monarch, the Acadians were viewed by the British with great suspicion in the lead-up to the French and Indian War.

That war, which culminated a century of New World colonial conflict, would result in France's loss of her New World colonies. But the tragedy was much more personal for the Pitres and other Acadians. The British forcibly removed the French Catholic Acadians in *Le Grand Dérangement* (The Great Upheaval), burning their homes and deporting over ten thousand Acadians to the American colonies, to England, or to France. Their land would later be given to British loyalists who had fled to Canada after opposing American independence.

Many Acadians were restless and unsatisfied with the idea of simply returning to France. Perhaps they had gotten used to the freedom, wide-open spaces, and self-reliance of frontier living. And so an offer from the Spanish Crown to settle the sparsely populated Louisiana, a wild land of natural bounty where they could freely practice their Catholic faith far from the battlegrounds of colonial conflict, intrigued many of the displaced Acadians, who would come to be known as Cajuns. They included my ancestor Pierre Pitre and his son François, who in 1765 were some of the first Acadians to arrive in Louisiana, settling in the Opelousas District, which remains my extended family's dwelling place to this day.

One of the unique things about the United States is that, apart from our Native American brothers and sisters, everyone who comes here has an exodus story of some kind. My ancestors' journey, carrying with them the traditions of Acadia to their new home, was a modern-day *Aeneid*, commemorated in Virgilian hexameter by Henry Wadsworth Longfellow in his epic poem *Evangeline, a Tale of Acadie* (1847).

The clichéd phrase "nation of immigrants" is too thin a term for the profound spiritual significance of coming to America, weighted with mythic and biblical meaning for the significant majority of new Americans from the Abrahamic faiths. Under a range of circumstances—some coming freely, others fleeing persecution, some compelled in chains—Americans have had the experience of leaving the Old World and journeying across the water. For many of them (including my Cajun ancestors), what they found when they arrived was not the land of milk and honey but a harsh and dangerous wilderness. Yet it was to them the Promised Land.

My family's story is why I've never had any time for the reactionary idea that America's ideals of pluralism and religious liberty are some-how fatal liberal flaws that cannot help but lead to secularism, unbelief, and pushing God out of the public square. In Acadia, my family could have had British liberty but not their faith. In France, they could have had their faith but not their liberty. In American Louisiana, they found both and built a legacy of fierce independence, generous community, and deep devotion that has lasted for centuries. In Louisiana, which is to this day organized not into counties but into parishes, it was the God-given freedoms guaranteed by the Constitution that created the space to develop a unique culture shaped by French heritage, the Catholic faith, and life in the Louisiana forests and bayous. The Cajuns never found any conflict between being fully Catholic and fully American.

Cajun Country

For generations upon generations, the Cajuns preserved their culture, faith, and language. Loyalty to family meant more than anything else, and Cajuns were raised among their extended kinfolk. Over a lifetime, people became enmeshed with networks of cousins, aunts, and uncles, and everyone was related to everyone else anyhow. Cajun French and the Catholic faith amid the English Protestant surroundings helped create a sense of distinction that cemented the community, and when my grandparents moved back, you'd still mostly hear Cajun French in the streets and shops of the parish. Few people in Opelousas spoke English. My Methodist grandmother described it as living in a foreign country (originally from a schoolteacher's family in Illinois, she may also have had a higher standard for what counted as "speaking English" than the local Creoles and Cajuns could meet).

PaPa Pete returned to work as a roughneck at Esso, later ExxonMobil. He'd hitchhike to the coast for a boat ride out to the rig, working seven days on, seven off. It was some of the physically toughest work there is, but he took pride in it and in supporting his family (as an older man, he became a foreman at an Exxon facility onshore).

PaPa Pete was a man's man—strong with gnarled hands, a genius at fixing anything mechanical. He was not stoic but not especially expressive, either. He liked to work hard and to enjoy the company of friends, a cold beer, and a baseball game. We whiled away afternoons together watching the Atlanta Braves on TV. And he took full advantage of living in "the Sportsman's Paradise," fishing with the best of them.

But he was also gentle and faithful. He was an old-fashioned gentleman who believed in taking care of womenfolk, my grandmother first of all. And I remember many a time working in the yard with PaPa Pete on a Saturday afternoon and being ordered to wash up: we were going to Confession. The family never had much, but my grandfather always had an envelope for the offering plate at Mass, which the whole family went to every Sunday.

Like many Cajun men, PaPa Pete had a special devotion to the Virgin Mary. He always had his rosary at his bedside. And he remained devoted to his widowed mother (my great-grandmother), visiting her almost every day of her long life.

My grandfather was the opposite of sentimental about what it meant to be a Cajun. He had grown up amid the worst parts of Cajun culture: the drinking, the insularity, the family dramas, the indifference to education. But he stood for all of the best, an irreplaceable way of life in the fabric of America and a source of real strength throughout my life.

When, as a nine-year-old boy, I found myself fighting against a vortex of familial chaos and pain, it was PaPa Pete and Grandma Betty who would save my life. They proved unfailingly consistent and unfailingly loving. My grandfather in particular stepped in as a role model, a man in my life I could count on. I needed the stability, normalcy, and constant love they provided. As the bottom dropped out of my home life, I clung to my grandfather and grandmother the way you might lash yourself to a bald cypress in a hurricane. I didn't appreciate then how deep their roots went, how much I owed the stability I desperately needed to a tradition and a faith that stretched back centuries and to all of those who had kept the fire burning along the way.

The Uniparty wants to discard or destroy all of the institutions that formed my grandparents, that gave them the strength and the virtue and the love that would save me. I bet if you reflect on the institutions and traditions that have made the most difference in your life, you'll find that they are under attack today, too.

Gratitude toward my three patrimonies—Catholic, Acadian, and American—leads me to continue to protect them, to nurture them, and to preserve them. What exactly does this entail?

Traditions live in and through our own lives. My grandparents and so many others of blessed memory initiated me into a way of life, handing to me the torch of my traditions, which I must carry, nourish, and fuel in how I live my life. If I don't, it will not only die out for me: it may die out altogether.

Most important, a tradition must be handed on. My parents and grandparents did that for me, so Michelle and I do that for our own kids (and hopefully will for our grandkids). Yes, we can and should do so with words and instruction. But how we spend our time and care has taught our kids most about what our family values. Give us a mountain sunset with the sounds of a creek nearby, with the family together, no screens, no music, no distractions—just us and our Creator—and you will find us all smiling, in awe of the simple but too infrequent act of appreciating His grandeur.

Tradition, like fire, is an embodied force, not an abstract idea. Traditions, like fire, die out when they are not tended. The modern conservative movement, founded as it was in the midst of an ideological fight with Soviet communism, has had a tendency to focus on getting ideas right. Too often, the health of our institutions—of *specific living, breathing institutions*—has been ignored. What made the difference in my life was faith, hope, and love: the faith of my fathers, hope in God's plan for my life, and the love of my family and my community. The difference between my life and those of so many lost and broken men in southern Louisiana was not another government program; it was a role model in my grandfather. It was a deep sense of who I was, of my story from my culture. It was a place where I belonged and a people I belonged to.

The state has only wards. It has no sons and daughters. It cannot love.

Moreover, there's another problem with the progressive vision: government handouts do not motivate the gratitude and the *pietas* that an inherited tradition or familial assistance do. And they cannot give you a role to fulfill and a future to fight for, the way that children and property of one's own do. It is because conservatives know what the government cannot provide that we believe in restrictions on government size and activity, to prevent it from crowding out or destroying the families, churches, civil society associations, and free enterprises that make up the topsoil of American life. The government by itself cannot give you a stake in the future.

For too long, American society has been mired in nostalgia. Too often, we have a better sense of what we don't want to change than of what we *must* change, a keener grasp of what has been lost than of where we ought to go. A country that is oriented exclusively toward the past cannot maintain the sacred fire.

Reagan the Creator

Restoring the permanent things will be a multigenerational project, and it will require every tool of statecraft available.

What concretely will it take for Americans to once again "look forward with confidence to the future," as President Reagan put it?

The biggest reason I left the great state of Texas to come to the swamp of DC was that I felt that the conservative movement had lost sight of what was important, of the need not only to conserve but to build. Every political community must have a vision for its future, or it is already dead. This ethos lies at the heart of the Party of Creation.

Ronald Reagan understood that. No other Republican president has so married a passion for our heritage with an excitement about our future. Reagan was not mired in nostalgia. He hated the idea that someone like his friend John Wayne might be called "The Last American Hero." Reagan believed that we were still a frontier nation and that our shared institutions had a role to play in creating a basis for American prosperity.

He understood that carrying the fire was about creation, not destruction. Nothing summed up Reagan's optimism like his unabashed embrace of "the next great frontier": space exploration. The historian John Logsdon dubbed him "the most pro-space president in American history." After a decade of budget cuts and lowered visions of the US space program, Reagan expanded NASA, shepherded the revolutionary space shuttle to completion, and pushed forward new research programs for a hypersonic passenger plane, the Strategic Defense Initiative, and the permanently crewed orbital Space Station *Freedom*. Reagan's interest in space was both personal and political. He spent more time talking to astronauts in orbit than any president before or since. He saw the United States' return to space as a vital symbol and sign of its broader national renewal.

Reagan had announced that there would be a program for civilians to ride on the space shuttle and that the first such passenger would be a schoolteacher, inspiring America's children to take up the mantle of pioneers to the stars. On that first civilian passenger flight, tragedy struck. Shortly after launch on January 28, 1986, Space Shuttle *Challenger* broke apart in midair. Millions of American schoolchildren saw it happen live on television. That night, President Reagan delayed his State of the Union address in order to address the nation.

It could have been a moment of turning back, a retreat to the security of unmanned space exploration or a promise to investigate and regulate space travel until it was "safe." But Reagan matched his mourning for the dead with a determination to carry on, comparing the astronauts to early American pioneers and the great explorer Sir Francis Drake. He promised, "Nothing ends here; our hopes and our journeys continue," adding, "The future doesn't belong to the fainthearted; it belongs to the brave."

In the face of a setback, he doubled down. For Reagan, space exploration was not about rivalry with the Soviets but about the spirit of the country. In a later speech, he said, "It is mankind's manifest destiny to bring our humanity into space; to colonize this galaxy; and as a nation, we have the power to determine whether America will lead or will follow. I say that America must lead." He then quoted the full text of the poem "High Flight," which he had immortalized in his speech after the *Challenger* disaster. Read in full, its mood is not elegiac but exuberant, even ecstatic, with pioneer spirit: "Oh! I have slipped the surly bonds of Earth / And danced the skies on laughter-silvered wings."

After Reagan, we downsized our aspirations. Clinton canceled the hypersonic travel program and reduced the Space Station *Freedom* program to a global partnership in the International Space Station. America's manned space program languished, to the point where, under President Obama, American astronauts going to the space station were forced to hitch rides on Russian rockets.

But the fire is rising again. Reagan would have absolutely delighted in the United States' return to space, this time with government playing a supporting role to an array of founders, explorers, and pioneers. Yet we need to match these extraordinary technological achievements with a political rhetoric and cultural mythmaking that point beyond them to the deep-rooted traditions they embody and the bright American future they portend. We at Reagan's think tank stand with the Gipper: it's time to build America's future again.

The Second American Revolution

Since Reagan left office, the American conservative movement has too often concentrated on fighting battles over abstract ideals and has forgotten that ideas must always be in the service of real institutions and people. In every instance, a focus on philosophical argument has allowed a class of rootless, globalist elites—including many who tout their "conservative principles"—to exert more power with less accountability.

As more and more Americans have rallied against these corrupt elites in recent years, the groundswell of support has had an unmistakable historical parallel to the decades before 1776. I believe we are living at the dawn of the Second American Revolution.

What is a revolution but an attempt to overthrow the institutions of society? Akin to our Founding Fathers, today we confront a far-off elite that is actively seeking to establish in the United States "new modes and orders" to achieve a Machiavellian overthrow of our constitutional system in favor of new institutions controlled by the Uniparty. In some ways, our situation is even more dire than during the First American Revolution.

Our elites today are further removed from the realities of American life than the British ever were from the colonists. Yes, it could take upward of six weeks to travel from England to the colonies at the time of the revolution, but our elites might as well live in a world apart. They own houses in different neighborhoods from the ones where you rent yours, they fill up—sorry, charge—their cars at different stations, they shop at different grocery stores, eat at different restaurants, vacation in different locations, and take their kids—sorry, dogs—to different parks than you do. Their language, filled with tortuous political correctness and managementese, is more different from the English of ordinary Americans than British English ever was from Colonial American dialects.

Like the First American Revolution, the second began when a corrupt ruling class sought to overthrow the existing institutions of American life. But whereas the British passed laws and imposed colonial officials, our elites have been more subtle. Over the span of decades, they have substituted a growing network of institutions (public and private) that allow them to exert control without accountability, leaching away power from our constitutional order and installing it in the Deep State, in woke corporations, massive foundations, and more.

The good news is, patriots across the country are already coming together, organizing the groundwork of resistance, and fighting back. Much like the Sons of Liberty, who banded together to spurn British goods more than a decade before shots were fired at Lexington and Concord, everyday Americans are once again boycotting the corrupt elites, from Bud Light to Target, and building a parallel economy. Indeed, the Daughters of Liberty have grown up and become Moms for Liberty. And though their spinning bees have turned into things such as classical school board meetings, American Heritage Girls chapters, and parent organizations keeping kids safe from digital technology, they're fighting for the same freedom. They're tending the same fire.

The New Conservative Movement

Today these forces are uniting into a powerful political force; we call it the New Conservative Movement.

Someone asked me what the focus of the New Conservative Movement ought to be. The three legs of the old conservative fusionism were social traditionalism, free enterprise, and anticommunism. The legs of the New Conservative Movement are Mom, Dad, and kids. And the focus of "family-first fusionism" is the modern-day hearth: the dining room table.

Family-first fusionism calls on conservatives to finally let go of the Cold War framework we've been operating in for thirty-plus years and work toward building an alliance against the greatest threat facing our country today: the Uniparty's war on the American family.

Like the first fusionism—that alliance among traditional conservatives, libertarians, and war hawks against a godless, collectivist Soviet communism that was threatening to take over the world—family-first fusionism must be a big tent with plenty of room for disagreement. If the old fusionism was built to fight an *ideological* war with Soviet communism by disseminating American ideas about freedom and capitalism, family-first fusionism must be equipped to fight an *institutional* war with our Uniparty elites by encouraging the formation of new American families and providing them the infrastructure they need to flourish.

Family-first fusionism aims to bring together men, women, and children to defend the institution of the American dinner table, the successor to the hearth in which the sacred fire of liberty yet burns.

A full dinner table used to be commonplace in our county, but today it is an increasingly rare spectacle. More and more people are choosing not to get married or have children. Many who do get married end up divorced, and many moms end up raising their kids on their own. On top of that, families that do stick together often struggle to make ends meet. More and more, both parents are forced to work, and as a result, there's simply not enough time to prepare a home-cooked meal. And why should they try, anyway? On those odd occasions when Mom or Dad does go the extra mile, everyone else seems to prefer the company of their friends on social media to that of their closest kin. With budgets tightening and the birth rate falling, is it any wonder that in August 2023 the *Wall Street Journal* reported that the average size of new homes has shrunk by 10 percent since 2018, with many floor plans now featuring no dining room at all?

Some might say that this is a good thing, that people's "consumer preferences" are being met. If building houses without dining rooms means that we can build them more efficiently, what's the big deal? This is the conservatism that Russell Kirk identified with "the dragon Fafnir lying upon his hoard of gold," hissing "Let me rest: I lie in possession!"

We have to fight that dragon because he lies indeed. The decadent conservatism of accumulation is fit for cold-blooded lizard people. Men are best understood as sons, husbands, and fathers, not as rational autonomous individuals. And while they certainly have a natural right to freedom, men are actually born as helpless babies who can't survive even a few hours without the nourishing love of their mothers, much less pursue their own destinies. In neglecting the dinner table, we turn our country inward toward self-gratification and narcissism.

The dinner table is the place where we learn who we are. It is the place where we grow from babies to boys and from boys to men. It is the place where we learn to be truly free by setting everything else in our life aside for a couple hours to break bread with our family and friends. It's the place where we go to serve others, in gestures as small as passing the table salt. It's the place where we gather to laugh, to cry, to bear one another's burdens, to pass on wisdom, to get advice, and to pray.

President Reagan, in his farewell address, said, "All great change in America begins at the dinner table." With gratitude in our hearts, the New Conservative Movement will fight for the future of the American dinner table. We will set aside ideological dogmas of a bygone era in exchange for an unremitting focus on the institutions that are under attack from the Uniparty, first and foremost the family. We will save the institutions that we can, start new ones wherever needed, and unapologetically destroy those that are hostile to our flourishing. And we will build a majority coalition of husbands and wives, fathers and mothers, brothers and sisters, sons and daughters, that will make its mark on the next century of American politics.

CHAPTER 3

Family-First Fusionism

To be happy at home is the end of all human endeavour.
—Samuel Johnson

F or most Americans, 1983 was the year the Reagan Revolution began to pay off, when dawn broke over the land once more. Inflation, interest, and unemployment rates were all in free fall. It was the year when America felt as though it was roaring back, as though it was sloughing off the malaise and stupor of the 1970s, of Vietnam, of stagflation, of the Iran hostage crisis, of the lines at the gas station, of burnt-out, drugged-out, dropped-out cityscapes. The year 1983 was a great year for America.

And it was the hardest year of my life.

I was born in Lafayette, Louisiana, the youngest of three. From as far back as I can remember, life at home was turbulent. There were a lot of good times, but my dad was an alcoholic, and he and my mom often fought. When I was four, my parents divorced.

It was the height of the 1970s, what Tom Wolfe dubbed "The 'Me' Decade," when the therapeutic mindset arrived for the American middle class. The new culture, popularized by elite influencers of every stripe, taught that happiness came not from loving others or living up to your duties to your neighbor and to God but from "finding yourself" with self-actualization, self-esteem, and self-care.

In the 1970s, such trivial institutions as marriage or organized religion seemed like pointless obstacles to the power of "finding the real me"!

My mom echoed what everyone else was saying in those days: "The kids will be just fine." Freed from my father and his troubles, she believed she would find a happiness that would make us kids happier, too. I remember hearing that argument on *The Phil Donahue Show* and seeing it on magazine covers at the grocery store checkout. But I knew that that was a lie. I knew we weren't fine, we weren't going to be fine, and nobody was really happier. Even today, I have a gut reaction whenever someone talks about divorce like that. There is a certain kind of rage and hurt that perhaps only the children of divorce know.

In a divorce, especially an acrimonious one, all of the forces that hold a marriage and a family together work in reverse to rip it apart. The shared project of the marital estate becomes the zero-sum division of assets. Uniting forces such as fidelity and shared children unravel into ugly feelings about new romances and custody agreements. Binding love becomes blinding hate. As William Butler Yeats wrote, "Turning and turning in the widening gyre . . . the centre cannot hold."

Aggravating the chaos at home was my family's deteriorating financial stability. My mother, who had always intended to stay home and raise us, was forced to take a full-time job at Sears, Roebuck to make ends meet. Like many low-skill service sector jobs, it paid hardly enough to support a family of three children. We moved into subsidized housing and started getting free lunches at school.

In an older America, a raft of social institutions—family, church, community, school, state, even employer—would have stood up to encourage my parents to stay married. But by the Me Decade, they had already been hollowed out and enfeebled.

It didn't just feel as though the wheels were coming off my own family's life; the whole region was in a funk. The same forces that had brought the United States roaring back in 1983 had devastated our region. Lafayette and its surrounds relied heavily on the energy economy, especially the oil and natural gas coming off the Gulf of Mexico. Tens of thousands of Louisianans worked in all of the different parts of the oil industry, from prospectors and drillers developing new fields to roughnecks (such as PaPa Pete) working on offshore rigs in the gulf to equipment operators and engineers at the refineries and petrochemical plants transforming crude into useful products.

While the rest of the United States had struggled to pay for gas in the 1970s, southern Louisiana had boomed, as investment capital and new jobs rushed in to boost the United States' domestic energy production.

Now, with oil prices plummeting into the 80s, it was our turn to be walloped. Plants closed, energy companies laid off workers by the hundreds, and a deep economic contraction set in. Soon, men whose families had lived in the region for centuries were packing up to look for work elsewhere. My family would eventually be forced to do the same.

Around that time, I remember seeing a car with a bumper sticker that summed up the city's mood: "Will the last person who leaves Lafayette please turn the lights off?"

But it wasn't the hardship of divorce or the economic downturn that made 1983 the hardest year of my life.

My older sister and brother had handled my parents' separation differently. My sister, Lori, now almost done with high school, had increasingly checked herself out of life at home. She had a popular social life with friends and without parental attention to rein her in became a bit of a wild child.

My brother, Doug, used baseball as an outlet. He was a phenom, a promising young first baseman. Being good at baseball gave him something to focus on and a clear place he belonged when things were messy at home. He had also become close to my stepdad, a younger man my mom had quickly married a few years after the divorce. They used to hang out and go shooting at the range or wherever else they could plink down some targets.

The brokenness at the heart of our family's life came to a head in November 1983. It was perhaps the deepest, darkest chapter of my parents' long divorce.

My father had remarried and started a new family with my stepmom. My parents refused to speak to each other, which contributed to tensions over their jointly raising kids. My siblings and I acutely felt ourselves to be a burden. Things got even worse when my mom divorced again, splitting from our stepdad. Of all of us, my brother felt that second divorce—the second loss of a father—most deeply. As a parting gesture, my now ex-stepdad let my brother keep the handgun they had gone shooting with.

One night, my brother was out carousing with his friends from the baseball team. Like many southern Louisiana teenage boys before them, after a few drinks they decided it would be a good idea to go out racing. Predictably, things went awry, and my brother crashed the car—my *mom's* car—into a light pole. He was ruffled but basically unharmed. But the car was in a bad way. It wouldn't start again. His friends went to get help or at least a tow rope.

We can't know what was going through my brother's head. Perhaps he was worried that the cops would come, that his baseball career would be over before it began. That the expense of fixing the car would be yet another way he was just a burden. Maybe he felt doubly fatherless, doubly adrift.

He must have felt abandoned, hopeless, alone, that he had somehow wrecked not only Mom's car but his life. High on adrenaline and drunk on liquor, sitting in my mom's wrecked car, my fifteen-year-old brother took my ex-stepdad's handgun and shot himself.

That night, I was staying at my dad's place with my stepmom and half siblings. I remember waking at 2:00 a.m. to the sound of my father shouting over the phone to my stepmom. "They're saying the gunshot is self-inflicted. There's no way. It doesn't make any sense." Like a bat out of hell, my dad drove us down to Lafayette General Hospital, Intensive Care Unit. I sat in the waiting room all night, some aunts and uncles trickling in about sunrise.

Like any nine-year-old boy, I thought my older brother walked on water. He was strong, athletic, popular. Nothing could happen to him.

And so I sat in total disbelief as the doctor came out and said to our waiting family that everyone needed to go and say goodbye. Even now it's hard to picture in my mind's eye the anguish and devastation on the faces of my kin as they shuffled into that room. I could see the deep woe in my grandparents' eyes. Yet they stood tall and strong as they went to bid my brother farewell.

Pain Which Cannot Forget

If our family had been a plane just managing to stay airborne in the years after the divorce, with my brother's suicide that plane disintegrated in midair; it was the kind of total family devastation that simply cannot be conveyed in words. It would reverberate over many years. It took decades for us to forgive one another and to forgive him.

Christian theology teaches that suicide results from spiritual despair and oppression, the foreclosing of the possibilities of one's future, including the possibility of future grace and redemption. Suicide happens when there's a truth you don't feel you can live with and that you don't believe you can (or will or should) be forgiven for. This oppression is often contagious in the wake of the void of hurt opened by a suicide, meant by the Evil One to be so. One person's suicide can ignite a spreading fire of despair.

Even though it may have been an impulsive act, a catastrophe such as the suicide of my brother, Doug, was the product of years and years of cultural decay, lies, and neglect. So many of the authority figures who should have sheltered and formed him passed the buck. Or they assumed that it was someone else's job. Or they were obsessed over their own problems. It took a village of institutions losing their way to make his death possible.

Yet I came to feel then, and still feel now, a deep sense of peace amid all my family's sorrow.

On the morning of my brother's death, PaPa Pete and Grandma Betty took me back to their house from the hospital. I was down in the back seat of their car, physically exhausted but also just numb with pain. Looking out the window, I took in the most beautiful sunny Louisiana dawn. And I then felt what I can only describe as the presence of the Holy Spirit, filling me with the peace that surpasses understanding.

In that moment, I knew that God was with me and all would be well. That was when my faith became unshakable.

I didn't have a whole lot of reasons to be optimistic about the future, my future. But I saw the faith my grandparents had. And it ignited my own, through the grace of God.

That faith, and the faithfulness of my grandparents and others, would bear fruit in surprising ways over many years. It would result in familial healing, restoration, and hope I scarcely would have thought possible at the time. Out of enormous tragedy would come new life.

Family Is the Foundation

Family breakdown doesn't happen in a vacuum. When this institution breaks, the damage spreads out to everything else in society, causing hopelessness, aimlessness, and contagious despair. The number one challenge Americans face in the twenty-first century is the crisis of family formation.

Over the past sixty years, the foundations of the American family have come under sustained assault, and rates of marriage and child-bearing have reached historic lows with no signs of reversal. Since the 2008 financial crisis in particular, the bottom has fallen out from underneath the American family.

Demographers predict that an astonishing one in three young adults will never marry and one in four will never have kids. American women are now expected to have an average of 1.66 children each, a far cry from the baby boom's 3.77 children per woman. Never have the rates of marriage and childbearing in the United States been so low.

That's a problem because a childless society becomes decadent and nostalgic. Aging, barren societies literally become consumptive, taking on higher levels of debt and depleting savings as they pay foreign workers to keep things going. They become less and less capable of innovation (a young person's game) and more and more stuck and decrepit every year. Their traditions, culture, and way of life die out, with nothing to hand on and no one to hand it on to. A culture of childlessness is, in the final analysis, a culture of despair.

Getting married and having kids, on the other hand, gives you skin in the game for the future of your country. It forces you to grow up, give up childish things, and live in the real world. It grounds you, gives you a sense of purpose in life, and helps generate community, gratitude, and joy. A culture of children is a culture of hope.

Unless we reverse our growing culture of despair, we will face insurmountable trade-offs. Every other challenge to the American way of life that we face this century will become more and more difficult. There are already fewer and fewer citizens able to support retirement programs, serve in the military, take care of the elderly, and maintain critical infrastructure. Soon we will be forced to choose between a total dependence on immigrants and a prolonged national senescence.

The good news is that our current birth dearth is not due to a lack of desire. A recent study by the National Survey of Family Growth found that women born in 1995 to 1999 want to have 2.1 children on average, just like women born in 1965 to 1969. But today, many more women are not able to have the families they hope for.

The New Conservative Movement can give Americans what they want and restore family formation in our country, but only if we are ready to take radical action. Our North Star must be striving to once again make a middle-class lifestyle available to every hardworking American family on a single-breadwinner income.

Just as essential, we must rebuild a culture of hope that celebrates children, encourages marriages, lifts up parents, cherishes extended family and community, and restores the civic fabric of our nation.

We're going to kill the snakes that are strangling the American way of life and build an abundant future for America's families. To restore abundance to America's families, the Party of Creation needs to fight and win on economics, technology, and culture. It will be an uphill battle. The alternative is national suicide. But before we propose solutions, we must answer this question: Why are Americans not forming families *even though they want to*?

The First Snake: Cost Disease Socialism

The first snake to kill is the economic crisis the American family faces, especially in housing. The median price of a single-family home in California was $859,800 in late 2023. If that sounds unaffordable to you, that's because it is. The middle class in California is effectively priced out of homeownership, so much so that 40 percent of Californians say they're considering leaving the state, with 60 percent citing the cost of living. But even with huge numbers of people moving to greener pastures (281,000 in 2021), housing prices continue to rise.

To staunch the bleeding, the Democrat-controlled state government has turned to massive subsidies for certain homebuyers. Since 2022, Sacramento has spent $315.3 million to help "preserve 1,364 affordable homes." Governor Gavin Newsom has also announced an additional $159.9 million intended to "preserve 638 affordable homes" for "lower-income Californians priced out of the market." That works out to an incredible average of *$237,362 of California taxpayer-funded support per home.*

Such an approach is self-defeating.

The issue is what economists call cost disease: when things get more expensive over time (even when adjusting for inflation) without getting better or more efficient. Over the past twenty years, Americans have been facing a form of cost disease on steroids. Since the year 2000, inflation-adjusted prices of consumer gadgets such as laptops and cell phones have plummeted, but prices of basics such as health care, housing, education, and child care have skyrocketed. Demand for these essential goods is "inelastic." That means that people are limited in their ability to reduce their need to buy them, even as prices rise. And so middle-class Americans' budgets have been getting squeezed, year after year.

In addition, cost disease creates a vicious cycle with the "two-income trap." For any individual household supported by a single income (normally the husband's), a second income would greatly contribute to purchasing better housing in a better neighborhood and better education for the kids. But as more and more women enter the workforce, it just contributes to bidding up the price of housing, child care, and education higher still, leaving everyone worse off.

Of course, there is one clear way to reduce your need to purchase health care, housing, education, and child care: have fewer children or no children at all. And Americans have been doing just that in droves.

"Cost disease socialism," as it has been labeled in an insightful Niskanen Center report by Steven M. Teles, Samuel Hammond, and Daniel Takash, is nothing short of a direct attack on the American family. In economic terms, cost disease socialism is a vicious cycle wherein the government subsidizes demand without doing anything about limitations on the growth of supply, thus pushing prices higher and higher. Even worse, by making every taxpayer pay a little bit, cost disease socialism distorts the self-correcting function of prices in free markets.

For decades, Republicans' conventional economic playbook has led them to try to reverse these trends by choking off consumer subsidies. As Teles, Hammond, and Takash pointed out, however, traditional budget cuts *cannot* lower spending in many areas but merely result in accounting tricks that hide mounting costs. What they suggest instead is a fiscally responsible approach that addresses the *regulatory* and supply-side sources of cost disease.

For instance, Medicare already makes up about 3.7 percent of GDP (and is expected to rise to around 6 percent of GDP by 2040) and accounts for almost 15 percent of all federal spending. Traditional approaches to cutting these costs, such as lowering reimbursement rates, end up lowering quality and shifting costs onto private sector insurers.

That's because regulatory burdens are the real culprits driving up Medicare costs. Government predictions of a doctor *surplus* in the 1980s and 1990s led to a decades-long moratorium on additional slots in medical schools, for example. Now the United States produces far fewer doctors per capita than any other nation with our level of health care spending. Meanwhile, needless state and federal regulations limit what nurse practitioners and physician assistants can do, even when evidence suggests an equivalent treatment result.

Addressing these supply-side issues can lead to massive savings. The Trump administration proved as much, according to the Niskanen Center report. Taking on the dialysis industry, which accounts for roughly 7 percent of Medicare spending at $87,000 per patient per year, Trump and his team made small reforms such as increasing incentives to donate kidneys and advocating for in-home dialysis treatments that led to almost $4.2 billion in savings. Better still, those changes improved quality of life for patients, who often prefer in-home treatments, and likely gave almost thirty thousand people another year of life.

You can find similar forces at work in every other area where the middle class is being priced out of the American Dream. Education costs, for example, have been driven higher and higher because of an increasing thicket of regulations that impose a staggering administrative burden. According to data from the National Center for Education Statistics, between 2000 and 2021, the number of teachers in public schools increased by 9.27 percent, but the number of principals and assistant principals increased by 36.70 percent and the number of school district administrative staff increased by a whopping 77.09 percent.

The same dynamic is at play in higher education. A Heritage Foundation report, "Diversity University: DEI Bloat in the Academy," revealed that the University of Michigan was spending $18.1 million on more than 163 DEI personnel, almost six per every hundred faculty members and more than twice the number of faculty teaching history.

NEPA-tism

How did the situation get so bad? The hidden mechanism driving so much of the strife in our country's life, including the decline of marriage, is that we've made it basically illegal to build things in much of the United States.

The Reagan Revolution called for "supply-side economics," which made the United States a great place to invest and build a business in again. But since Reagan left office, Republicans have lost the plot. They forgot to ensure that investment actually builds productive capacity—the only thing that will create abundance and good jobs.

Even progressives are beginning to realize that cost disease socialism threatens their ostensible goals of building the "electric vehicle transition," the Green New Deal, or a socialist paradise. Moderate supply-side progressives such as Ezra Klein and Matthew Yglesias have started to pop up, arguing for limited deregulation for infrastructure projects, though Reihan Salam pointed out in the *Atlantic* that few people in the Democrats' electoral coalition agree with them.

The granddaddy of abundance-strangling regulations is the National Environmental Policy Act (NEPA), passed in 1970. The act itself has largely been made redundant, between later state and federal regulations that actually protect the environment and a huge number of categorical exclusions. But it limps along as a zombie, imposing massive compliance costs on *virtually everything done with federal money*.

As passed by Congress, NEPA was intended as a kind of reality check for projects. It requires that federal projects assess the impact they will have on the environment: it's just a procedural step with no actual impact on project decision making or legality. And initially compliance was easy, with short environmental impact statements (EISs). According to Eli Dourado of the Abundance Institute, EISs have grown from as short as ten pages in the 1970s to an average today of six hundred pages plus a further thousand-plus pages of appendices. The federal government completes almost three hundred EISs a year, but under NEPA it also has to complete twelve thousand preliminary environmental assessments, 98 percent of which find no significant impact.

What this also means is that paradoxically, when Congress decides to support building something because it is important for the national interest, it automatically imposes a massive additional regulatory burden. The CHIPS and Science Act, passed in 2022, had some major flaws. But despite all of its problems, it was supposed to actually do at least one thing: provide badly needed subsidies to rebuild the United States' domestic semiconductor production capacity and secure our supply chain from China, including the $52 billion CHIPS for America fund.

All of this funding is stuck right now. Not a single shovelful of dirt can be moved until the NEPA process is complete.

NEPA is the tip of the iceberg. But a recent analysis by the Foundation for American Innovation's Thomas Hochman highlighted other regulations that impose subtler costs, including the Resource Conservation and Recovery Act of 2023, the Clean Water Act of 1972, and above all the Clean Air Act of 1970. During the Trump administration, the Department of Commerce polled American manufacturers about the specific regulations they viewed as most burdensome: NEPA didn't even make the top ten.

America can't build anything because it has a giant regulatory monkey on its back, a vetocracy that highlights the costs and risks of projects to the exclusion of benefits and opportunities. Permitting and regulatory reform is one of the most critical political issues the New Conservative Movement should fight for, something vital for our national security and vital for our abundance agenda. It will make a real difference in the lives of ordinary American families.

First Comes Love; When Comes Marriage?

You can see these economic forces eating at the material foundation of the American family.

In 1980, a young couple (call them Mike and Lisa) thinking about getting married and starting a family is wondering what their life together will be like. Having lots of friends who are also getting married would help shape their thinking, of course, but there are also practical considerations. Mike and Lisa might consider how much a home and a car would cost, weigh whether to pursue a college education, and think about whether Lisa would keep her job or work at home raising the kids. They wouldn't worry about the cost of health care: in 1980, fewer than half of employees were required to contribute *anything* to medical insurance costs.

Overall, they would find economic and social conditions favorable to marriage. At a median 1980 home cost of $47,200, Mike and Lisa could pay off their mortgage in principle with only 2.25 years of work at the median American income ($21,020). If they chose to go to college, they could earn a four-year bachelor's degree from a public university for $9,308 in *total* tuition, room, and board, which could be paid off with five months of work at the median income. They could purchase the cheapest new car (a two-door Chevy Chevette) for $4,057, only eleven weeks of the median income. If Lisa chose to stay home with the kids, they'd have no trouble supporting themselves on Mike's income alone.

What would the same arrangements have looked like for another young couple, Jake and Emily, getting married in 2020? At the median income of $56,287, buying the median American home, which costs $267,693, would cost them almost twice as much time (close to five years). Unlike Mike and Lisa, Jake and Emily would definitely have to think about health care. Family insurance contributions had risen to $5,588 as of 2020. The cheapest new car (a Chevy Spark Hatchback) costs $14,095 (thirteen weeks of income). Four years of college at a public university would set them back $85,348 (three times as much as in 1980 and double again if they both went). With Jake working at the median wage, they would struggle to make ends meet. Emily is likely to look at working at least part-time and putting her babies into day care, at a significant cost.

Rather than fighting the factors restricting supply and driving up costs, America's cost disease socialism has been kicking the can down the road. Jake and Emily will be encouraged to take on student loans for their education, a substantially higher debt burden for their home, and credit card debt to handle their day-to-day expenses. Rather than fixing the sources of exorbitant health care costs, we have mandated that young adults can stay on their parents' insurance until age twenty-six and increased the employer-subsidized share of insurance premiums.

Is it any wonder that fewer young people than ever are getting married and starting families and that the ones who are do so later and later? When the mountain they must climb to achieve financial maturity gets higher and higher, it becomes easier and easier to justify an extended period of adolescence.

Now, that's not to say that being a spouse and a parent is ever easy. But it was a lot easier in 1980 than it is today, in terms of both culture and cost, especially for Americans without a college education.

Our models of inflation assume that if people pay more for higher-quality goods, no real inflation has taken place. Some DC economists even have the nerve to say that when people spend more on health care, new cars, new houses, child care, and education, it reflects consumer choice. But that's not true.

A couple that takes on a crushing mortgage to move to a "nicer" house because their neighborhood is being overrun with crime and their existing school district is terrible is not really making a choice. A family that scrapes together a car payment for a "nicer" vehicle when their old one dies is not thriving on the benefits of improved quality. This is obvious because it is the most affordable entry-level goods that experience the greatest demand relative to supply. It is even more obvious when you talk to ordinary Americans about their household budgets.

The truth is, changing regulatory demands and Uniparty managerial control exert much more influence over the markets for health care, new cars, new houses, child care, and education than do consumer choices. That's why when the Trump administration instituted policies that reversed globalization, lowered regulatory burdens, and unleashed investment, the long stagnation of American working-class wages briefly lifted. But since then, Bidenomics, rampant spending, and a crackdown on energy production have sent inflation soaring, dragging real wages back to pre-2015 levels.

Why do many elites in the Uniparty not recognize this problem? Probably because they're members of a wealthy, educated class that insulates them from such challenges. Elites don't live in a culture of family breakdown, so it's easy for them to claim that marriage doesn't matter.

Marriage was once something that transcended class, but today that's no longer the case. According to the General Social Survey, 58 percent of college-educated Americans ages eighteen to fifty-five are married, compared to *39 percent* of people without college degrees. Moreover, having a college degree is *the single greatest predictor of avoiding divorce*: the divorce rate among those with a college degree is 22 percent, compared to 37 percent for people without a college degree.

Social scientists aren't sure about the exact relationship among marriage, education, and income. But according to the Pew Research Center, over 40 percent of never-married adults earning less than $75,000 per year say that financial instability is a major reason they aren't married, double the 21 percent earning over $75,000 who say the same. And how could it not? Since 1983, life for a working-class family has become more expensive, even as wages for working-class men have stagnated.

In 1980, it took a man with only a high school diploma, working full-time at the *median wage* ($13,832), 3.4 years to earn the cost of the median home, 42 percent longer than the equivalent man earning the median college-educated wage ($19,552). In 2023, it would have taken him seven years, an astounding 82 percent longer than someone with a college degree. And the reality is even worse than these data alone suggest.

This economic malaise is tanking working-class marriage rates—and America's well-being along with them.

But does it really matter if Americans are having to defer marriage? Isn't it true that good things often come after hard work, perseverance, and—crucially—waiting? Actually, the delay matters a lot.

The renowned University of Virginia sociologist and head of the

National Marriage Project Brad Wilcox pointed out in his book *Get Married: Why Americans Must Defy the Elites, Forge Strong Families, and Save Civilization* that the falling fortunes of marriage in America are the top reason why happiness rates in this country are hitting record lows. Raj Chetty, an esteemed Harvard economist, tells us the biggest reason the American Dream is out of reach in communities across America is that there are too few two-parent families. It's a finding that the economist Melissa S. Kearney confirmed in her book *The Two-Parent Privilege: How Americans Stopped Getting Married and Started Falling Behind*, which chronicled with study after study that on basically every metric, children benefit tremendously from living with their married parents, even when controlling for parental education, income, and other factors.

It is literally a matter of life and death: among the white working class experiencing lowering life expectancy, rising deaths from despair (from pills, fentanyl, cirrhosis, suicide, and the like) are almost entirely confined to unmarried men and women.

You've read my story; you'll know that this is viscerally personal for me.

After my parents' divorce, circumstances forced us to rely on government programs temporarily. And I am grateful for them, as far as they go. They were a merciful safety net that slowed our descent into what could have been a fearsome, damaging sort of poverty and enabled my mom (now a single mother) to get things back on track.

But I didn't just want housing; I needed a home. I didn't just want food in my belly; I needed a provider, a father. I didn't just want an education; I needed a culture worth learning about. I didn't just want a job; I needed a purpose.

Doing whatever we can to restore American marriage is essential to everything else, because so many of the problems our country faces come back to the breakdown of the American family. Every year, the evidence gets stronger and stronger that family structure—whether a child is raised in a home by his or her married parents—is a better predictor of economic mobility, education, criminality, psychological disorders, suicide, and dozens of other variables than *any other single factor*, including parents' education, wealth, race, or anything else.

It's not surprising that the Party of Destruction has repeatedly suppressed these findings: they suggest that no government program could possibly be effective enough to override the influence of the independent institution of the family.

But many DC conservatives have been almost worse, because they give lip service to the ideal of marriage and do nothing to bolster the institution. They won't stand up publicly for the reality of a one-man, one-woman marriage, the reality that every child needs a mother and a father, or the reality that men and women want different things in marriage.

And they wring their hands when you talk about materially supporting working families, easing their burden, recognizing the real cost and difficulty of raising kids, supporting women who want to be homemakers, or building an economy of stable jobs for marriageable men.

Under these conditions, the recalcitrance of many wax-museum conservatives to support the American family with any policies besides aggressive tax cuts for big corporations is truly shocking and shameful. If the New Conservative Movement does not take responsibility for the dire state of America's working class—which starts with admitting that some of our policies were part of the problem—all our other success will eventually come to nothing.

An Abundance Agenda for American Families

A family should not be a luxury good. The way out of our decadence, however, isn't austerity and rigidity but abundance and dynamism. Today, we must be willing to remove as many barriers as possible to building in the United States: new housing, new schools, new energy, new industry, new agriculture, new technology, and more.

In other words, we cannot simply budget cut our way out of the bind we are in. Decades of neglect have created an emergency that directly endangers America's future. We can't simply stop further increases in costs and regulation: we need to invest in positively reversing them.

It's time to build.

A supply-side approach to family formation means a supply-side approach to everything families need, starting with affordable housing. That doesn't mean imposing artificial rent controls or some other progressive policy that makes housing affordable for a select few. Housing should be affordable for all, simply because there is so much of it.

We might find inspiration in a surprising place. Out of desperation, California has become the national leader in rapid housing deregulation. It's gotten so bad that the Golden State even wants God on its side. In 2023, the state legislature passed a Yes in God's Backyard (YIGBY) bill, which allows a religious institution or independent institution of higher education to build a housing development project on its property "by right." Other legislation has mandated that localities act to update their housing codes and approve or disapprove projects, in some cases allowing projects to go ahead *automatically* if local boards are standing in the way of growth but not offering anything positive.

But housing prices are shooting up in red states, too, partially because families can't afford to live in California anymore, and conservatives need to do more than pat themselves on the back for having less regulation than California (a low, low bar). Part of the problem is that America's capacity to build basic infrastructure—roads, trains, houses, factories, and so on—has not improved in almost seventy years. In fact, economists at the University of Chicago found that construction productivity has *declined by as much as 40 percent* since 1970, compared to steady growth in other sectors.

We need to apply supply-side thinking to a whole host of industries: encouraging energy investment and drilling to lower energy costs, reforming emissions rules to allow electric companies to upgrade facilities with new equipment (instead of modifying old equipment forever), getting the FDA to loosen restrictions on importing high-quality baby formula from Europe (but not from China, where formula is often contaminated), importing South Korean nuclear reactor and Japanese bullet train know-how with technology transfers and joint ventures, channeling federal research dollars away from genderqueer zoology studies and toward construction productivity research—anything we can do to lower costs for the essentials that families need to survive and thrive will help further the abundance agenda.

Marginal improvements are not enough. In the New Conservative Movement, moneyball approaches to family policy (attempting to calculate the minimum viable cost per extra child born) will be considered unserious, as will arguments that put the onus on everyday Americans to have more kids while letting politicians in Washington who have the power to make it easier to start a family off the hook. We need to make marriage and family more attractive as institutions, shaping our policy to the concrete needs of actual American families and not the abstract economic pronouncements of some long-dead Austrian aristocrat.

What you see in countries that have successfully maintained fertility rates or even reversed fertility declines, including Israel, Hungary, and the Republic of Georgia, is that they combine serious family policy with a culture that cherishes children and upholds a mission of national renewal. They don't just try to use technocratic tax incentives to nudge parents into having more kids, nor do they just use cultural messaging to talk about having kids without putting their money where their mouth is.

They place the family at the *center* and do both. They use massive public expenditures to send the explicit message that the family is the most important thing for the future of the nation. Today, Hungary, the world's leader in family policy, spends up to 6 percent of its GDP on measures to encourage family formation and the raising of children. But these policies, where they work, operate not by nudging parents but by changing the culture.

To change the culture, we must put *everything* in the service of enshrining the American family at the very heart of our civilization, including vastly reshaping the economic incentives supporting the

American family. *We have to do everything. It has to be our number one priority. We need to pull every plausible lever, economic and cultural; local, state, and federal; public sector, private sector, and civil society.*

Family policy needs to be at the heart of everything the New Conservative Movement does.

Stingy spending on families today is penny wise but pound foolish. Family policy is fiscal policy. The easiest way (maybe the only way) to deal with the looming national debt and insolvent entitlement programs is to grow our way out of them. There is *no realistic scenario* for resolving our fiscal crisis that does not involve having more American families. We need to be family formation supply-siders!

Family policy is innovation policy. Economists have shown that innovation is a young person's game: as a population ages, its ability to innovate and generate new ideas and inventions declines. The more children we have, the more young people we will have to help solve the problems of tomorrow.

That's also why family policy is national security policy. We can't defend our interests at home and abroad from a position of decay and decadence or without the able-bodied young men and women needed to protect our country. Significant population aging practically requires large numbers of immigrants to serve as caretakers and nurses and keep the economy going. It's important that we secure our border. But no amount of strength along the wall will be enough if we do not regenerate our nation at home the old-fashioned way: through family formation.

Finally, family policy is good conservative politics. Younger Americans are much more likely to identify as liberal than older generations were. That's not simply because of cultural Marxism or progressive universities, which are more the symptoms than the root causes of our current crisis. It's because they have been denied a stake in the system. They've been denied access to the things that one takes pride and responsibility in: marriage, family, homeownership, and the like. They've been denied the need to prepare for and fight for a concrete future for their children.

For the past few decades, America has been pursuing what might be called a decadence agenda: cheaper consumer goods, foreign credit, the increasing cost of family essentials, growing numbers of DINKs (double income, no kids). It's an economy that provides more luxuries to fewer workers. It's an agenda with no future and no hope.

We must pursue an agenda of abundance, not decadence.

Wax-museum conservatives in government have not been willing to practice what they preach. And I don't just mean the hypocrisy of philandering "family-values" congressmen. In the year of our Lord 2024, how are there still marriage penalties embedded in our tax code, not to mention in our welfare system? Depending on the state and the programs in question, working-class Americans are penalized, sometimes to the tune of more than ten thousand dollars a year, if they get married. And red states are some of the worst offenders!

In 2017, Republicans in Congress fixed many marriage penalties via the Tax Cuts and Jobs Act—but only for upper-middle-class Americans. Marriage penalties, including substantial ones, remain for the working class, falling hardest on families earning between $35,000 and $65,000, sometimes costing them up to 30 percent of their real income, compared to if the couple had not gotten married. Conservatives can rightly disagree on the wonky particulars of how we can make marriage and family an attractive institutional and economic proposition. But in the New Conservative Movement, it will not be acceptable for policy makers and thought leaders to simply dismiss the question.

As every parent knows, raising a child well is real work and a huge investment of time and money. Yet the nation as a whole benefits from the work of parents. Our tax code should recognize this by expanding the child tax credit and ensuring that support begins from conception (at least through a retroactive refund or a newborn bonus).

We should consider even more radical measures such as adopting a successful Hungarian policy that gave low-interest-rate loans to never-before-married young newlyweds, with the proviso that a large chunk will be forgiven for each child they have. We already subsidize student loans to the tune of billions of dollars; why not move some portion of that over to family formation? Much like President Trump's decision to expand the use of 529 tax-advantaged savings plans from postsecondary education only to K–12 in 2017 and apprenticeship programs in 2019, this policy would simultaneously punish America's corrupt colleges and reward families. On the one hand, by aiding working parents, we'd be helping create the material conditions for family life; on the other hand, we'd reverse support for bloated college tuitions and weaken the cultural norm for parents to obsess over how to pay for college.

Another proposal the team at the Heritage Foundation is batting around would create a family flexible savings account (FFSA). Each family would be able to deduct up to $10,000 a year per child from its income taxes to put into this account. Working families on welfare would be able to receive $10,000 a year in lieu of other welfare program eligibility. Married couples would be able to deduct substantially more so that we would be heavily incentivizing marriage, with a bonus for every third child or more. Families could use their account to pay for education expenses, health care, housing, child care, and college/apprenticeships, and savings could grow tax free (as in a Health Savings Account).

We are still figuring out the best approaches to family policy, the best levers in government and civil society, to bring abundance back to marriage and child rearing. We know that we must balance the critical need for more American families with fiscal prudence and evidence-based policy. But we have our sharpest thinkers and wonks on the case.

The Second Snake: Culture-Shaping Technologies

The second snake strangling the American family has often escaped our notice. Conservatives sometimes take the naive view that new technologies are just the products of the "invisible hand" of the free market. But while private sector companies create products consumers want, the scientific breakthroughs leading to the most revolutionary technologies often originate in political projects. The birth control pill (the first hormonal contraceptive) was the product of a decades-long research agenda paid for by the Rockefeller Foundation and other eugenicist and population control–oriented groups. All of the basic technologies underlying the smartphone emerged from US government and military research programs, the economist Mariana Mazzucato has shown. The surge in electric vehicles and infrastructure is being driven almost entirely by federal government subsidies. New technologies are not the random by-products of the free market's natural selection but the results of careful efforts by powerful people intended to reshape society.

We need to understand what could be called contraceptive technologies—revolutionary inventions that shape American culture away from abundance, marriage, and family—in the same vein. They shift norms, incentives, and choices, often invisibly and involuntarily. Conservatives inveigh against no-fault divorce, the Sexual Revolution, and the destruction of a culture of hope without recognizing that these cultural changes are all downstream of technological ones.

Here's the thing: we like to think of our desires as springing from thin air or from our deepest internal being. We want what we want because we want it. In fact, human beings are highly mimetic creatures, which is to say, we mimic the priorities of the culture around us. Look at your friends and peer group. How different from them are you, really? If you change a culture, you change the desires of the people in that culture. If you change a culture on a profound level, you can break the most basic functioning elements of civilization.

In the case of contraceptives, we are a society remade according to a research agenda set by the Party of Destruction. From the 1920s until the present day, groups such as the Rockefeller Foundation, the Ford Foundation, and the Bill and Melinda Gates Foundation have poured billions of dollars into developing, testing, marketing, and distributing chemical contraceptives in the United States and around the world, with little pushback or alternatives from conservatives.

It's true that contraceptives give families more control over when they have children. But the creators of the technologies wanted to go much further than controlling a natural process; they wanted everyone in our culture, regardless of their beliefs or choices about contraceptives, to believe that having kids is an optional individual choice instead of a social expectation or a transcendent gift. Formerly, we thought that *rejecting* children meant consciously resisting life's natural progression; now we are more likely to describe *having* children as a divergence from life's natural progression. Children aren't an inevitability; they're an optional add-on.

This may not sound radical to you, but consider: one technology has convinced humanity that extinction is natural and procreation is unnatural. Maybe we're not the freethinkers we think we are.

Even those who reject chemical contraceptives for religious or health reasons are now seen as *choosing* to do something that was entirely natural before: what first seemed to be freedom for individuals was actually a cultural revolution for everyone (not to mention the growing concerns about artificial hormones infusing the water supply).

Once you understand this pattern (individual choice masking cultural upheaval), you will see it everywhere. In vitro fertilization (IVF) seems to assist fertility but has the added effect of incentivizing women to delay trying to start a family, often leading to added problems when the time comes. Investment in improved hormonal birth control has masked a growing range of autoimmune and other disorders such as endometriosis and a lack of medical and scientific attention to solving them. Experienced infertility specialists say that increased commercial emphasis on IVF and other invasive (and profitable) treatments is creating a generation of doctors who actually don't know how to perform older, noninvasive, but quite successful methods of restoring fertility.

And of course nowhere is this more extreme than in the case of abortion. As other kinds of contraceptive technologies spread, abortion rates went up, not down. Why? Because technological change made having a child seem like an *optional* and not *natural* result of having sex and destroyed a whole series of institutions and cultural norms that had protected women and forced men to take responsibility for their actions. It's why, despite the supposed increase in "choice," the proportion of single moms in the United States has quintupled since the 1960s.

The same pattern (individual choice masking cultural upheaval) is reflected in the fact that as the prices of basic goods needed to raise a family have gone up, prices have plummeted and "quality" has soared for all kinds of mindless entertainment: video games, huge high-definition TVs, social media, pornography, and more. These technologies aren't thought of as contraceptive, but that's what their effect is in American life: they make young men lazier and more impotent (literally) and less inclined to be husbands and fathers. One study even estimated that the improvements to video game and computer quality alone accounted for half of the drop in working time for men aged twenty-one to thirty between 2004 and 2015, which decreased by 203 hours (12 percent). With virtual reality, infinitely extendable games, and AI-generated personalized pornography on the horizon, many more men will consider dropping out of the rat race and becoming shut-ins living in their aging parents' basements (already an epidemic in Japan).

Procreative Technologies

No number of economic incentives alone can reform a culture that shapes people's hearts not to want children. Technology isn't going away. But we should be aware that we're not fighting a "neutral" market; we're fighting an intentional plot against family formation, carried out through technology. Beginning to take the power of technology as seriously as the Party of Destruction does requires going beyond tax policy tweaks or cultural diatribes. It means that the Party of Creation should invest in true next-generation technologies that will protect and valorize the traditional family.

Whereas contraceptive technologies such as Tinder trap users in a vortex of "situationships" that don't lead anywhere, entrepreneurs in the Party of Creation will build in the opposite direction. For instance, Keeper is not a dating or hookup app but a *marriage* app, designed with unique paths for men and women. It uses expert matchmakers and artificial intelligence to present its users with a single match at a time, based on an extremely thorough initial questionnaire. Keeper is already making a dent, attracting further investment, and growing like gangbusters among a generation scarred by the Sexual Revolution and eager for real connection. According to Keeper CEO Jake Kozloski, 25 percent of the first dates scheduled so far have resulted in long-term relationships, and the first Keeper wedding was last November, with several more in the pipeline.

Some of these procreative technologies will be truly cutting-edge. Remote work and online marketplaces have made it easier for some families to live near their relatives or in tight-knit communities while still making a good living. The internet has made it easier than ever for homeschool parents to swap best practices and lesson plans. And tools such as CNC milling and 3D printers have restored the economic viability of workshop production, at least for specialized products. Advanced technology is an important element of rebuilding an American society in the shape of the family.

But some of the most powerful "technologies" at our disposal are not scientific novelties but ancient cultural practices. Our culture no longer values observing a Sabbath. We're so attuned to technological thinking that it seems like a waste of time. Couldn't we be working? But keeping the Sabbath actually represents a conscious choice to prioritize faith, family, and rest over work—in other words, to relinquish control. For centuries, Sabbath closing laws protected a space of communal and familial life. The laws were simple, but they served a radical purpose: they reminded Americans, in the midst of our hustle and bustle, of the importance of rest, of community, and of thanksgiving. Little by little over the course of the twentieth century, the Party of Destruction abolished the Sabbath rest. Now burnout, including of parents, is reaching epic proportions.

We cannot expect a harried, restless, and anxious people to "be fruitful and multiply." The Party of Creation should fight to restore the Sabbath rest. In government, we should advocate for mandatory overtime pay on Sundays, for reducing Sabbath commercial hours, and for more pro-Sabbath policy choices.

The same applies to our local communities and our own lives: For many families, the Sabbath becomes busy not with work but with travel sports and the like. We can fight at the level of the little platoons to build a Sabbath rest again; to put down the screens for the day, worship God, and invite some friends over; to rest, for ourselves and for our families.

We have to make the choice to reject workaholism, consumption, and decadence and embrace "inefficient" rest. We have to trust that God will reward this commitment. Many Americans have started practicing a "digital Sabbath" that involves structured time away from screens or social media. In Hyattsville, Maryland, members of the community are taking things even further, with a few dozen families taking the "Postman Pledge." Named after the famed media historian Neil Postman, they agree to keep their kids off of social media and smartphones and to limit the ways in which digital tech shapes their families' home lives. This technology temperance is in service of doubling down on the real world, "to foster friendships among our families in the natural, traditional ways human cultures have always done."

These efforts, even if small scale, can have an outsized impact. That's because family choices are most shaped by particular subcultures—the beliefs, norms, and incentives of particular places. As the journalist Timothy P. Carney argued in his book *Family Unfriendly: How Our Culture Made Raising Kids Much Harder than It Needs to Be*, these subcultures are highly determinative of whether people will get married and have kids. According to Carney, what matters is that the pillars of pro-natalist traditions reshape the environment around them for everyone. This includes the physical landscape: pro-natalist subcultures minimize the distance between work, church, school, and home, with parks and walkable paths that are safe for children at play.

What you find is that even if many of these subcultures are dominated by a particular religion, there are huge spillover effects. Secular Israelis have "only" an average of 2.2 kids in a society where large Orthodox families are normal. Catholics living in Mormon Utah have more kids than Catholics anywhere else do.

The Party of Creation can make the Sabbath its own sort of subculture. Slowly but surely, its effects will be contagious, and soon we will find Americans resting, gathering around the dinner table, and enjoying family time throughout the week once again, learning to master the technologies that support their flourishing.

The Third Snake: Antifamily Propaganda

Conservatives need to recognize that American family culture hasn't simply drifted away. There was a culture war, and we lost—in some sense before we ever started fighting.

Several years before *Roe v. Wade*, plotlines about unwanted and unexpected pregnancies started popping up in the most popular television shows across all of the major networks. To this day, American media (now including social media and tabloid websites) are dominated by messages extolling a glamorous carefree child-free lifestyle and mocking the traditional family.

In an era of globalized competition, this kind of spiritual warfare has gone international. Last summer, a TikTok video went viral, accruing tens of millions of views. It depicted a young, happy blonde eagerly putting her hand out for her off-screen beloved to slip on an engagement ring. But as she did, she experienced a vision of future domestic toil: mopping floors, folding laundry, and cooking while holding a baby. She took the ring off.

Soon after the clip exploded, suspicious internet sleuths starting digging into little details that seemed a bit off: tile patterns, T-shirt brands, architectural features, and more. They quickly proved where the video came from: it was Chinese antifamily, antinatalist propaganda made with a foreign actress, produced for an American audience.

Uniparty elites know that these messages are for chumps. College-educated, wealthy Americans (including liberal ones) are the most likely group to be raising their kids as married parents. Our elites are actively antagonistic to promoting normal family formation in the common culture (they don't want to "exclude" or "shame" anybody!), but of course they practice married parenting in their private lives. In the 1980s and '90s, conservatives fought for the common culture, especially regarding the family, but for the last twenty years, it has seemed as though we have given up. We can't afford to.

An overtly child-hostile culture permeates cities such as DC and San Francisco. That was driven home to me when I walked by Swampoodle Park in a hip neighborhood in DC. It's a tiny park, less than a quarter of an acre, and on its edge sits a long, narrow caged-in structure. The structure is about twenty feet tall, and inside it is a labyrinth with platforms and nets. This is the "playground"—the other 90 percent of the park is an open area set aside as a dog park.

This image—children cooped up in a literal cage so that the canine "progeny" of childless "dog parents" can run about—perfectly sums up the antifamily culture shaping legislation, regulation, and enforcement throughout our sprawling government.

We have a culture *and* an economy that are hostile to family formation. Neither the private sector nor the government takes the need to encourage family formation into account in decision making: on the contrary, both the public and private sector do much to damage family formation in service of other priorities. The way things stand now, federal regulations demand that builders study the impact of a major construction project such as a pipeline, highway, or dam on the future population of an animal such as the Kings River pyrg snail or the snail darter fish but not its impact on the future population of America's own children.

The time is ripe for the Party of Creation to take the offensive in the culture war, in defense of the traditional family and, frankly, of the happiness of a desperate and lonely generation that has been sold a bill of goods and increasingly knows it.

Making a Home Is Real Work

Winning the future for America's families requires more than tax tweaks; it requires elevating the dignity and purpose of the home.

Having more women working has often been presented as the forward-thinking option, supporting women's desires. In fact, we've course corrected so far that we've ignored many women's actual preferences.

Some "conservative" economists blindly set the number of women in the workforce as a universally positive goal, the same way that the Biden administration and the Party of Destruction do. But having more women working isn't axiomatically good, because large numbers of women with kids at home *prefer* to support their families as homemakers or to work part-time (over 70 percent, according to one recent study from the Institute for Family Studies). The Party of Creation supports mothers who choose to stay home with their kids and families that live off of the income of a single traditional breadwinner. Women should be able to work if they want to, but what the Uniparty refuses to admit is that we're now in a society full of women who feel as though they have to work when they'd prefer to orient their life around their family. The polling data back this up.

The problem is that we live in a country that has systematically devalued household work. In a republic, the familial hearth (and the role of mothers in particular) was to be exalted. But the Party of Destruction has ensured that women are ignored by the tools that policy makers use to understand and manage the economy and everything else. According to Lyman Stone, "our data collection institutions are structurally biased against home-producers, disproportionately mothers: their production of goods and services doesn't count for anything in official data." He points out that if a mom were to start a small business and charge her husband for all of her services, measured GDP would rise, with no real change in economic activity.

This isn't an accident. The Left meticulously constructs policies that favor two-income households and constantly promotes a culture that discourages women from working in the home. Under the guise of "equality," our culture, educational system, and economy reward and incentivize work outside the home over work within it.

The Left's approach to family policy is simple: to pretend that women's work at home counts for nothing and should be actively discouraged, and so build policies that actively reward two-income households and child care in state-regulated day cares.

We need to take the opposite approach, ensuring that family policy proposals don't punish traditional single-breadwinner families (*under any circumstances*) and finding ways to recognize and encourage home production (and reproduction!). Whereas the Left is fighting for corporate-run day cares and advantages for woke capital, we should advocate for policies that advantage family-run in-home day cares and remove regulatory barriers from home businesses, especially those involved in food production.

Even as we fight back against the erasure of American women at home, we need to serve families in which Mom continues to work. Employers are disincentivized from making it easy for moms to have their kids close by at work. It's not a matter of the noise—especially since the rise of great noise-canceling headphones, this is hardly a problem! The issue is that between the onerous regulations of child care centers and the poor tax treatment for on-site day care and nannies, employers are incentivized to force the separation of the women working for them from their children. Those who bear this burden most acutely are not high-powered girlboss executives (who can afford a nanny or au pair) but working-class moms at the other end of the pay scale. We also need to fight regulations that trap women into coming back to work. Today the Family and Medical Leave Act (FMLA), which provides for unpaid maternity leave, punishes mothers who choose to leave the workforce afterward, requiring them to pay back thousands of dollars of medical care premiums (whereas someone using FMLA for an injury has no such requirement).

Tax breaks or subsidies for families, by themselves, cannot move the needle on improving fertility rates (though the evidence suggests that they can induce would-be parents to get married). In a review of family policy around the world, Heritage Foundation scholars found that while government policies that penalize parents can have a dramatic effect on lowering birth rates, reversing these policies or offering even generous public benefits to families does not significantly induce parents to have more kids; inevitably, these benefits amount to a tiny fraction of the total cost (including labor) of raising kids.

The biggest headwind against fertility is not this or that government policy but prosperity itself: the wealthier a society is, the greater the opportunity cost involved in raising kids. Choosing to bring children into the world in developed societies is not an economic calculation but an act of faith and love.

Rejecting decadence means making a conscious choice not to maximize our own comfort, efficiency, and independence. In a culture in which everyone else is making the opposite decision, forming a family feels like a risky choice and not a natural one. We have to do all we can to make it easier for parents to make that choice. The more we do that, the more we can win the cultural norms back from the Party of Destruction's antifamily propaganda.

The Party of Creation is literally more (pro)creative. As the economist (and mother of eight) Catherine Pakaluk showed in her beautiful study *Hannah's Children: The Women Quietly Defying the Birth Dearth*, choosing to have a large family is ultimately about valuing children in and of themselves above "a more comfortable lifestyle," usually done as an act of faith. As the rest of America hastens toward decadence, conservatives and religious believers are increasingly diverging from the herd with higher levels of marriage, lower rates of divorce, and larger numbers of children.

And so, even as we kill the economic and technological snakes strangling the American family at the material level, we must also cut off the snake that tempts us in the same way the serpent did in the Garden of Eden: by tempting our hearts away from worshipping and upholding the right things. We must embrace the home as not just a place where two parents and 2.1 kids happen to reside but as a sacred site of immortal value and irreplaceable work.

Creative Abundance over Nihilist Decadence

The good news is that the seeds of renewal are scattered across the country and many have already taken root. There are so many people, from young couples getting married and having children to sitting US senators, who are working to renew the American family.

For every antinatalist would-be girlboss or carefree playboy, there is another twentysomething who has seen through the charade and wants to set into the deep in search of meaning, connection, marriage, and children. In magazines and online social spaces where they gather, the case against the hookup culture, dating apps, chemical contraception, and other liturgies of the culture of despair is stronger than ever.

I know this is true because when I arrived at the Heritage Foundation in 2021, I was determined to place us at the center of that work.

Before we could lead, though, we had to take a cold, hard look at our own policies. Over the past few years, we have doubled our paid maternity leave policy to what I think is the most generous of any conservative think tank. We also increased paternity leave, so fathers have the chance to help their wives recover from labor and spend those precious first weeks at home with their children. We adopted policies that include some work-from-home and part-time, flexible solutions, so that young Heritage Foundation parents have the choice to do what is best for their families.

Already, it's paying off in a big way. Over the past couple of years, there has been a Heritage baby boom, with baby showers and new birth announcements almost every week. At the same time, we are retaining more brilliant, young, talented conservative thinkers, who could make more money elsewhere or in the private sector but who value our family-first culture and mission.

Now we are working with partners at the state level, where a lot of the outstanding work in family policy has been going on already. As of 2023, twenty-four states have removed all sales tax on disposable diapers, including Colorado, Indiana, and Virginia. Tennessee, under

Governor Bill Lee's leadership, has become the first state in the nation
to provide free diapers to families on TennCare (the state Medicaid program), offering half of the diapers a baby needs for the first two years
of life. Since the *Dobbs* decision, many states have also been working
to expand Medicaid for needy pregnant mothers and babies. And in
2021, Massachusetts introduced the country's first universal tax credit
for children and other dependent family members, which has since been
expanded with bipartisan support to remove the cap on the number of
children it provides for.

Moreover, states are partnering with the vast network of pregnancy
resource centers that the pro-life movement spent decades building.
These centers provide new moms with loving encouragement as well as
tangible support with everything from pregnancy tests to ultrasounds,
parenting classes, adoption referrals, diaper banks, help signing up for
social services, and more. Beginning with Mississippi in 2017, at least
eighteen states are now partnering with these networks and providing
them with tax credits or state social spending. Florida, for example,
increased its support for these centers from $4.5 million to $25 million from 2022 to 2023 alone—and Tennessee from $3 million to
$20 million.

But this is easier said than done. As in so many other areas, conservatives have long extolled the *idea* of the family while neglecting the forces
undermining and tearing apart so many *actual* families or preventing
them from being formed in the first place. Unfortunately, some of them
still don't understand what time it is. When confronted with data on
the crisis of family formation and working-class men's marriageability,
some want to celebrate this as freedom: "Americans have voted with their
wallets. . . . More women have professional aspirations, more young adults
want to spend more time childless and single, and more adults of all ages
prefer a more comfortable lifestyle that often requires two incomes," wrote
Scott Winship, a former director of the Social Capital Project. Ignoring
the loss of meaning, unhappiness, and loneliness (not to mention the war
on a conservative pattern of life), wax-museum conservatives point to
consumer choice and wealth. They betray no understanding of the stakes.

Thankfully, the decadence of wax-museum conservatives dooms them to obsolescence. American parents of all stripes support an agenda that recognizes their vital service to America's future and supports them. A recent study by the Ethics and Public Policy Center found massive support for a pro-family agenda by Democratic, independent, and Republican parents alike, with substantial majorities of Republicans approving not only cultural interventions such as banning smartphones in classrooms and age verification for access to online pornography but also generous economic benefits for working families, such as state property tax credits for families, a state-funded paid leave program for new parents, and state-funded education savings accounts for kids. A head-in-the-sand approach to family policy isn't just wrong on the merits; it is also political suicide.

But family policy is about a lot more than just policy and politics; it's about spiritual renewal. We have built a society that alienates each generation from the previous one. Many young American adults today have never seen a dead body and never held a newborn baby. Becoming a parent fills you with a real sense for the impermanence and fragility of life. Sociologists such as Mary Eberstadt have shown huge correlations among singleness, fatherlessness, childlessness, atheism, and revolutionary anger and, inversely, among marriage, family, children, growing faith, and a conservative attitude toward social change. The victory of abundance over decadence begins in that spark of transcendent hope that comes with holding your new baby in your arms.

Neither the cost disease socialists nor the wax-museum conservatives can deliver on the abundance agenda. The New Conservative Movement's vision of an America brimming with flourishing families, raising their kids, and working productively, with affordable housing and other necessities, full of babies and of Sabbath rest, is enormously attractive. We shouldn't get in our own way in articulating that vision to the American people, celebrating it in our culture, and adopting the policies to help it happen.

CHAPTER 4

Schools Should Teach Piety

The only foundation for a useful education in a republic is to be laid in Religion. Without this there can be no virtue, and without virtue there can be no liberty, and liberty is the object and life of all republican governments.

—Benjamin Rush

'll state it extra clearly for the FBI: I am a parental rights extremist.

The single most important thing we can do for education is to ensure that every taxpayer dollar spent on education—federal, state, and local—follows a child to the school of his or her parents' choice.

For most parents, universal school choice is important because it helps them do right by their kids. But for our country, the stakes are even higher; it's a battle for the future of America.

What may surprise you to learn, then, is that as strongly as I care about parental rights, I don't think our current educational crisis is just *about parental choice*; we're fighting to reassert our rights because of a deeper crisis.

The current educational crisis does not really arise from a fundamental disagreement about rights, about whether a parent or a teacher should educate a child. In a healthy society, it would be both. The problem is that our schools have been transformed from institutions designed to cultivate children's souls into godless assembly lines meant to shape obedient little comrades who think morality is a construct and nature is an illusion.

Right now, parents' rights must be jealously guarded because America's teachers have gone insane. The reason many parents are having to reassert their rights is that teachers are trying to enforce a truly radical agenda, one that assumes that reality is a social construct.

We have to restore reality-based education.

In my heart, I'm an educator. It's a vocation more than it is a profession or a job. In my case, a contemplated career detour from a university job into an administrative role at a prestigious college prep school turned into a calling from God: to start a classical Catholic school in my hometown of Lafayette, Louisiana.

As a historian, I've always drawn inspiration from America's profound heritage of education. In many ways, education made this country. Our first university, set up so that America would have its own learned clergy, was founded only sixteen years after the landing at Plymouth Rock. Only a few years later, we had our first printing press and the first book printed in British America, the *Bay Psalm Book*. Then in 1647, the Massachusetts colonists passed the Old Deluder Satan Law, establishing the first public education in the New World, aimed at ensuring the literacy of the citizenry.

The Puritans recognized that education was a matter of the highest public importance, vital for the spiritual health of the commonwealth. Learning to read meant learning to think for oneself, to draw inspiration and direction from God's Word and the wisdom of the ages, and to participate in an increasingly skilled and commercial society. Broad literacy was the precondition for a republican form of government in which ordinary citizens had a real say in political debate.

The early American colonists understood what every wise person throughout history has realized: that at the end of the day, all education is moral education. Our forebears believed that school wasn't just about memorizing facts; it was about shaping character.

But sometime between the Old Deluder Satan Law and the twenty-first century, we forgot this truth.

During the covid-19 pandemic, public schools around the country went remote. With families stuck at home under strict lockdowns, kids logged on to Zoom from their kitchen tables. For many parents, it was their first time experiencing what was going on inside their kids' classrooms, and it alarmed so many of them that it almost single-handedly led to a revolution in schooling in America.

Honestly, for most parents, the wokeness they encountered—critical race theory in history class, gender ideology in biology—was only the tip of the iceberg. They saw their kids struggling and failing to learn from teachers who were strung out and unprepared at best, indifferent, jaded, and crazed with outlandish ideas at worst. They experienced the bizarre methods that "education experts" prescribed to teach math and the surreal vacuum at the heart of how reading and writing are taught.

It's easy to think that the problem was just remote school. But the truth goes much deeper.

Though few parents were themselves teachers, they intuited that something was fundamentally rotten about this whole enterprise.

They were right.

A Century-Long Conspiracy

It might seem to average American parents as though our current educational environment is a passing fad. In fact, it's the result of a hundred years of plotting by progressives who want to create generations of obedient drones. For more than a century, the Party of Destruction has zeroed in on the education system as the key institution of social transformation. From Plato's *Republic* on down, philosophers and revolutionaries interested in remaking the world in their image of utopia have realized that reshaping young minds is a prerequisite for success.

The Party of Destruction's long march through all of America's institutions emanates from its biggest stronghold: the public education system, teachers colleges, and universities. They are led by a group of administrators, donors, education theorists, and teacher foot soldiers of the sort C. S. Lewis called "the Conditioners" in his warning about dystopian progressivism, *The Abolition of Man*.

Beginning in the early twentieth century, an entirely alien and hostile philosophy of education began its march through our institutions of education, led by Conditioners such as John Dewey. Those Conditioners—who claimed the title of Progressives at the time—realized that the tradition of American education, steeped in the Bible, Anglo-American history, and Western culture stood in the way of their aspiration to use the education system, in Dewey's words, as "the fundamental method of social progress and reform." The Conditioners took on the role of cultural barbarians, burning to the ground—mostly figuratively but increasingly literally—the statues, icons, and touchstones of our cultural inheritance.

The Conditioners first mounted a direct assault on the tradition of American education, and only partially succeeded. In that round, they took control of almost every teachers college and many public schools, but they failed to make public education compulsory or to mandate the total removal of anything touching Christianity in public classrooms (though they made a concerted effort on both fronts).

But the Conditioners' indirect effort was much more successful. The soft underbelly of American civilization has often been its commitment to what is immediately practical and "useful." So the Conditioners realized that if they set aside their overt social engineering for a moment, they could make the case that the liberal arts and the Western tradition were not *useful* to a modern industrial society and that schools should instead focus on teaching methods and skills such as critical thinking and training in science, technology, engineering, and mathematics (STEM). Once education had been sufficiently emptied of anything substantive from the American tradition (in the name of mere technique), a new philosophy of moral formation could quietly take its place.

This philosophical shift has led to creating new generations of shallow people who don't value the permanent things. It's bigger than just a few bad apples or underfunded institutions; it's a pervasive philosophical problem. The political theorist Patrick Deneen discovered that his students, even at enormously selective schools, were brilliant know-nothings with a "pervasive ignorance of western and American history, civilization, politics, art and literature." That wasn't an accident but the successful outworking of an educational system that aimed to produce "cultureless ciphers who can live anywhere and perform any kind of work without inquiring about its purposes or ends," ideal cogs in a globalist, Uniparty economic system. "In such a world, possessing a culture, a history, an inheritance, a commitment to a place and particular people, specific forms of gratitude and indebtedness . . . are hindrances and handicaps."

While Deneen was writing about his students at an elite university, you can see the same phenomenon at work in Oregon's public schools. According to the state's 2021 K–12 Social Science Standards, traditional US civics instruction accounts for only a sixth of the overall graduation requirement. The rest is taken up by modules in areas such as Ethnic Studies, Tribal History, and Genocide Studies, focused on concepts such as "identity" and "resistance," in which teachers are instructed to "discuss incidents and types of oppression," making sure to "attend to trauma-informed and social emotional learning." One student I spoke to said that in lieu of a traditional freshman history class, his Portland high school had imposed a yearlong seminar on the radical leftist historian Howard Zinn's *A People's History of the United States.*

Thus, when students graduate and become antifa activists tearing down a statue of George Washington, throwing Molotov cocktails at police stations, and shouting anti-Semitic slogans, the problem is not that they didn't pay attention in school; it is that they did.

In the same year that he wrote *The Abolition of Man*, Lewis wrote an allegorical story or "fairy-tale," *That Hideous Strength*, reflecting the same themes. *That Hideous Strength* and *The Abolition of Man* are often regarded as Lewis's major statements on modern science and technology and on the roots of totalitarianism.

Yet both works are centered on traditional institutions of education. That was not simply Lewis, an Oxford don, writing about what he knew. Lewis foresaw that a totalitarian rewiring of society required not just new technologies of society control but also the inculcation of a fundamentally revolutionary vision of the human person through the educational system. Society would literally need to be reprogrammed to accept its new masters.

Rule 1: Tradition Is Oppressive

What every faction of the Party of Destruction shares is the belief that all human values are ultimately arbitrary; that the ideas, symbols, traditions, and morals shaping a human society are something made up by that society and therefore something that can be remade to transform society. This is why the first rule of progressive education is that education is about "breaking free" of tradition.

Progressives are willing to do anything to make sure people get with that program. My family would know. In Louisiana, Progressivism came hard after the Cajun way of life. Today, Governor Huey Long (1893–1935)—"The Kingfish," as he liked to call himself—is often regarded as a kind of populist. And certainly he had the common touch in his campaigning. But he was at heart a Progressive: he made his start suing large corporations, using new antitrust laws passed by Progressive reformers, and he supported the Progressive John Parker for governor before turning against him as a rival. His causes were Progressive causes.

What's ironic is that leftists like to pitch themselves as champions of "unassimilated" minorities. The reality is that they've always been brutally imperialist in their efforts to erase "oppressive" conservative beliefs. Certainly, some of the traditions (such as dirt roads) that Long swept away needed changing. But he was hostile to the Cajuns. He viewed our way of life as fundamentally backward, part of what made Louisiana so "medieval." And he hated our resistance to the centralization of power (for our own good, of course), our indifference to "modernization," our holding true to our language and our faith.

To teach your children a way of speaking is the same as to teach them a way of seeing the world. In our proud French heritage, the Party of Destruction saw a resistance to assimilation and participation in the broader US economy. In our Catholic faith, it saw mere superstition. In our strong communities, it saw a suspicion of outsiders, a bulwark against openness and cosmopolitanism. In our rural way of life, it saw nothing but inefficient industry and a waste of human capital.

And so it tried to destroy us. The Louisiana Constitution of 1921 (overseen by state elites, including the Progressive governor) had banned Cajun French from being taught in schools. Huey Long went a step further.

One of his claims to Progressive fame is that he gave away free textbooks to all students and increased the percentage of students going to public school dramatically. But my own grandfather, PaPa Pete, remembered it a bit differently. The textbooks were exclusively in English, and the public school reforms were designed to undermine Cajun culture and the system of Catholic diocesan schools.

PaPa Pete remembered the humiliation when, in the first or second grade, all of the textbooks were switched out one day. It wasn't that he couldn't speak or read English (though Cajun French was his first language). It was the message it was sending to the ordinary folks of Opelousas: you're backward, your people are nobody rubes, get with the program, we're in charge. He hated Huey Long for it till the day he died: "In our own state that *we founded*, this sonofabitch was telling us we didn't matter."

Pat Buchanan, writing twenty years ago, saw that the Conditioners aimed to do to all of America what Huey Long and the Progressive movement had tried to do to the Cajuns. Of the cultural carnage wreaked by the Left's march through our institutions, Buchanan observed:

Destroy the record of a people's past, leave it in ignorance of who its ancestors were and what they did, and one can fill the empty vessels of their souls with a new history, as in *1984*. Dishonor or disgrace a nation's heroes, and you can demoralize its people. . . .

Many of the institutions that now have custody of America's past operate on the principles of Big Brother's Ministry of Truth: drop down the "memory hole" the patriotic stories of America's greatness and glory, and produce new "warts-and-all" histories that play up her crimes and sins, revealing what we have loved to be loathsome and those we have revered to be disreputable, even despicable. Many old heroes have not survived the killing fields of the New History. [The] Ultimate goal: Destroy patriotism, kill the love of country, demoralize the people, deconstruct America. History then will no longer unite and inspire us, but depress and divide us into the children of victims and the children villains of America's past.

It's no coincidence that no region in the country delivered a higher percentage of votes for Buchanan in the 1992 election than did Acadiana. We knew exactly what he was talking about. It just took the rest of the country thirty years to catch up.

Rule 2: Dishonor Your Parents

If you stop to think about it, it may seem odd that "Honor your father and mother" is considered important enough to feature in the Ten Commandments, surrounded by warnings about murder and adultery. But on reflection it makes perfect sense; our entire posture toward life is determined by whether we have proper respect for the deeds of the past.

That's why, at first glance, there is something deeply strange in the fact that the areas of education that have most given themselves over to the Conditioners are not the hard sciences (the strongholds of skepticism and the Party of Destruction in Lewis's day) but fields such as English and my own discipline of history.

After all, these subjects, by their nature, *demand piety*. The humanities should naturally resist the progressive educational goal of rejecting the past, because the humanities are *traditional*, dealing in the language, stories, and symbols handed down to us. What is a language but a tradition of speech? Almost by definition, the utterances we use to make words and the rules that form a grammar are arbitrary—indeed, there are thousands and thousands of human societies, each of which does them differently. Similarly with history: going back into the mists of time, billions of things have "happened." The stories that we tell about where our people come from are part of a tradition of storytelling about our history.

It's a sign of how corrupt our modern education system is that the humanities are the most antitraditional fields now. When the humanities are oriented toward *piety* and reverence, along with a desire to move through a particular society's traditions toward the permanent things and big-T Truth, they attract the sort of teacher who inspires his or her students toward love and gratitude of their inheritance. Looking back later in life at my own education in a Lafayette public school, I realized that that had been the spark of my own love of learning: teachers whose love of Shakespeare, Greek mythology, and Civil War history was sincere and infectious.

In an educational system premised on piety, schools act *in loco parentis*: they are tasked with taking responsibility for the kids in their charge with the same fidelity and care that their parents would demonstrate. But the Conditioners have a very different idea of *in loco parentis*: they want to *replace* parents, to replace the tradition parents are trying to hand on with a very different one, like a cuckoo kicking another bird's babies out of the nest to replace them with its own. What unites the various educational factions of the Party of Destruction is the abolition of inheritance. No longer are students the dignified heirs of a culture and a way of life that form a foundation upon which they can stand; instead they are taught that their value is now as cogs in an economic apparatus or as minirevolutionaries serving some utopian vision or another.

Precisely because the humanities are where an important handing on happens, the Conditioners seized on them as a tool of social manipulation: disrupt how language, culture, and history are handed on, raise children whose attitude toward their inheritance is one of scorn instead of gratitude, and you can destroy a tradition in a single generation.

Of course, in the process, these academic fields will wither and die. If not motivated by a sense of the past as a cherished storehouse of wisdom, the study of literature, history, and art becomes nothing more than an instrument for criticizing society, not something valuable in its own right. The result of critical race theory approaches such as the 1619 Project (now in thousands of schools) is not kids who love a *different* history but kids who don't see the point of history at all. Lewis wrote of the self-defeating nature of this enterprise, "To 'see through' everything is the same as not to see."

It should also go without saying that institutions unprepared for moral education are also unprepared for the education of any other aspects of the human person. Even measuring the wrong things, as public schools do, national progress in eighth-grade math and reading reversed around 2012 before plunging as never before after the pandemic. Teachers' unions, protecting their own convenience over the well-being of America's children to keep lockdowns and remote school going (for *two years* in some places!), threw kerosene on a fire that was already raging.

Rule 3: The Rules of Nature Are Made to Be Broken

Given the Conditioners' rejection of any unchosen authorities (including tradition and reality), it's unsurprising that they eventually got around to discarding nature itself. What is a man? What is a woman? To the Party of Destruction, these created beings are merely arbitrary lumps of matter to be rearranged at will. It was inevitable that gender ideology would infiltrate and take over our schools. It's not really the product of cultural Marxism or a conspiracy but something more fundamental.

To say that man is *for* women and vice versa, even simply biologically or grammatically, is to make a claim about the meaning of life, the nature of the family, and the purpose of the body. Such a claim is necessarily limiting. It implies that men and women can't lead exactly the same kind of life, that kids need both of their parents, that institutions that support a man, a woman, and their children have a kind of priority that no other configuration can possibly have. The so-called gender binary *is* "exclusionary" in the sense that any truth is exclusionary of falsehood. If you are committed to "inclusion" above all else, and if you define public schooling in terms of total inclusion, your system is committed to disintegration from the start.

Gender was simply the last domino to fall, after the community, the nation, the human person, the faith, the West, and every other value had already been bulldozed.

By reimagining the human person as merely another animal free of any spiritual core, we've also eliminated the ideas of meaning and dignity. In *The Abolition of Man*, C. S. Lewis called the products of this kind of education "men without chests." The Conditioners sought to remake our children in their own perverted image and were surprised that their experiment produced not a Nietzschean Overman but a confused, anxious, ignorant generation. As Lewis wrote so powerfully, "We make men without chests and expect of them virtue and enterprise. We laugh at honor and are shocked to find traitors in our midst. We castrate and bid the geldings be fruitful."

In Lewis's description, the castration (of virtue, honor, and vitality) was intended to be symbolic. We have sunk so far that it is, in states such as Oregon, not a metaphor. The ultimate poisoned fruits of our public education system are the kids with sullen eyes and purple hair who know all about "their pronouns" but don't know how pronouns work in English grammar. Lewis's "men without chests" have been joined in a twisted mirror by "women without breasts."

What gender ideology has done to an American generation is something so damaging that it serves as a condensed symbol of the bankruptcy of the entire institution. America's public school system, as a whole, is beyond saving.

What the Party of Destruction doesn't want you to know is not just that American parents have had enough but that they're fighting back—and winning—all over the country.

Yiatin Chu never had any intention of becoming an education activist. But when New York mayor Bill de Blasio announced a plan to scrap the traditional merit test–based admissions to New York's elite public magnet schools in the name of racial equity, she decided she had to get involved. De Blasio's plans went beyond just scrapping the standardized test for New York's best public high schools; he also sought to defund New York's public gifted and talented programs.

As with similar efforts in San Francisco and northern Virginia, those changes were justified in the name of racial equity. The Conditioners hate these programs, because they expose the manifest failures of public elementary education and underline the importance of family structure and culture on student outcomes.

But Yiatin and many others like her couldn't help but notice who specifically was being punished: the Asian families who qualified for the programs in disproportionate numbers, despite (in New York City) experiencing identical rates of poverty as blacks and Hispanics. And she fought back, running for and winning a school board seat and cofounding PLACE NYC, a nonprofit that organizes parents to fight for merit-based public school programs in New York City. They successfully stopped de Blasio's machinations in their tracks.

There are parents, especially moms, all over the country who were radicalized by the experience of public education over the past several years, fighting and winning school board seats in order to advance curriculum transparency, ban Critical Race Theory from classrooms, protect merit-based programs, prevent teacher activists from concealing children's "gender transitions" from parents, and otherwise restore parental rights.

Yiatin was able to fight back inside the system. But she's in a minority. In huge numbers, parents are opting for an even more radical solution to do what is best for their kids: withdrawing them from the public school system altogether.

In 1973, there were fewer than thirteen thousand American kids being schooled at home. During the pandemic, more than 11 million kids were homeschooled. And parents, encouraged by the wealth of resources now available for pupils, liked what they saw: even accounting for the temporary surge, homeschooling is up 30 percent since before the pandemic. And while the original homeschoolers were largely those with highly defined religious or philosophical values who were ill served in public schools, homeschooling has gone mainstream, with parents expressing a wide variety of motivations.

Studies suggest that the public school population has dropped a substantial 5 percent since the pandemic, representing millions of students who have exited the broken public school system and are beginning to fundamentally change the culture of education in America.

I didn't have a revolution in American schooling in mind when I started John Paul the Great Academy in Lafayette, Louisiana, along with my good friend Father Bryce Sibley, a brilliant theologian and parish priest with a rock-ribbed commitment to the Catholic faith. But we stumbled into a small role in a much more important movement, one that, it is no exaggeration to say, may help save Western civilization.

The implicit American understanding of education is that it's meant to shape children to the needs of their future careers or a future, more "progressive" society, who will evolve beyond their parents, past, and faith. Even conservatives often talk about growing up as though it's about separation and accumulation.

Classical education restores an older understanding of education. It's about honoring your parents, not superseding them; carrying the torch of tradition, not burning down the family home. Drawing inspiration from Greek and Roman academic traditions, classical education seeks to ground students in the good, the true, and the beautiful. Its highest aim is to form virtuous students grounded in the best of the Western canon.

Classical schools instruct students through the sequence known as the *trivium*, guiding them through grammar, logic, and rhetoric. Students first establish a knowledge base, then learn how to evaluate arguments, and finally learn how to express their thoughts articulately.

At the heart of classical education is its view of the human person. It sees students not as learning machines or future cogs in some great industrial gear but as precious beings made in the image of God. Students must be led to the font of knowledge by the involvement of all of their faculties: their intellects, yes, but also their morals, their sense of beauty, and their affections. Classical educators see ourselves as shepherds of our students, ultimately leading them toward a knowledge of the heart and not merely of the head. We want to teach our students the right things to love.

Classical education steeps students in the great works of literature, philosophy, history, and science—what the poet Matthew Arnold called "the best which has been thought and said." Instead of Critical Race Theory and Marxist claptrap, children learn about Greece and Rome, William Shakespeare and the Renaissance, Jane Austen, Emily Dickinson, and the glory of the American founding.

Classical education is interested in more than forming good students; its charge is forming students who are good.

This movement is designed to recover the past, but it's essentially forward looking. If you look through the roster of the thousands of classical schools and the institutions established to support them, I don't think you'll find a single one older than fifty years old, with the vast majority founded in the last thirty years.

I don't think my story, and the story of John Paul the Great Academy, is atypical. Father Sibley and I did not set out to establish a classical school per se; we felt a divine calling to restore the tradition of Catholic education in our corner of Louisiana after the devastation wrought by Hurricane Katrina. But as we developed the concept of the school and its curriculum, we realized that we were facing an unexpected problem: even though parents rejected the moral values of modern schools, they hadn't unlearned the incentive structure of progressive education.

As a headmaster, I was shocked by how deeply progressive philosophy had penetrated even into communities of informed, educated, devout parents. They were parents who viscerally opposed political correctness and cultural Marxism, who were (or thought they were) conscious of the Conditioners' machinations against their kids. But they had an Achilles' heel: "college preparation."

What does college preparation mean, practically? It doesn't just mean mastering reading, writing, mathematics, science, and so on up to a certain level. In secondary education, "college preparation" means preparing to excel at the mechanics of going to college, including being admitted to elite and selective schools and gaining college course credit. Though seemingly innocuous, "college preparation" has established an institutional chokehold on the best schools and the most educated parents, regardless of their espoused education philosophy or religious values.

Before he founded the Classic Learning Test (CLT), Jeremy Tate was a college counselor at a prestigious Catholic school near Baltimore. He recalled his immense difficulty in getting his students to take courses on philosophy and Catholic apologetics, taught by some of the best teachers in the school. Despite their avowed interest in the subjects, his students demurred that there were no Advanced Placement (AP) exams for them. If they took them, not only would they be sacrificing college credit, they would be lowering their GPA even if they got an A; their school, like many others, awarded extra GPA points for AP classes.

When he looked around, Jeremy realized that almost everything by which his school measured and defined success was controlled by one entity. It wasn't the parents, the teachers, the school's board, or even the archdiocese; it was the College Board, whose power and influence over American education is subtle but immense. Like many college prep–focused schools, including Christian ones, Tate's school prided itself on its SAT scores, the number of its National Merit Scholars, and the number of AP courses it offered—all of which were controlled by the College Board.

As a headmaster, I found myself often referencing Archbishop J. Michael Miller's "Five Essential Marks of Catholic Schools" in his book *The Holy See's Teaching on Catholic Schools*, one of which is that Catholic schools "are genuine communities of faith" that represent the greatest alternative to our "individualistic society"; genuine communities, shaped by the bonds of relationship, duty, and love in which the inculcation of culture really happens.

But when I looked at the AP course standards, I realized that there was no way I could let our community be controlled by the College Board's puppet strings. The AP United States History course has no use for the biographies of American statesmen such as Benjamin Franklin and James Madison. Its English Literature and Composition exam requires no knowledge or love of any literature from our beautiful tradition, focusing solely on cultivating "critical thinking" skills; Shakespeare and Chaucer are optional. The AP European History course has no use for the inconvenient centrality of Christianity, except for highlighting the rise of the liberal state out of the supposed Protestant and Catholic bloodletting of the Thirty Years' War (what the theologian William Cavanaugh calls "the myth of religious violence").

(But while the College Board has no interest in letting American parents have a say in what shapes their kids' heads and hearts, it's tripped over itself to seek input from the Chinese Communist Party. An extraordinary investigation by the National Association of Scholars revealed that the College Board had partnered extensively with the CCP on the development of the AP Chinese Language and Culture Course and even cosponsored the CCP's Confucius Institutes, propaganda outfits hosted in American colleges and high schools.)

One of my hardest initial battles was to convince parents that the formation of their kids, and of their souls, was more important than what passes for "college preparation"; in other words, the subordination of the lessons, curriculum, homework, and lectures to a value system other than the pursuit of truth, goodness, and beauty. We succeeded only because, as a "genuine community of faith," we knew that we could choose to worship only one God, and so we chose the true One.

It goes without saying that, motivated by a love of wonder and of excellence, our kids also did great on the standardized tests.

For this reason, one of the most exciting and important signs of the seriousness of the classical education movement was the development of the Classic Learning Test by Jeremy Tate, which aims to displace the SAT by 2040. It provides rigorous testing of student performance but draws on the best of the classical inheritance, not merely whatever deracinated slop can pass the College Board's sensitivity committee (a real thing). Florida recently announced that its public universities will accept the CLT, and more states will soon follow.

The CLT is only the tip of the iceberg. A forest of institutions is blooming, with a number of national-level associations promoting the movement, Hillsdale College's Barney Charter School Initiative providing resources to help start classical charter schools, the Classical Academic Press publishing textbooks and teacher training, the Paideia Institute (among others) offering online Greek and Latin for homeschools and emerging classical schools, and much else besides. The classical school movement is building an institutional foundation for the next century of American education.

Free Education for a Free Country

One of the things I love about the United States is that it guarantees the finest education in the history of the world to everyone, regardless of birth, family situation, or parental involvement. Throughout history, it has said a lot about society as to which people it believed were "worthy" to be educated. One of the strongest evidences that America was founded on the Christian notion of human dignity, that "all men are *created* equal" (in dignity, by God), has been the country's commitment to realizing the ideal of universal education.

The most powerful tool we have in realizing the ideal of American education is universal school choice, ensuring that every single tax dollar (local, state, and federal) follows a student to the school of his or her parents' choice. School choice is an idea whose time has come, and the progress we are seeing as we go on the offensive is nothing short of breathtaking. The journalist Cara Fitzpatrick even entitled her book on the subject *The Death of Public School: How Conservatives Won the War over Education in America* (from her lips to God's ears!).

Like many other hopeful signs, the turnaround in education began almost without anyone's notice. Probably the apex of the Conditioners' contemporary power was the passage of the No Child Left Behind Act in 2001 and the subsequent attempts to create a Common Core curriculum imposed on school systems all across America, centralizing federal power over education to an unprecedented degree. But because the *money* was still local (despite the Department of Education's increasing attempts to use the purse strings to control American schools), and because features of those actions brought some visibility and accountability to teachers unions, they proved immensely unpopular. In 2015, a bipartisan consensus stripped out the national control elements of No Child Left Behind, and power has increasingly swung back toward the states as parents fight for it.

In a sense, the biggest ally in our fight for universal school choice has been the teachers unions. One can say of them what Burke said of the French revolutionaries: "In the manifest failure of their abilities, they take credit for their benevolence." But while they claim the humanitarian mantel of "professional educators," the teachers unions have been so transparently self-serving, so unconcerned about parental voices and desires, so callous about what is best for students that they have been by far the most effective marketing for universal school choice. Many a red state governor went all in on school choice after being sued by the teachers unions to keep schools closed during the pandemic.

As a result, political pressure toward school choice has exploded. Ten states have passed universal education savings account programs since 2021 alone. In 2023, lawmakers in fifteen states passed bills establishing school choice programs or expanding existing ones, with dozens more states introducing legislation.

The desire to encourage and direct this momentum led us to introduce the Education Freedom Report Card at the Heritage Foundation, now in its third year. The report card tracks educational choice across a number of policies, transparency around curriculum, friendliness toward homeschooling, public school choice, teacher freedom, DEI bureaucrats (that's a negative variable), value to taxpayers, and more. Florida has led the rankings so far, but other states are racing to catch up, with Iowa and Arkansas showing leaps-and-bounds improvements even since last year.

But contrary to the critics of school choice, it does not actually aim at the death of public *schools*. It will disrupt and destroy a public school system that has grown insular, corrupt, and incompetent (as shown by falling test scores across every metric for the past decade almost everywhere in the nation). Universal school choice lifts all boats by ensuring that parents are supported to make the decisions that are best for their kids and creating meaningful competition and market signals to all schools, including public schools.

It's clear why this should be the case just by reasoning from first principles. But social science evidence is already coming in that validates this hypothesis. One big study published in February 2020 as a National Bureau of Economic Research working paper found that increased competition due to school choice led to higher standardized test scores and lower absenteeism and suspension rates in public schools, especially for students with lower family incomes and lower maternal education levels. The Heritage Foundation will continue to monitor student outcomes and advocate for policies that serve parents and students, not the teachers unions.

Just a few years ago, no states had universal school choice. Just this year, there are more than a half-dozen states that have established universal school choice, with more on the way, not to mention dozens of states with more marginal improvements toward parental choice. A revolution in American education has begun.

Education and Piety

Progressive critics have lately charged that support for classical schooling is only the latest Republican plot to undermine teachers unions and
destroy America's public schools. For instance, one such critic, historian
Erin Maglaque, asserted that "the Christian nationalists and neoliberal
free marketeers whose interests have coalesced in the cause of classical
charter schools don't actually care about Petrarch."

These critics have it exactly backward. Everything we are doing,
public and private, to enable school vouchers and parental choice (including public charter schools) is in service of the underlying mission
of the classical education movement. We don't merely seek an exit from
the system; we are coming for the curriculums and classrooms of the
remaining public schools, too. We seek to return American education to
a tradition that encourages the love of beauty, awakens wonder, teaches
gratitude for our republic, and instills piety toward our nation, even as it
teaches a prudent and circumspect history of its flaws. We fight for this
regardless of whether your kids are in a public school, a charter school,
or a private school or homeschooled. Caring about Petrarch is way more
dangerous to the Conditioners than is the illusion of parental choice
in a system whose educational philosophy is secretly controlled by the
College Board.

But for now, we will start with universal school choice. As the classicist James Hankins said in reply to these critics:

> Thanks to the classical education movement, some children,
> at least, will not have to live their lives unable to perceive the
> beauty in Shakespeare's sonnets, Michelangelo's *Pietà*, or Handel's
> *Messiah*. It's a pity so many, trapped in politicized schools, will
> have to endure a diminished humanity. But the door to the
> classical school is open.

In this cataclysmic battle for our remaining institutions, there is no
room for half measures. The single best way to equip men and women

to contend for America's future is to immerse them in the intellectual traditions of the West. This is armor against the modern age of decadence and incoherence, for it reminds us—inspires us—to build and rebuild while our opponents are hell-bent on destruction. It's an education motivated by love and gratitude, which you grasp as soon as you meet the young men and women who are the products of these new institutions of American education.

Our successes in education fill me with tremendous hope for the future of America. We are already on the offensive.

CHAPTER 5

The Economy Should Serve the Country, Not the Other Way Around

As many as possible should share in the ownership of the land and thus be bound to it by economic interest, by the investment of love and work, by family loyalty, by memory and tradition.

—Wendell Berry

The US economy today bears the same resemblance to a system of free enterprise as a movie set does to a real stock exchange: it's a facade.

The Uniparty elite have been selling out the American middle class. Worse, they have been using ordinary Americans' hard-earned savings to do so. Globalization and the hollowing out of the American heartland are not the result of some economic law but of political choices made by our corrupt elites and the avowed enemies of the American way of life in Davos, Brussels, and Beijing. Behind the mask of supposedly capitalistic corporations lies the specter of social control and the destruction of our liberty.

That the "free market process" kept sending American wealth and jobs to China, kept repressing wages, kept driving up the price of assets faster than regular Americans could acquire them, kept bolstering woke corporations and undermining small enterprises, wax-museum conservatives hold not to be a matter of public concern, not something you should actually *do* something about via any actionable policy lever, lest you interfere with the "free market process."

We talk a lot about "the economy," but anyone who studies political language knows that broad words often conceal fuzzy thinking. When was the last time you heard someone ask what the economy was for? The thing we've forgotten is that money and prosperity aren't about mere accumulation and consumption; they're about creating a world in which children can thrive, traditions can continue, and faith can flourish. In other words, the economy was made for people, not the other way around.

The Uniparty will tell you that there's nothing that can be done to stop the war on ownership. The New Conservative Movement recognizes that even as we seek to prudently use the best tools to shape it, having an economy that upholds our way of life is very much an appropriate subject of political action. We must disassemble this sham economy that is funneling money to the parasitical enemies of the American way of life and reassemble the great, productive American economic system of free enterprise and meaningful work, the dynamic engine that drove our prosperity and that is our future.

Globalist Corporatism and Socialism Are Functionally the Same

If socialism descends upon America, where will it come from? In his classic book *Capitalism, Socialism, and Democracy*, famous for introducing the idea of "creative destruction," the economist Joseph Schumpeter (1883–1950) had a surprising answer: the modern corporation.

Schumpeter's analysis focused on a transformation in the business world in the early twentieth century called the *managerial revolution*.

Before the managerial revolution, companies had tended to be run by the families of the entrepreneurs who had started them or at least by people personally trusted by personally involved owners. By the end of the nineteenth century, the United States had some pretty large companies, especially in manufacturing, oil, transportation, and finance. But they were still usually run by the families that owned them (including famous names such as Rockefeller, du Pont, Morgan, and Vanderbilt). The senior ranks tended to be filled with men who had risen through the business, often engineers or salesmen who had in some cases started on the factory floor. And each company was rooted in a particular place and community where it had its headquarters or carried out substantial production. And it went without saying that each was an *American* company, with a vested interest in the continued prosperity and growth of the United States.

The managerial revolution transformed how those companies were run and who was running them. As corporations grew larger and more complex, they required more professional expertise to run; the science of management was born. At the same time, blossoming financial markets and the passage of time led to the diffusion of ownership, with shares in companies held by the general public, institutional investors, and descendants of the founders, who were more interested in high society living than running the family firm.

The result was that power over everyday business decisions passed from entrepreneurs with skin in the game and ties to particular companies and communities to managers and executives whose loyalties rested not in the corporations that employed them but in the profession and process of management itself.

That professional mindset, Schumpeter saw, diverged from capitalism in some important ways. For one thing, it had been developed not in the rough-and-tumble world of business competition but in the college classroom. Universities and business schools initiated would-be titans of management into a rational, scientific, white-collar profession and taught them that their real peers were their fellow managers in business, government, regulatory agencies, philanthropic foundations, and more.

Whereas earlier American executives had cut their teeth in the field, the new managers looked down on blue-collar work. In 1942, only a portion of the leaders of the United States' largest companies had a college degree. By 2017, according to one study, 96 percent had a degree, with 41 percent having a degree from one of a small number of elite schools.

Not only did this new managerial class have no loyalty to the companies they ran (caring more about what their peers were doing), they also had no loyalty to capitalism, to the United States, or to the family. Because they already ran somebody else's company, it didn't really matter who the nominal owner was, whether shareholders, a foreign bank, or the government.

For an entrepreneur, the future of the firm was the future of *his family* and *his community*—each needed the other. For a manager, having a family is a career negative, and if a manager does have kids, the priority isn't getting them to run the business but getting them into an elite university to ease their ascendance within the managerial class. A top manager can't even consider remaining rooted in a local community, when his next opportunity might be a new position in his company's Tokyo office or a lateral move to a new company in New York City.

Schumpeter argued that the managers' rootlessness and disdain for the working class would enhance the popular demand for socialism. Meanwhile, the shell of the modern corporation would supply the practical infrastructure for socialism. Dispense with meaningful private ownership of productive property but keep the managerial process, the rational administration of the firm, the elite university education of the management class, and the perks and rewards that accrue to executives, and the managerial class would keep things humming just fine. The socialist state's overseer is just another "stakeholder" for the managers to please, and besides, they probably went to Harvard together.

During his lifetime, Schumpeter never saw his prediction come true, because history intervened. Faced with the totalitarian threats of Nazism and communism, US businessmen stepped up in the service of their country. During World War II, senior executives voluntarily cooperated with one another and the government to transform the US economy into an "arsenal of democracy." Dollar-a-year men such as former General Motors president Bill Knudsen and the construction magnate Henry Kaiser applied their genius to the production of B-29s and Liberty ships. After the war, they helped build a US economy that was good for families, good for communities, and good for the world.

In the Cold War that followed, even as the managers continued their slow ascendance in American society, there was no question that they needed to stand with the United States and the Free World, if only because the United States' ongoing strength promised to continue to open up new markets and protect their holdings. A Communist revolution in a country such as Vietnam or Cuba tended to be bad for business and detrimental to the value of one's investments. The United States, democracy, capitalism, and corporate profits rose and fell as one.

The New Road to Serfdom

Ironically, it was the United States' victory over communism that set the stage for Schumpeter's vision to come true. After the Cold War ended, not only the Berlin Wall but all kinds of other walls fell, too: fair and reciprocal trade barriers, limitations on financial flows, loyalty to communities, and more. In a process called globalization, US firms sought to make profits all over the world by expanding into new markets, sending factories overseas, running money through international tax havens, developing global supply chains, and employing other new strategies, with the Chinese Communist Party in particular using all kinds of legal and illegal methods to draw in US companies. The interests of corporate managers increasingly diverged from what was good for the United States, its families, and its communities. You can guess which one they pursued.

In an extremely undeveloped society, productivity is plagued by nepotism. The important thing is who you're related to. In the era of globalist corporatism, eventually you end up with the same problem; it's all about who you know. Corporate managers get ahead by making inside deals with would-be regulators, by winning the support of asset managers, and by coordinating with fellow managers at their erstwhile competitors to ensure that competition doesn't take too much of a bite out of profits. It's another *conspiratio*—elites "breathing together" in the sauna or ski chalet.

This pathway is lower risk and higher reward (for the managers) than breaking new ground is, which is one key reason why global growth has been slowing down. According to a US Senate report, "American Investment in the 21st Century," by Senator Marco Rubio, corporate investment in capital equipment and basic research is lower than it's ever been in modern America. Instead, corporations try to dominate their markets, roll up competitors, squeeze suppliers, build regulatory moats, cut deals with governments, and otherwise avoid competition.

In the era of globalist corporatism, outsourcing isn't always about finding cheaper supplies or labor. In many cases, US corporations decide to shutter factories or cut jobs because they've wrangled a special tax break or government handout in another country or because they know that in that country, environmental or safety regulations won't be enforced.

Behind the seemingly capitalist facade of globalist corporatism lies, simply, socialism. The most sophisticated analysts of socialism, including Schumpeter, have understood that some elements of classical socialist ideas, such as public ownership of the means of production and centralized economic planning by government boards, are incidental to its essence. What is important is its aspiration: the effectual control and micromanagement of production decisions to achieve social goals and reengineer society.

The *ends* toward which socialism works have proven to be remarkably flexible, encompassing August Comte's scientific society, Karl Marx's proletarian paradise, Paul Ehrlich's demographic doomerism, and Alexandria Ocasio-Cortez's Green New Deal. Socialism's polestar is its *means*: bureaucratic management oriented toward "rational" planning objectives decided upon by a technocratic elite perched on the commanding heights of society.

Rather than wasting time on organizing the proletariat and other "deplorables" via a popular revolution, social engineers have gotten smart. Using the shared loyalty of the managerial class, they can now engineer a revolution from above.

Step one: Create environmental, social, and governance (ESG) and diversity, equity, and inclusion (DEI) social credit score systems and tie them to investment decisions, inclusion in index funds, or loan terms. Reinforce this with influential and wealthy leftist organizations such as the California Public Employees' Retirement System (CalPERS), the Norwegian sovereign wealth fund, and the Bill and Melinda Gates Foundation demanding that their money managers follow suit.

Step two: Get the managers of the world's largest corporations to declare that due to the principle of maximizing shareholder value, they have no choice but to fully adopt DEI and ESG goals into their business decisions, lest they be penalized by "markets" (money managers), banks (more money managers), and other "stakeholders" (other kinds of managers). Insist that DEI and ESG metrics track suppliers and business partners, so that large corporations can enforce them on small businesses.

Step three: As it becomes impossible to access insurance, a bank account, a loan, equity, or corporate customers without bowing the knee to DEI and ESG, start ratcheting up the process. Exclude whole sectors, such as fossil fuels and firearms. Start including not just diversity or green energy goals but reparations for "historical harms" and "climate injustice" in metrics.

Congrats, comrade manager, you're well on your way to "building socialism." Where is the money to do this coming from? The middle class, out of their small businesses and 401(k)s through slumping growth and out of their pocketbooks through massive inflation. The elite managers, as always, will do just fine.

The Managerial Revolution's Costs Are Invisible Because They're Immeasurable

Despite some first-blush similarities, an entrepreneur and a manager are as radically different as a parent and a babysitter. Because he is an *owner* whose life is wrapped up in his enterprise, the entrepreneur cares about the health of his business as a whole, not simply the bottom line or a quarterly return. But the managerial revolution has separated those overseeing a business from those actually operating it, sometimes by thousands of miles. Bureaucratic management goes hand in hand with a fixation on the measurable. "What gets measured gets managed," right?

Over the past forty years, we have increasingly talked and thought about our economy in terms of a handful of numbers: gross domestic product (GDP) up, inflation down, unemployment down. But it's too easy to game the numbers, to overlook their limitations or what they ignore; to look only at the surface and not into the heart of things.

A number of developments that, when measured by the permanent things, are bad, appear as neutral developments on our usual measures. GDP, for instance, is value neutral. When the CCP opens a Confucius Institute, GDP goes up. When a mom who wants to stay home can no longer afford to do so and joins the workforce while paying someone else to watch her child, GDP goes up. When a municipal government uses taxpayer money to house illegal immigrants in a hotel for months, GDP goes up. When a meth addict breaks a car window to steal camera equipment and the beleaguered photographer dips into her savings to repair the window and buy new equipment, GDP goes up. In fact, almost any time spiritual decay in American life requires the government or private sector to do something that our culture and community once provided, GDP goes up.

Today, economists are baffled: unemployment numbers are near all-time lows; inflation is "being managed." Yet in late 2023, three in four Americans said the economy is "not so good" or "poor."

As usual, the American people are onto something that the professionals have missed. Not ensconced in the ivory tower, they see the changes that have happened even within their own lifetime. They know that the *kinds* of jobs they can now get are not as fulfilling, don't pay as much (once inflation, especially in housing, is priced in), don't offer the kind of stability or growth needed to build a flourishing human life as they once did. They're not the kind of jobs the American Dream is made of. The managers who are running things, focused on pleasing Wall Street analysts and meeting DEI metrics, don't want them to be.

Ordinary Americans know that if they want to start a small business, they'll face an increasingly uneven playing field, competing with Big Tech and politically connected monopolies that have constructed regulatory moats to protect their turf. Every year, the burden of these "rents," the cut of the pie that the government, monopolists, and Big Tech can extract, has been increasing.

Americans know that somehow and in some way, the bar to *own* something that matters—a home, a small business, a work truck, a piece of land that's yours—seems to be a little more out of reach every day.

This isn't an accident. It is all is plainly described on the World Economic Forum website, though pointing this out is labeled by our media as a "conspiracy theory." I suppose in the sense that a conspiracy is supposed to be hidden, it isn't strictly one.

Our globalist elite managers have been pushing us toward a "Great Reset" of the world economy, after which "you'll own nothing, and you'll be happy."

Once, the vast majority of the country's wealth was held in *stuff* that people owned: real estate, productive machinery (capital), valuable commodities, shop inventory, mineral rights, and goods destined for market. While in some cases there might have been deeds, stock certificates, and other financial paperwork, they merely pointed to the ownership of that solid stuff, which was the valuable thing. Those assets were, in the language of finance, illiquid: hard to sell or convert into cash quickly (of course, we remember what Jesus said about building a house upon liquidity). And it was stuff that you had to take care of, that prioritized careful personal attention and maintenance if it was to maintain its value or to grow. Because it was real stuff that existed in a place for a people.

What Carol Roth described as a "new financial world order" seeks to "liberate" the world from being bound to stuff. Ownership of things will be a privilege afforded only to asset supermanagers such as BlackRock and large corporations such as Apple, whose Uniparty loyalty can be depended on. For everyone else, the ability to access a bank account, rent a home, hold down a job, open a business, and more will be determined by a social credit score of the kind China has already deployed. As we saw during the coronavirus pandemic, all of this can be implemented without a shred of "government interference" by corporations' merely following along with the social and political dictates of the Uniparty at the commanding heights of our global financial system.

A Fake Economy Creates Weak People

The biggest problem with this kind of economy is not material and economic; it's spiritual and social. It's like raising kids who never play a real sport, just video games, in which all the consequences are hypothetical. Sports and jobs shape us because their consequences and responsibility are real and personal.

Responsibility makes us grow up. Our republican form of government demands people who take responsibility, both for themselves and for the common good of the republic. It demands institutions that build virtuous habits of working together to solve collective problems without demanding that the dead hand of government fix everything. It demands an economy in which ordinary people have the liberty to meet their own needs and those of their community through their own efforts. Especially since the 1990s, we have been building an economy that is moving farther and farther away from these principles.

A company dominated by managerialism breeds an attitude of fear, compliance, and conformity. The mantra of the owner is "The buck stops here." The mantra of the manager is "I'm sorry, it's company policy."

You can see this subtle transition, which has slowly taken place all over the country, in the career of a software entrepreneur named Andrew Crapuchettes. After a few successful jobs early in his career, he moved to Moscow, Idaho, with some capital to invest and the determination to grow a company in this beautiful college town. A family man and Christian, he wanted to build the kind of company and culture that he wanted to work in. He describes wanting to build a company that blessed its customers, blessed its employees, and blessed its shareholders, in that order. Through friends, he was introduced to some local economists who had a small consulting company of three employees, Emsi. He joined them.

With an initial goal of creating fifty jobs paying over $50,000 in that little town, over the ensuing years, Andrew and his colleagues built a company with more than 250 employees providing labor market data and related services to employers and colleges. Along the way, Emsi had a number of investors: a small private equity investment that helped it scale up, an acquisition by a much larger company (CareerBuilder.com), and then a spin-off. Each of those moves was motivated by sound financial practices and a desire to keep creating more value and growing the business.

In 2018, Emsi was spun off from CareerBuilder.com and sold to Strada Education Network, a $1.2 billion nonprofit foundation. Strada seems to do good work in improving access to higher ed and employment, including things such as cost transparency and skills training. But it's also a classic Uniparty entity. It used to be rooted in Indianapolis, but it's increasingly tied into national elite networks. It controls a huge purse of unaccountable money, and the people it has to keep happy are other Uniparty elites: college presidents, politicians, coastal elite potential donors.

After Strada acquired Emsi, things went great for a while. And then 2020 happened. During the George Floyd riots, the Sauron-like eye of the Uniparty turned on all things DEI. Strada, of course, put out a statement vowing that it would do more to advance racial equity, and it started to pour money into antiracist initiatives. And it asked all of the companies it had invested in to do the same.

Andrew Crapuchettes refused. That unexpected resistance seemingly caused Strada managers to look more closely at the company they had bought; they were alarmed to find that it had a culture that had not been totally HR-ified. People worked together, but they also prayed together and hung out together after hours. At Christmas, the company held a huge community Christmas decoration contest. During covid-19, it refused to impose a vaccine mandate or force its employees to choose between supporting their families and holding by their beliefs. The company had an ethos, and it wasn't a woke one, and that frightened Strada's Uniparty managers. They gave Andrew an ultimatum: you are allowed to be a CEO who is a Christian, but not a Christian CEO.

Andrew chose his faith over his C-suite salary. The reason he had the courage to resist wasn't an accident. His was a character shaped by ownership. He'd had to make thousands of choices before that point where the consequences had been real and immediate, and each challenge and choice had strengthened his resolve, character, and courage.

And Strada sort of blinked. According to Andrew's account, rather than immediately firing him and courting controversy, and having gotten what they needed out of Emsi, it sold off the company to make Andrew someone else's problem.

Unlike Emsi's previous buyers, this one had goals other than simply growing the company or creating jobs. The KKR Global Impact Fund incorporates environmental, social, and governance (ESG) factors into decision making, in support of the United Nations' Sustainable Development Goals. Translation: KKR Global Impact uses middle-class people's retirement funds to advance Uniparty priorities and support for woke companies over profitability, part of an effort to tilt the global financial playing field against free enterprise. By Andrew's telling, the fund engineered a merger for Emsi with one of its portfolio companies doing similar work and—sensing the presence of an unassimilated man—gave Andrew the velvet boot.

KKR wasn't just "advancing equity," though (at least not of the social justice warrior kind). The fund was reportedly in the red in its investment in Emsi's rival company Burning Glass, in part because of the competition. By merging the companies, KKR consolidated the industry and created a little monopoly that also greatly improved its returns on paper, competition be damned.

Why Everything Is Coordinated

Here's a hard truth, though: wokeness isn't the real problem. If it wasn't wokeness that corporations were pushing, it'd be some other crazy anti-human philosophy. The problem is that the very shape of corporate managerial life, which is totally alienated from reality, makes inhuman activity nearly inevitable. It's the underlying institutional revolution that has made wokeness possible—one that replaces hardy free competition, open discussion, and personal ownership with managerial cowardice, hidden coordination, and quiet consolidation; one that allows woke virtue signaling to cover up a total loss of corporate vision and innovation, a turn to decadence and corporate bloat—that is the real threat to our way of life.

What shocked me during the George Floyd riots was not that some woke companies would have something to say but that everyone was coordinated, instantly. It felt like *Invasion of the Body Snatchers*: frozen yogurt chains, sports teams, beer companies, and too-big-to-fail banks, all speaking and walking in lockstep.

What kind of infrastructure lies behind this? The same mechanisms driving instantaneous conformity to BLM drove it for covid-19 vaccine mandates and for "Pride Month" and are in place to do it for whatever the next Uniparty crisis is. But it's not just woke politics; Uniparty managers use the same tools to impose environmental and safety rules (above and beyond what is legally required), to coordinate price increases, to repress wages, to box out potential competition, and otherwise to control the economy outside of free market competition and democratic process.

The puppet strings: a revolving door of college-educated managers with more class loyalty than company (or country) loyalty; networks of Uniparty institutions, especially Fortune 500 companies, consulting firms, business schools, and data brokers, that coordinate ideas and practices; standards and regulations, both private and public, that impose bureaucratic control over all kinds of things; and this managerial stitch-up now undergirded by information technology that makes data sharing, constant surveillance, and hidden coordination easier than ever.

There's a political dimension to this, too. Companies know that even if they make policies that harm the American way of life, wax-museum conservatives will back them to the hilt based on "free market principles." Meanwhile, the Left is raring to regulate and control them, *unless* companies buy them off by preemptively ceding control and by using corporate social responsibility money to fund woke nonprofits and armies of foot soldiers (who do you think pays for all those community organizers?).

This phenomenon has an international component. Globalist corporations go out of their way to please EU regulators and avoid angering the Chinese Communist Party, while taking no heed of what's good for the United States. They'll blackmail US states not to pass religious freedom legislation but won't post a rainbow flag on social media in the Middle East.

As long as there are both the puppet strings of the managerial revolution and this deep political and national asymmetry, our political economy will continue to be possessed by the Uniparty.

The New Conservative Movement is going to send a message: protecting American families and rebuilding a dynamic American economy of productive ownership and family-supporting jobs are more important than movement sloganeering or ideological purity.

At the state level, some leaders are beginning to wake up to the problem. After decades of sending tens of billions of dollars to New York City financiers with no strings attached, adding fuel to the fire of woke capital, last year the state of Florida instituted sweeping restrictions on state investment funds that are designed to protect the interests of everyday Floridians, especially by eliminating ESG investments. Legislators in more than twenty states have introduced bills reclaiming proxy voting power and amending fiduciary duty laws for state retirement systems.

The Great Reset is socialism wearing the modern corporation as a skinsuit. And God-fearing Americans who value their property and liberty have been duped into defending it under the guise of capitalism and free markets. It's time to get real and defend our country, our communities, and our kids.

A Revolutionary Response

What would the Founders have made of the modern financialized corporation? They risked their "lives, fortunes, and sacred honor" in their defense of "life, liberty, and property" (at least before Thomas Jefferson swapped in the more egalitarian "pursuit of happiness") as the fundamental purposes of republican government. But in their day, the largest business enterprises were rooted in particular places and communities: farms, merchant banks, and small factory concerns. There was no analogy to the globe-spanning multinational monopolies of today that derive their value from predatory, anticompetitive regulations and cozy relations with governments.

No analogy except one: the British East India Company. Shortly before the American Revolution, the EIC was in serious difficulty, its profits endangered by turmoil in Bengal and Europe and its fat payments to the Crown. Just like today's managerial elite, the officials of the company had close ties to the British government, the company counting dozens of MPs among its shareholders (Nancy Pelosi would approve).

British prime minister Lord North's solution was a scheme of political and social engineering, the Tea Act of 1773. Trouble had been brewing for years over increased British interference and taxation in the American colonies, including the Townshend Act tax on tea, which clever American merchants had avoided by smuggling in cheaper, poorer-quality Dutch tea. At a single stroke, the Tea Act, which allowed the company to sell tea directly in the United States without paying even the tariffs American importers had to pay, would bail out the East India Company, crush America's thousands of independent merchants, and recondition the American subjects to the Townshend Act tax on tea, which paid the salaries of the Crown's colonial enforcers. We know what the founding generation thought of the East India Company based on their brave actions in Boston Harbor on December 16, 1773, which turned seawater-soaked tea into the fuel of revolution.

The Founding Fathers recognized that globe-spanning corporatist cartels are a thing apart from real American businesses and acted accordingly, in defense of meaningful self-government and free enterprise. And so have great American statesmen ever since.

As governor of New York and later as president, Theodore Roosevelt had to contend with industrial monopolies and large trusts that, much like today's, operated by creating unfair, government-protected advantages and suppressing competition for the benefit of foreign investors, squeezing American businesses and hurting American families. In a 2019 speech, Senator Josh Hawley, a Roosevelt historian, distilled TR's vision into an eloquent phrase: "a republican nation requires a republican economy."

The Founders and Theodore Roosevelt alike were steeped in the West's republican tradition. Thinkers from Plato to Montesquieu taught that the force that destroys republics is corruption, understood as people with power abusing their authority to advance their private interests and destroying the *res publica*, the common good. When the Founders warned against faction, they weren't just talking about political parties: today, we might interpret their concern as being about "special interests." And when those special interests are not just American but globalist, we are in exactly the moment of peril that George Washington warned about in his Farewell Address.

The Future of Our Prosperity

What kind of economy can reinvigorate the American spirit?

The best conservative approach toward unions, government interference in business, and woke capitalism works toward one goal: the restoration of American ownership in dynamic companies founded in real communities.

The good news is that America's fundamental strengths remain: some of the best, most industrious people in the world, workers and entrepreneurs with skill at and dedication to problem solving, an enormous natural bounty, a robust network of trading partners, a world-leading scientific education system, and a nation that is not afraid to build the future.

The problem today is large corporations that are more beholden to globalist managers than to the American people. The solution has to be a radical reclamation of a republican political economy.

It's got to be dynamic: we want more start-ups, more small businesses, more nimble companies weighted down by fewer regulations and external impositions and the managerialism that come with them.

It's got to be capital intensive: we need to rebuild productive capacity, strengthen supply chains, and invest in technologies that will drive down manufacturing costs and keep high-value jobs here, even as we realign our trade policy with our national interest.

It's got to be good for American families: our goal has to be more jobs that can support raising a family on a single income. That also means labor conditions that support parents' investing their time and energy in their kids.

Such an economy would be a return to real American free enterprise. Ironically, years of ideologically blinding ourselves to the rise of globalist corporatism have not only hurt our country spiritually but also weakened its economic base, shuttering profitable factories, weakening supply chains, and hampering innovation. There will be short-term sacrifices, including higher prices for some consumer goods, but the alternative is worse. Would you rather be a free man without a few luxuries or a slave with an eighty-inch TV?

Such an economy would also ameliorate many of the labor troubles that are convulsing America. Restoring meaningful competition among companies would force them to compete more on wages, working conditions, even company culture. Rebalancing the playing field toward small and medium-sized businesses and start-ups and toward patriotic American management will naturally allow workers to feel more heard in the workplace.

The Ownership Society

One of the reasons I am bullish about and hopeful for our country's future, if we fight for it, is that as I go around the country, all of the smartest, most energetic, most talented people seem to be flocking not to rich and powerful incumbents but to start-ups and upstarts. Not for the first time, our republican tradition faces the challenge of intertwined governmental and private power seen in the revolutionary period and the era of Theodore Roosevelt. And as in those prior fights, my money is on the underdog.

Almost by virtue of the scale of their success, globalist corporatist companies attract the people most motivated by what the philosopher Alasdair MacIntyre called "external goods": wealth, power, status, fame, and other rewards that convey obvious privileges in society. You'll still find very smart, very talented, very driven people motivated by external goods; this is the human capital that the Uniparty uses to sustain itself.

But explorers and innovators are never motivated primarily by external goods. The reason is that it is never obvious or guaranteed which new ideas, techniques, products, or visions will unlock massive value and change the world. And so, if your motivation is wholly external, you'll never develop the passion and obsession to fully invest in something genuinely innovative and creative. At some level, you have to do it, in the words of Michael Jordan, for the love of the game.

In the United States today, by virtue of the dominance of the Uniparty and the strategies the corporations it controls use to cement their power (such as consolidation, cartelization, regulatory capture, DEI mandates, and ESG), the best, brightest, most creative, most obsessive explorers of worlds and builders of empires are becoming aligned against the Uniparty. The companies that will displace Uniparty bastions such as Google, Goldman Sachs, Raytheon, Anheuser-Busch, Unilever, and the Walt Disney Company may already have been founded.

Founded by entrepreneurs such as Andrew Crapuchettes. After he was forced out of Emsi, he could have retired to a life of midmorning tee times and leisurely hours with his lovely family. But instead, he looked around and saw that woke corporate policies were an opportunity. He founded RedBalloon, a recruiting start-up aimed at helping companies that want to hire for pro-America values and for mission, as Emsi once did. Companies with strongly held values (especially conservative ones) have a hard time navigating the employment market and are especially at risk of lawsuits and regulatory action aimed at forcing them to adopt the same woke HR policies as everyone else. RedBalloon works with companies to find hires who are a great fit for the company culture. It's received a big boost of interest from job seekers looking for work in red states or at companies that allow medical autonomy or respect faith commitments.

Some of its customers are conservative groups or religious organizations that were kicked off of Big Tech platforms such as LinkedIn because they insisted on hiring according to their faith principles. But most of its customers are regular American businesses that are sick of bad culture hires and want to support the kinds of jobs our republic needs. And because the Big Tech firms are so bloated and decadent, RedBalloon is able to identify customer needs and build matching products and services much more quickly (it helps that RedBalloon actually doesn't hate its customers).

Companies such as RedBalloon are going to get a boost from a major global shift that is now under way and that will pop up a few places throughout the book, one that began picking up steam under President Donald Trump's pathbreaking leadership. Supply chain disruptions in China and elsewhere, along with rising labor costs, the increasing attractiveness of the US-Mexico-Canada Agreement (USMCA) trading area, energy cost increases in Europe, and some important policy choices in China and the United States, have combined to make the United States a more attractive place in which to make things again.

Companies that went all in on China are increasingly realizing the nature of the Chinese Communist Party, as it arbitrarily closes off supply chains, restricts profits from leaving China, throws tech executives into jail, and otherwise reexerts itself. The country's experiment with free markets (which was always a sham) is coming to a close. And the companies that colluded with the CCP will be left holding the bag.

That's why it is such an important moment for the New Conservative Movement: there is a short window of flux and uncertainty in which to work to restore a republican economy for the twenty-first century and beyond.

Rebuilding the Economic Order of the Republic

Doing so will require defining vigorous and innovative policies and ideas equal to the moment we are in. It will involve breaking some eggs.

To conserve the republic against globalist corporatism, against special interests, against woke Great Reset ecosocialism, we need to restore the proper use of the government to disperse power, level the playing field, help the free enterprise system do its job, and put the American people, communities, and families first again. How can we do that? Here are some principles and ideas that should guide the New Conservative Movement.

Reverse the Managerial Revolution

One of the biggest things we can do to both reverse the Managerial Revolution and take down the stronghold of woke academia is one of the simplest: reduce the *automatic* advantage that a college degree gives you.

Notice the word *automatic*. As a former college president, I know how valuable and transformative a college education can be. And I believe the education we delivered at Wyoming Catholic College made our students better citizens, better community leaders, and better employees. But as a college president, I also paid close attention to what was going on at other schools and universities. And for every great institution such as Hillsdale College or the University of Texas at Austin (Hook 'em, Horns!), there were a dozen institutions coasting by on huge subsidies in the form of student loans and credentials inflation while failing to deliver a transformative education experience for their students. Many students waste their years in school and end up learning on the job anyway.

That's why the Heritage Foundation recommended, in our Project 2025, that Congress pass legislation prohibiting automatic algorithmic filtering by educational level in hiring, at least for positions in which a professional degree isn't required by law (such as nurses, medical doctors, and structural engineers).

I am not suggesting that employers not be able to take educational credentials into account, even to require them of their new hires. But since the advent of the internet, the vast majority of hiring has occurred using systems that use algorithms that filter out candidates and in many cases *won't even let someone without a BA apply for a job*, even if they're otherwise qualified and the company would have hired them. This is unjust and unfair to the millions of Americans with serious work experience and qualifications who happen never to have finished college. And politically, it's a free handout to the woke university system, which knows that students need the BA credential, even if they don't learn anything in school.

In addition to banning the BA box, states can work to reverse degree inflation by reducing the minimal education requirements for government and contractor jobs. The states of Maryland, Alaska, California, Colorado, New Jersey, North Carolina, Ohio, Pennsylvania, South Dakota, Utah, and Virginia have taken big steps in this direction since 2022. President Trump issued an executive order in 2020 to reduce degree requirements in the federal government, but Congress should take further action at a federal level and in the District of Columbia (for instance, annulling DC's outrageous requirement that *day care workers* have a college degree).

Even as we lay siege to the ivory tower, we need to make sure we're investing in the skills American industry needs. The federal government spends more than $100 billion per year subsidizing higher education but less than $2 billion supporting people on noncollege pathways. With student loan forgiveness on the Democrats' policy agenda, you can expect them to spend hundreds of billions of dollars more without a dime going to working-class Americans who invested in their own business or a trade instead of going to college.

After decades of pushing every student to go to college, we now face a situation in which critical industrial and artisanal skills, not to mention the trades, are in ever shorter supply. Investing in Americans' skills is a vital aspect of rebooting a republican economy; many of these jobs convey the dignity, self-possession, and literal or figurative ownership that builds republican virtue. And we need these skills to make our manufactures competitive again and drive down the costs of building and repairing infrastructure, a key requirement of the Abundance Agenda.

Thankfully, states are leading the way. In Minnesota, a strong bipartisan majority passed legislation funding high school construction training programs, in which students learn in-demand skills on real home-building sites while actively contributing to ameliorating Minnesota's housing crisis. In West Virginia, State Treasurer Riley Moore worked to create a Jumpstart Savings Program that is a 529-style tax-advantaged route to saving to start a blue-collar business or learn a trade. We should expand this federally.

It will be just in time. After two centuries of new technologies favoring brains over brawn, white-collar work over blue-collar, we are finally at the cusp of an important reversal with the advent of artificial intelligence (AI). Many of the worst aspects of the managerial revolution—endless reports, bureaucracy, oversight, check-in meetings, and so on—can be significantly automated. And for small-business owners, it will be easier to scale up a company when there are fewer managers clogging up the works.

Entrepreneurs will find ways to use AI to outsource and automate many bureaucratic and administrative functions. We need to ensure that our regulatory framework allows them to do so, that the Uniparty doesn't use regulation to protect make-work HR jobs and impose woke commissars throughout the corporate economy (the current status quo). Preserving open-source AI not controlled by woke companies is especially critical for our future.

Make Ownership Great Again

Ownership in a society positions a citizen to consider the common good. We need citizens who feel empowered to participate in the setting of the course of their own lives, who have the time and resources to invest in intermediary institutions, family, civil society, and the workplace.

We'll never free ourselves of Uniparty control unless we reduce the unfair regulatory burdens that create moats for globalist corporatist companies. In this sense, I depart from some of my friends in the so-called New Right who are friendly toward the proactive use of government regulation. For me the issue is less about interference in the free market and more about political control. One of the things that might not be apparent to those who don't own their own business is that whenever the Democrats come back into power, they immediately start tightening regulatory screws on small-business owners, using various executive agencies' enforcement discretion.

For example, in the wake of the 2008 global financial crisis, Congress passed the Dodd-Frank Act, supposedly in order to rein in the too-big-to-fail banks and the lending practices that had been responsible for crashing the mortgage securities market. But it had the opposite effect. While Dodd-Frank did increase compliance costs for big banks, as a percentage of revenues, it increased them even more for smaller banks. Large banks, in building out their new compliance desks, also built more ties to Washington and a revolving door of compliance jobs for former government employees, actually increasing their political influence. As a result, community banks, which should be the biggest sector of the banking industry (they once were), have closed or consolidated, while the three or four largest Wall Street banks have gotten even bigger and more systemically important, and the number of new bank charters in the entire country has dwindled to a handful since 2010.

The next Republican president needs to use administrative and rule-making powers to significantly limit executive agencies' abusive use of enforcement discretion (and especially of abusive, nebulous guidance documents). But a real fix will require labor agencies to use their authority under the Regulatory Flexibility Act of 1980 to exempt small businesses from regulation where possible. Congress should also enact legislation increasing the revenue thresholds at which the National Labor Relations Board asserts jurisdiction over employers to match changes in inflation since 1935 and should also exempt small-business, first-time, nonwillful violators from fines issued by the Occupational Health and Safety Administration.

More important, we should pursue a two-tier system of federal regulation such that large businesses are subject to a heavier grade of regulation. Small and medium-sized businesses have actual owners, reducing the human distance between workers and owners (and their families and community). Small businesses are also less likely to create an unfair monopoly and exert coercive pressure on wages and work conditions.

The vast majority of Americans will not be owners of businesses. So it matters that they work in places that invest in them, give their work a sense of dignity, and allow them to feel ownership of it. Andrew Crapuchettes's example is inspiring: in the economic order of the republic, after blessing his customers, a company leader's next duties are to his employees and their families, before he blesses his shareholders (with profits).

The reality is that the vast majority of owners who are involved in their businesses feel enormous responsibility for their employees. Remember, "the buck stops here." Despite a small number of bad apples, many of them make enormous personal sacrifices rather than leave their employees high and dry.

But the farther owners are removed from everyday interactions with workers and their families and communities, the more it seems as though some kind of labor voice is needed. And as the scale of work in an industry increases, direct ownership becomes less and less feasible. So we need ways to provide workers with a sense of ownership and agency, even where complex management is an operational necessity.

Personally, I think unionization is not the right answer; in almost every case, something like a workers' council could do the same job at lower cost and without coercive measures. In any case, national-level unions are often part of the problem and part of the Uniparty. Surveys show that that's how most working-class Americans see it, too.

But I think that conservatives need to be clear-eyed about the problems that the Managerial Revolution presents for workers' well-being and sense of ownership in their society, especially when globalist managers are involved (remember their mantra: "I'm sorry, it's company policy"). Oftentimes, in companies owned by financiers in Frankfurt, Riyadh, or Beijing, the only folks standing for American values, American jobs, American families, and American communities are the workers in those enterprises. I don't have a lot of time for the United Auto Workers—but I do have a little, because in 1999, during China's move to enter the World Trade Organization, it was just about the only national institution to stand up for the American worker against the Uniparty and the CCP. That's a sobering truth that conservatives need to chew on for a minute.

Especially when it comes to Big Tech and big banks, we need to consider the nuclear option. I am skeptical about the use of antitrust powers to micromanage the "right" amount of competition or market structure. But I am not skeptical about their proper use, as envisioned by Teddy Roosevelt: to rein in globalist corporatism that threatens the republic. Uniparty managers, modeling themselves on the East India Company, pursue scale to destroy local competitors and then prostitute themselves to the Deep State to avoid accountability to the American people for the destruction they cause to American families and communities. Burning down companies such as Google and BlackRock by breaking them up will be good for America.

Create "an Active Commerce" for the Twenty-First Century

In *The Federalist Papers*, No. 11, Alexander Hamilton made the case for "an active commerce" as a vital national interest. The arguments he made sound eerily familiar today: powerful geopolitical rivals were endeavoring to divide and conquer American commerce, squeezing production and value out of the new states and back to their own shores. In the extreme case, they could impose a passive commerce in which supply chains, finance, and high-value manufacturing were controlled from abroad and the American economy was at the whim of foreigners. Sound familiar?

Our laws regarding corporate finance, tax, trade, and accounting encourage companies to reap massive paper profits for strategies that, in the end, ship jobs overseas, make supply chains fragile and vulnerable to our foreign enemies, and reduce innovation at home. We've been selling off our birthright for a bowl of pottage (cheap Chinese consumer goods).

For example, when it was founded, Apple Computer made its products in the United States at a highly automated plant in Fremont, California. But after normalization of trade with China, it shifted almost all of its manufacturing operations to the People's Republic and induced its suppliers, such as Corning Glass, to do so, too, even when doing so created massive national security risks. And even though its products proudly proclaim that they are "Designed in California," for tax purposes,

Apple declares that all of its international profits belong to a subsidiary in Ireland, a strategy that has cost US taxpayers hundreds of billions of dollars. Just between 2009 and 2012, a congressional investigation found that Apple had hidden $74 billion from the IRS that way. It's no coincidence that Apple chose Tim Cook as Steve Jobs's successor: he led Apple's courtship of the Chinese Communist Party.

We need to pursue an Active Commerce for the twenty-first century. That means taking back control of our global supply chains and using all the powers of the United States—our governments, industries, and communities working in concert—to restore our economic sovereignty. While the hardest work of all will come from our entrepreneurs, workers, investors, merchants, and innovators, it will also require the use of the immense powers of our federal and state governments, in total alignment with the American tradition prior to the 1990s.

We need to reverse what our federal policies ruined by encouraging viable businesses to invest in America. Industrial policy isn't about industry; it's about restoring a republican economy. It's Family Jobs policy. It's Defending Our Country policy. It's Make America Great Again policy, which is one of the reasons why, against the screeching of the wax-museum conservatives, President Trump had so many successes beginning the work of getting our country back on track.

Restoring our Active Commerce is about more than just the material. Our indebtedness to others is weakening our American spirit (in so many senses). The same wax-museum conservatives who poetize about the United States' global leadership (by which they mean continuous war, not real leadership) also criticize an active pursuit of American commerce as against our "free enterprise system" (making smartphones in Chinese slave camps). But of course, the more in hock the United States is to the global managerial ruling class, the more timid and deferential we have to be. It's un-American and humiliating.

Corporations can no longer have their cake and eat it, too, lecturing Americans about wokeness and bossing around their small-business suppliers and customers, all the while manufacturing their wares in smog-ridden Communist China. As we will explore more fully in chapter 10, various trade barriers can be used to level the playing field, penalizing corporations that seek to take advantage of modern-day slavery, unfair environmental practices, and other kinds of regulatory arbitrage and encouraging them to bring American jobs home. We can coordinate at the state or federal level to end the practice of corporations pitting states or localities against one another for special government tax handouts or bullying them not to pass laws that protect their values.

Conservatives need to wrestle with this uncomfortable truth: there is no world in which the creative destruction of capitalism, left to its own devices, will be able to fend off the Great Reset. American capitalism faces a parasitical strategy designed explicitly to hijack "free enterprise" toward socialist ends. Unless we recover the republican tradition of confronting globalist corporatism exemplified by the Boston Tea Party and Teddy Roosevelt, our way of life will be lost.

CHAPTER 6

Freedom Requires Order

Greater love than this hath no man than that he lay down his
life for his friend. Here were nineteen-year-old boys ready to lay
down their lives to stop a mob from molesting old people they did
not even know. And as those boys took back the streets of Los Angeles,
block by block, my friends, we must take back our cities, and
take back our culture, and take back our country.

—Patrick Buchanan on the 1992 Los Angeles riots

A lot of classic Hollywood westerns are really parables about politics. In a lawless land, a good man has to figure out the best way to impose order so that civilization can flourish. In John Ford's *The Man Who Shot Liberty Valance*, for instance, Jimmy Stewart plays a lawyer from back east who is scandalized when he arrives in a frontier town that is held in thrall by the anarchic violence of the criminal Liberty Valance. Stewart understands that if "liberty" is let loose without law, a society will be unjust and anarchical. He starts learning to use his Second Amendment rights, and—well, you'll have to watch it to find out what happens next.

The foundation stone of American civilization is our ethos of *ordered liberty*. It is not an *idea* but an *institution*, a set of practices, habits, and symbols that provides our deepest sense of who we are as a people. It lives not in our heads but in our hearts.

What does it mean for liberty to be *ordered*, and *by whom* is it ordered?

Ordered liberty demands that each citizen cultivate within themselves an ethic of responsibility for their own liberty and that of the nation, and that they hold both themselves and others to that high standard. Self-rule begins at home.

Under ordered liberty, the role of the government is to protect the public peace and good order—imprisoning violent criminals, guarding the border, enforcing the law, and otherwise safeguarding the common good against antisocial actors. Having provided public order, the government steps back and calls ordinary Americans to take agency over their own lives, businesses, and communities, recognizing their ownership over their own flourishing. The only way to square the circle of an expansive sphere of liberty and a state that is not so powerful that it becomes despotic is if citizens *govern themselves responsibly*, beginning with their own personal behavior and spiraling outward to their families, their communities, and their towns.

When I talk to Americans around the country, there is a universal intuition that our ordered liberty is in danger. We see it in our communities and on the evening news every day. Is the problem simply anarchy or lawlessness? It is so much worse.

Anarchy is what happens when there's no established government. Government is then established by whoever has the biggest stick, so it's impossible for true peaceful civilization to exist in the chaos. But while such a "war of all against all" is inimical to "life, liberty, and the pursuit of happiness," because it is vulnerable to violent outlaws, it also does not *prevent* a militia of virtuous citizens from creating a self-organized peace. This has been the pattern of pioneer politics from Plymouth Colony on down. And so anarchy, while a low state of affairs, is not in and of itself *tyrannical* because it's possible for "ordered liberty" to exist.

What would be the direct opposite of ordered liberty? It would be a disordered tyranny, in which the government *forbids* ordinary citizens to take responsibility for the public order and exercising their liberties, all the while *permitting or even encouraging* the violation of the law and the looting of public order. Such a condition, called anarcho-tyranny, has now taken hold across American life. The rot is deeper than you may realize.

We can see this in what has changed in our culture in the last thirty years. In 1992, huge riots broke out in South Central Los Angeles. In the preceding years, LAPD chief Daryl Gates had resorted to increasingly militaristic tactics to rein in gang violence, and the black and Hispanic communities of South Central had correspondingly grown more and more angry at the police. The acquittal of four officers who had been seen beating the prostrate Rodney King in a widely broadcast videotape lit the tinderbox. The violence that followed was the most damaging and most costly breakdown in public order in US history (until the George Floyd riots in the summer of 2020, of course).

The rioters from South Central targeted not only the LAPD but also the community immediately to their north: Koreatown, where tensions ran high between Korean American business owners and their black and Hispanic patrons from South Central. Over the years, there had been occasional flare-ups between the communities, but the anarchy that took hold of the city in the wake of the Rodney King ruling was unprecedented.

Anarchy gives bad actors unique opportunities to fill the power vacuum. Amid the rage and rioting, the gangs of South Central saw an opportunity. The Bloods and the Crips called a truce, joined by Latino gangs such as MS-13 and Barrio 18. Rather than targeting one another, they began going after businesses that they held a grudge against or that simply looked vulnerable.

Koreatown was ripe for the plucking, and when the LAPD officers withdrew on the first day of the riots, the community was left to fend for itself.

But that's the thing about true anarchy: a vacuum of power also gives space for good guys to fight back. As looters started to attack their stores, Korean Americans organized to defend themselves. Many of them had served in the South Korean Army, some in combat, and the men of the community armed themselves with rifles, shotguns, and handguns.

They took their position on the parapets of a grocery store (leading to the moniker on the nightly news of "Rooftop Koreans") and used the Korean-language radio channel as an ad hoc command center. Marines from the Korean Veterans Association led armed patrols of the neighborhood. In many cases, they fired blanks or warning shots to scare the looters off (the thugs targeting them did not return the favor). They held their ground until the National Guard restored order in Los Angeles. Miraculously, no one died, although both the looters and those defending their homes were treated for gunshot wounds.

Make no mistake: that descent into anarchy was hugely destructive. Despite their best efforts, the Korean Americans and their businesses still ended up suffering more than $400 million worth of damage, about half of the total damage in all of LA. Businesses shuttered; some people never recovered. The state of California failed in its basic duty to provide order to the law-abiding residents of Koreatown and South Central who were the real victims of the riots. Needless to say, LA's leadership abandoned communities such as Koreatown in order to protect neighborhoods such as Beverly Hills, where rich Uniparty progressives live. But in the anarchy, at least the Rooftop Koreans could take up arms in defense of their lives, their fortunes, and their sacred honor.

The LA riots took place in an environment of anarchy. That's never a good thing, but there's one thing that's worse: anarcho-tyranny. To understand anarcho-tyranny, imagine for a moment how differently the 1992 riots would have played out in Gavin Newsom's California.

For starters, thousands more looters and rioters—many of them violent criminals—would have been out on the street from the start, as they were in 2020 thanks to Newsom's soft-on-crime approach and "prison reform" (letting violent criminals out of prison). Likewise, when the felons began looting Koreatown, its residents would have been left defenseless, since California has passed some of the most restrictive gun laws in the country.

To make matters worse, as chronicled in Zach Smith and Charles D. Stimson's exposé *Rogue Prosecutors: How Radical Soros Lawyers Are Destroying America's Communities*, California is now run by George Soros–backed progressive prosecutors such as LA district attorney George Gascón, whose city saw property crime increase by a whopping 49 percent during his previous tenure in the same post in San Francisco. In Gavin Newsom's California, as soon as riots begin, Gascón would likely stand up on television and insist that not only his office but the federal Department of Justice's Civil Rights Division would put every single claimed case of self-defense or excessive force on the part of California's rapidly declining number of police officers under a microscope to ensure that the rights of "mostly peaceful protesters" had not been violated.

Moreover, in 1992, the Rooftop Koreans were reported on by actual journalists. Today, selectively edited videos would be put out on social media, sometimes by the perpetrators themselves, leading to flash mobs overwhelming the overstretched police resources. At the same time, coastal elite reporters would run interference for the looters from thousands of miles away on television and Twitter, while Vice President Kamala Harris raised money for their bail.

Is it any wonder that in 2020, as California kept the state's restaurants and businesses locked down and forbade its citizens from going out in public unless they were protesting with Black Lives Matter, Adam Cho, the second-generation business owner of Ham Ji Park, which opened in Koreatown in 1989—told *Eater* magazine that "this is worse than the Rodney King riots. . . . We don't have millions of dollars saved up. If we're closed for dine-in for a month or two, we're shutting down."

A free republic without virtuous, self-governing citizens will soon devolve into either anarchy or an authoritarian state. Russell Kirk, echoing the classical republican tradition, held that the "inner order" of the soul and the "outer order" of the Republic are intimately linked.

The Party of Creation is not ashamed to take a stand for normalcy, peace, and good order, for the defined limits (including self-limits) that promote the inner order of the soul (like a trellis helping a vine to grow). And we make no apologies about using the power of the government to impose public order as needed, like a gardener pulling weeds to protect his crop.

It may seem like a paradox, but the truth is that liberty and order are not opposed but intertwined. That's why in US cities, where public order has broken down and progressive "freedom" runs rampant, ordinary people are no longer able to live lives of trust and freedom. The windows on their homes must have bars. Their schools require metal detectors and police officers. At their convenience stores, wares are locked onto the shelves. Assemblies at public parks require permits, lest "mostly peaceful protests" or gang fights break out.

That's why the Founders never wavered from their firm belief that the living practice of ordered liberty was a precondition for self-government. The Constitution's authors believed that the document they wrote and ratified would utterly fail if ordered liberty—forged in war, revolution, and frontier struggle in a hostile, yet bountiful land—was not written on the hearts of the American people. As Benjamin Franklin put it, "Only a virtuous people are capable of freedom. As nations become corrupt and vicious, they have more need of masters."

The Party of Destruction hates ordered liberty. It hates the idea of limitations on freedom; it deplores the "inequity" of a gardener discriminating against weeds and insects: "Why not let it all grow?" To continue the analogy, it hates independent gardeners. It hates the fact that well-ordered souls in a well-ordered society have little need of government programs and taxpayer-funded NGOs and little interest in utopian schemes for social "improvement." By undermining public order and promoting the rights of criminals over the rights of ordinary Americans, they also increase the power and resources they can wield in their quixotic campaign against the limitations imposed by reality and civilization.

Nothing illustrates the difference among ordered liberty, mere anarchy, and anarcho-tyranny better than the story of LA's Koreatown.

That's what defines anarcho-tyranny: when those who ought to pro-

The Government In:	Ordered Liberty	Anarchy	Anarcho-Tyranny
For Upright Citizens:	Encourages and protects virtue	Fails to provide order, leading to "frontier justice"	Punishes and "corrects" virtue
For Criminals and Scoundrels:	Punishes and corrects vice		Encourages and protects vice

tect public order and justice are at best negligent of the common good as they pursue their private interests and at worst hyperscrupulous of the "rights" of repeat criminals, violent addicts, and mentally disturbed vagrants while ignoring the rights of ordinary Americans to domestic tranquility and the use of their property.

It's the underclass looting the streets while the ruling class loots the state and the private sector. It's buying razed buildings for pennies on the dollar and texting your golf buddies on the planning commission to get a special zoning exemption to build on the plots. It's Gavin Newsom closing Adam Cho's restaurant but enjoying a private birthday party (indoors) for his lobbyist friend at the French Laundry (one of the most expensive restaurants in the United States). It's gated communities secured by a private police force while gangs of carjackers roam the city. It's public goods replaced by private bubbles. It's million-dollar villas sitting on private bluffs with private roads and private security overlooking slum towns and favelas. It's Rio de Janeiro, and increasingly, it's Los Angeles, San Francisco, Portland, New York, Philadelphia, and Washington, DC.

At its heart is a Uniparty that profits off the destruction of ordered liberty and the transformation of US citizens into distracted, compliant, weak slaves. Ordered liberty means accountability, citizens doing things for themselves instead of demanding that the state do them, transparent laws that reduce opportunities for graft, patronage, and special exceptions, and the provision of public goods for the common welfare. Anarcho-tyranny is a weapon by which the Uniparty can extract the wealth of the middle class while buying off the underclass.

Here's just one example of how this works. In 2018, San Francisco voters passed Proposition C, a ballot referendum doubling the city's business tax, with the money earmarked for "homeless services." The city's far-left activist and political class pushed for the measure, but they had one seemingly unlikely ally: the multibillionaire software entrepreneur Marc Benioff, the founder of Salesforce, who pledged to donate millions of dollars to their efforts.

It's obvious what the activist class stood to gain from Prop C. The tax created a massive fund with almost no accountability, controlled by the same activists and politicians and doled out to hundreds of NGOs and contractors. But was Benioff operating simply out of the kindness of his heart and a sense of public duty?

Bay Area insiders reveal that there's a more cynical angle to the story. Prop C also had some features that would hurt Benioff's competitors. Benioff's Salesforce was the biggest employer in San Francisco, competing with other tech companies for office space and software engineering hires, but challengers were rising. At the time, many of those rapidly growing competitors were financial technology companies, including two of Benioff's biggest competitors for downtown real estate and software engineering talent: Square (the developer of CashApp) and Stripe (one of the largest internet payments processors).

Prop C greatly increased the tax on gross receipts, or every dollar that comes into a business, regardless of the business's profitability. Salesforce's enterprise software businesses generate large profits. But as financial services companies, Square and Stripe were mostly moving their customers' money, making a fraction of a penny on every dollar they handled. Even though Salesforce was a larger, more profitable company, Prop C taxed its competitors far more. They left San Francisco after the tax was passed.

So for a few million dollars (half from Salesforce's shareholders), Benioff created an influential coalition of activist allies, won the support of leftists who might otherwise have targeted Salesforce, buffed his media image as a humanitarian progressive do-gooder, and literally chased his business rivals out of town.

Meanwhile, the beleaguered SF middle class was squeezed just a little bit more: slightly higher prices, a little less growth, a little less upward wage pressure, a little more street crime, a little worse place to raise a family. Anarcho-tyranny happens like bankruptcy: slowly, then all at once.

But Benioff bit off more than he could chew. As is often the case, he and other members of what the conservative philosopher Willmoore Kendall called "the Committee to Abolish Original Sin" failed to anticipate how addicts and criminals would respond to the concentration of free services and (thanks to the Soros-backed DA Gascón) the legalization of petty crime. And neither Benioff nor his woke activist allies fully appreciated what the massive shift among drug users from heroin to fentanyl would do to the exploding homeless population. Driving your competitors out of a booming market is a neat trick, but in the wake of covid-19 and the out-of-control streets, the suicide of downtown San Francisco is so bad that Benioff's Salesforce may also pull out of the city.

Of course, when things get bad, Benioff can just jet off to his Hawaii compound. It's San Francisco's middle-class residents and ordinary citizens who will have to clean up the mess.

This is the really sadistic thing: by destroying public goods and terrorizing ordinary Americans, the Uniparty's anarcho-tyranny *increases* the value of the privatized alternatives. It *increases* the demand for the gated community, the luxury shopping development with private security, the private jet, the exclusive clinic. It damages housing prices and quality of life in affordable neighborhoods while increasing the demand for precisely the exclusive and safe neighborhoods where the rich already live. Worse, these private alternatives penalize larger families, who benefit disproportionately from high-quality public goods.

Learned Helplessness

The effect of anarcho-tyranny on ordinary Americans is to establish a sense of learned helplessness, and it has more sinister roots than you might imagine.

In the dark days immediately after September 11, 2001, when Americans genuinely worried about Al-Qaeda sleeper cells unleashing even greater destruction, two air force psychologists conducted research into a phenomenon called *learned helplessness*, which they thought American counterterrorism officials could use to induce cooperation by captured terrorists.

Back in the 1960s, psychologists had accidentally discovered that a state of total apathy and compliance could be induced by subjecting someone to repeated bad outcomes (such as electric shocks) that they were not allowed to mitigate or prevent. Doing this breaks down what psychologists call *self-efficacy* and *internal locus of control*: the belief that even amid hardship, you can do something to change your circumstances. Despair sets in and apathy with it.

The scientists who originally worked on learned helplessness intended to develop methods to aid patients suffering from ailments such as depression by showing them that they had the power to take responsibility for their circumstances and act to improve them. But after 9/11, those air force psychologists persuaded counterterrorism officials that the techniques could be used in reverse: to design methods to *induce* a state of learned helplessness, after which suspected terrorists would become compliant. That was the birth of the CIA's controversial "enhanced interrogation" program, which included sleep deprivation, loud music, sexual humiliation, involuntary drug injections, partial asphyxiation (including waterboarding), and other techniques that reduced once proud jihadists to husks of their former selves.

Everything about enhanced interrogation is designed to induce learned helplessness by saying "You're not in charge. We are. You're not even in charge of what you put into your body or where you use the bathroom."

This is not the condition of free citizens but of slaves. And indeed, many slave societies have had institutions designed to induce learned helplessness among the slave population: not only the repressive violence of the plantation in the American South but also the autumnal Spartan hunt recounted by Plutarch in his *Life of Lycurgus*, in which the

Crypteia (a secret society of young warriors) would stealthily stalk and kill random members of the helot slave caste. (I'm sure the *New Sparta Times* editorial pages dismissed the tales of missing villagers as mere conspiracy theories promulgated by helot deplorables.)

Today, the Uniparty is applying these same psychological torture techniques not to radical jihadists but to the population of law-abiding everyday Americans. This torture method is the rampant violence and petty crime. It's the state forcing experimental vaccines into people's arms, lest they lose their jobs or businesses. It's forcing citizens to close their businesses and schools for months on end and to huff through itchy masks. It's the smug despotism of telling parents that schools are going to trans their kids whether they like it or not, or Child Services will take them away. It's the sexual humiliation of forcing teenage girls to change in the same locker room as biological men and of making their parents let it happen.

It all sends the same message: "You're not in charge. We are. You're not even in charge of what you put into your body or where you use the bathroom."

The habits of the heart that anarcho-tyranny leads to, most of all this learned helplessness, have real consequences for the lives of everyday Americans and their children.

No example better demonstrates the high stakes than the 2022 school shooting at Robb Elementary School in Uvalde, Texas. For an agonizing seventy-four minutes, the Uvalde Consolidated Independent School District (UCISD) police cordoned off the school and waited to confront the gunman, while children and teachers bled out and died inside; that despite knowing from their training two months earlier what police departments have known since Columbine: that confronting a gunman as quickly as possible is the only way to reduce loss of life in an active shooter scenario.

UCISD police officers not only utterly failed to do their duty but also used the color of law to force parents and community members who had showed up to stand outside helplessly. Parents pleaded for the UCISD police to confront the gunman and offered to risk their own lives to get their children out, but rather than listen, the UCISD police barricaded the school to prevent parents from attempting any rescue. They tackled, tased, pepper sprayed, handcuffed, and otherwise abused parents who tried to heroically intervene or who challenged their authority.

They did that to folks such as Ruben Ruiz, himself a UCISD police officer. His wife, Eva Mireles, called him and told him that she had been shot and was dying. When Ruben moved to risk his own life to find and rescue her, his UCISD comrades detained him and took away his service weapon. Eva Mireles died of her wounds.

The lawful innocent were forbidden to exercise their liberty for the common good, while the authorities permitted a lawless criminal to have his way for seventy-four minutes. That's anarcho-tyranny.

It is easy to tell ourselves that Uvalde was a unique disaster. But is that how it seems to you? Are the attitudes of the Uvalde police—prioritizing compliance over competence, legalese over liberty—foreign to you? They're not. All over the country, there are signs that our ordered liberty is giving way to anarcho-tyranny and the learned helplessness it leads to.

Fighting Back

The good news is that a vast swath of the American middle class, of all political backgrounds and party loyalties, is sick and tired of anarcho-tyranny. American patriots have, literally and metaphorically, been hitting the gym.

Remember that the root cause of our spiritual crisis is not our pathetic and petty "overlords" but the spiritual oppression, apathy, and laziness that encourage us to accept this state of affairs passively. Just like our bodies, we Americans have gotten out of shape in our exercise of ordered liberty: flabby from years of sitting in front of the computer or television instead of fighting in the arena or building something with our hands; overfed on spiritual junk food; easily fatigued when forced to exercise; anxious to avoid a reckoning with the scale. Yet I believe there is great strength in us.

I believe that the experience of the past few years has been radicalizing for many ordinary Americans. They saw playgrounds, schools, and churches forcibly closed while politicians labeled strip clubs and liquor stores "essential businesses." They saw public health officials justify lockdowns while excusing mass riots because "racism is a public health crisis, too." With everyone forced to homeschool, they saw the garbage that public schools were teaching their kids while failing to teach them basic skills, and they saw teachers unions defending the worst of it.

All of us have seen how easy it is to lose our liberties if we fail to fight for them. Thankfully, there are Americans who are fighting back, to preserve and restore ordered liberty for our glorious American future. Since the pandemic, more than a dozen states have strengthened laws protecting individual rights, in everything from vaccine mandates to constitutional carry.

Already, ordinary San Franciscans fed up with anarcho-tyranny have led the successful recall of Chesa Boudin, the city's Soros-backed DA. And under the banner of "GrowSF," they have begun the hard work of dismantling the grip of Party of Destruction radicals in the city's other elected offices.

Among many other important issues, the Cicero Institute, led by the entrepreneur and investor Joe Lonsdale, is working with state legislatures to destroy the power of radical activists and woke cities to impose anarcho-tyranny around public drug use and street camping. Florida has recently become the first state to fully overhaul its homelessness laws and claw back public space for common sense and away from radical activists, and more will follow.

But a restoration of ordered liberty will take more than better government policy. It requires personal transformation and working to restore the "inner order of the soul."

Think of the more than 100,000 men who have taken up Exodus 90 since 2015, for example. Designed to free men from the shackles of alcohol, pornography, gambling, social media, and other distractions and addictions, the program requires a ninety-day commitment to daily prayer and reading, weekly Sabbath observance, and a number of ascetic practices, such as cold showers, exercise, no unnecessary use of digital technology, no snacking or desserts, no alcohol, and so on. These simple commitments are ordered liberty in action, and the rapidly growing movement around Exodus 90, alongside a broader grassroots embrace of intensive fitness, emergency preparedness, and addiction treatment, has already helped thousands of men transform their lives.

What's more, when well-ordered men like these come together, they can change communities, thwart disaster, and even save lives. There's perhaps no better example of a group doing that than my hometown's Cajun Navy. Founded in the wake of Hurricane Katrina, the Cajun Navy is a group of volunteer patriots who work tirelessly to provide order and relief in the face of disaster. They are ordinary Louisianans who use pickup trucks, low-draft rigid inflatables with outboard motors, swamp boats, and more to go wherever they are needed, organizing themselves with increasingly sophisticated but voluntary and decentralized digital communications systems. Everyone from southern Louisiana knows that every year when hurricanes hit, the Cajun Navy will be there to help while the federal government is still fumbling with its keys. There is almost nothing that better embodies the battle between anarcho-tyranny and ordered liberty in my mind than the image of hapless Washington politicians flying over Louisiana's devastation while everyday Cajuns organized themselves, got into their boats, and started saving lives.

Our Uniparty elites hate people like this. They hate a man who is in control of himself. They hate a community that can rely on itself in the middle of a hurricane. Of course, they won't admit it openly, but they know that the sleeping giant of the great American middle class is beginning to rouse itself from its post–Cold War slumber, and they're scared to death. Just look at the way they treat anyone who refuses to sit there and take it; folks such as Daniel Penny, Todd Beamer, and Jack Wilson, who, not unlike the Rooftop Koreans, simply refused to accept the imposition of chaos and violence, who fought for their lives and those of the people around them.

In the case of Penny, woke journalists and activists (but I repeat myself) attempted to set the narrative early, surfacing any and every potentially right-wing opinion the former marine had held and writing hagiographic treatments of the man he had attempted to subdue during a violent outburst in a busy subway car in May 2023. But the "victim" who had verbally threatened to kill innocent New York City straphangers was not the carefree Michael Jackson impersonator of his posthumous *New York Times* profile but a seriously mentally disturbed drug addict with forty-two prior arrests and a history of violently assaulting subway riders.

The spiritual attack on men such as Beamer and Wilson is more subtle. Beamer was an evangelical husband and dad who, on September 11, 2001, helped organize the effort on United Flight 93 to take back the plane from Al-Qaeda terrorists. Wilson was a Texas church parishioner and security volunteer who shot dead a mentally disturbed junkie who pulled out a shotgun during communion and started blasting one Sunday morning in December 2019.

In the wake of those heinous events, only the radical left fringe of American media celebrated. But up until the moment they engaged in acts of terror, the media would have expressed far more sympathy for the perpetrators of those crimes (Muslim immigrants passionate about the Palestinian cause; a homeless man struggling with substance abuse and mental health issues) than the heroes who stopped them. Our Uniparty-controlled culture attacks, mocks, and denigrates normal, responsible American men in the mold of Beamer and Wilson relentlessly, at least until the moment it desperately needs them to push back against the evil the elites have allowed to fester.

We as a society have tried to forget that. But who would you rather have as a neighbor or a local official: Wilson and Penny or those they defended themselves against? And what does it say about our ruling class, the answer they would give (or pretend to give) to that question?

The Guarantor of All Other Liberties

First and foremost, it says that the Second Amendment is more important than ever. As the ultimate guarantor of all other liberties, Americans' tradition of keeping and bearing arms is more important now than ever. Indeed, it ensures that the US citizenry will not be deprived of its life, liberty, or property without a fight.

Critics often say that the United States' gun laws are unique in the world. What they fail to point out is that our tradition of freedom is just as unique. Long ago, our English forebears understood that liberty undefended was liberty unsecured. Thus among their several ancient liberties they always maintained that of bearing arms. There were some restrictions as compatible with the public peace (such as against carrying swords in churches) but on the whole, no leader attempted to systematically disarm the populace, for good reason: he would have understood it to be a precursor to tyranny and the destruction of their liberties.

President Joe Biden has articulated a common and smug dismissal of this principle, saying "If you want to fight against a country, you need an F-15. You need something a little more than a gun." But he's wrong. For starters, considering that Biden caved to the Taliban, I'm not sure what makes him think he can take on the Cajun Navy. More important, armed American patriots, protective of their rights, exert an influence on our government just by existing, even without needing to mount an armed resistance. By raising the potential cost of any government intervention, the Second Amendment creates a structural restraint on the growth of tyranny within our borders.

You can see this in a comparison between the United States and Australia, Canada, and the United Kingdom. Before the American Revolution, we all shared a legal tradition, including a tradition of public gun ownership. But in the twentieth century, those other countries largely gave up the right to bear arms. During the covid-19 pandemic, we saw the results.

During covid-19, Australia set up some of the strictest rules, locking down the entire country, restricting freedom of movement, and even creating internment camps for "quarantine violators." Canada similarly imposed severe lockdowns and vaccine mandates and used emergency powers to seize the bank accounts and create business blacklists of peaceful protesters. The United Kingdom introduced a vaccine passport through a government-mandated phone app and required it to attend so-called high-density venues. The government had considered requiring it even to visit pubs and shops before backing down to public pressure and parliamentary protest.

No jurisdiction in the United States used serious police power to enforce pandemic policies. American politicians know that the people (many of whom are well armed) will not put up with tyranny. Even California, where Gavin Newsom squeezed churches and small businesses with an iron fist while cheering on BLM rioters, did not attempt the kinds of enforced movement restrictions imposed by the state in Australia, Canada, or the United Kingdom. People who scoff at the liberty-inducing power of the Second Amendment should reconsider their position in light of the evidence. What ultimately prevented the establishment of Australia-style covid quarantine concentration camps was not good laws but good men with good arms.

Indeed, we can attribute the freedoms we maintained during covid to the Second Amendment. Americans are inherently dangerous and violent to tyrants relative to our sister civilizations, and the myth of man's neuterability, of his placability, can never take hold. A European, even an Australian, may be civilized, but an American is a dangerous creature. Because of that, the modern project of turning people into the slaves of the state is resisted at the level of physical violence, and our country, despite the Uniparty's best efforts, remains a global beacon of liberty, the one and only land to which the oppressed and downtrodden may yet lift their eyes for hope and inspiration.

Cultivating Order

In his memoir, *My Grandfather's Son*, Supreme Court Justice Clarence Thomas illustrated what the pursuit of ordered liberty might personally demand from us. He recounted riding in his grandfather's truck in the family's fuel oil delivery business. In 1956, after years of making do with an old truck, Myers Anderson, Thomas's grandfather, purchased a new GMC truck. The first thing he did was remove the heater from his truck. Why? Because he was in the business of delivering fuel oil in winter, and he sought to avoid anything that might tempt him to delay or shirk his duties (to stay in the nice warm cab of the truck). So on the shelf in the garage the heater sat.

The New Conservative Movement should look to people such as Myers Anderson, Todd Beamer, Daniel Penny, and the members of the Cajun Navy for inspiration and encouragement. Likewise, we can look to our Founders. It was George Washington, after all, who in his inaugural address insisted that "the preservation of the sacred fire of Liberty and the destiny of the republican model of Government are justly considered perhaps as *deeply*, as *finally* staked on the experiment entrusted to the hands of the American people."

For too long, those hands have been idle. And indeed, until we once again begin to wield political power for the explicit purpose of restoring America's tradition of ordered liberty, we will be fighting a losing battle. That's because the "inner order" of the soul and the "outer order" of the republic are intrinsically linked. As George Will once stated and then forgot, statecraft is, in fact, soulcraft.

Now, some so-called conservatives will retort, "You want to legislate morality." They're not wrong. I do want the New Conservative Movement to make America moral again. What the wax-museum conservatives are wrong about, however, is that there is some alternative to "legislating morality"—that there is some other universe in which everything is neutral and freedom reigns supreme. They couldn't be more wrong.

We're going to channel the American middle class's fury against anarcho-tyranny into a populist movement to take back control in our lives, in our schools, in our communities, and in our country. We're going to bust up the Big Tech companies that have short-circuited our children's nervous systems, spread Chinese propaganda, and addicted millions of people to porn. And we're going to (metaphorically) burn down the LA district attorney's office and run George Gascón out of town on a rail, along with all the other prosecutors who abuse their power to try to stop us.

We are going to restore America's ordered liberty. We're going to start by empowering the good folks in Koreatown and other small-business owners across the country to defend themselves rather than board up their windows the next time BLM decides to burn down their city. Moreover, we're going to stop merely defending our individual right to own a gun, and we're going to start reforming police stations and founding rifle clubs that will help all of us fulfill our collective duty to keep our communities free and safe rather than having to wait helplessly outside a school where children are in grave danger. We're going to put into place district attorneys who will enforce the law. We're going to support companies, organizations, and hospitals that will help people overcome their addictions to drugs, gambling, and porn. We're going to clean up our public spaces.

So much rides on defeating anarcho-tyranny and defending ordered liberty in our country today. Will we surrender to the chaos and control of the Uniparty, or will we reassert our ancient inheritance of liberty? We need to fight today so that tomorrow, our children can again sit in shade, peace, and comfort under their own vine and fig tree.

CHAPTER 7

There's No Freedom
Without the Frontier

The true point of view in the history of this nation is not the Atlantic
coast, it is the great West.

—Frederick Jackson Turner

Have you ever driven through a blizzard in Wyoming? Your field of vision doesn't extend more than twenty feet. There are only the storm and the road, except for the occasional butte or buffalo. Silence descends on the glacier-carved valleys as ice and snow pile up and muffle all sound. The grizzlies seek shelter. You want to do the same. The frontier is dangerous. It is majestic yet simple. It is imposing yet liberating. It is, in short, the most American thing there is. And like those ancient glaciers that permanently reshaped the landscape of the West, Americans have been carving civilization into the stone since the Pilgrim fathers' "errand into the wilderness."

Still, the frontier has changed us much more than we will ever change it. Land shapes behavior. Western blizzards formed a people with distinct habits and customs; westerners couldn't survive in such a land if they didn't have a spirit of perseverance, toughness, and adaptability. The very unavoidability of nature gave people a healthy appreciation of mortality and chance. Other American landscapes did the same. The Cajun culture of Opelousas, for example, is indelibly intertwined with the forests and bayous where my ancestors settled. The same is true of the descendants of the brave men and women who followed Daniel Boone through the Cumberland Gap and settled large swaths of Ohio, Kentucky, West Virginia, and Tennessee—and of the pioneers who pushed across the Great Plains, past the Rockies, and to the Pacific Coast. Those mountains made them.

As much as the natural diversity of her people, the variations of America's landscape created a need for federalism. As each group of people adapted to each unique landscape, America developed diverse local cultures, economies, and institutions that made federalism both necessary and sensible. At the same time, the experience of settling a wild yet bountiful land was common to them all. The rugged individualism and true grit demanded by the frontier forged the American spirit.

That's a big part of what makes America unique. Our frontier tends to shape explorers, astronauts, cowboys, and innovators. A frontier attitude is one of risk taking, hard work, and optimism. Our elites once understood this spirit. Andrew Jackson, Abraham Lincoln, even Barry Goldwater (who was born in the Arizona Territory) all came from the frontier. But this is no longer the case. For those who are stuck in big cities on the coasts, the frontier has become nothing but a setting for movies and video games, and federalism a hollowed-out idea from a dead letter.

So what happened? When did we lose sight of the American frontier, and how can we reclaim it? That story begins and ends in California.

That's because California wasn't always the progressive hellscape it is today. For most of its history, California occupied a particular place in the American and Western imagination: it was the end of the frontier, the edge of the Western world, the place where the sun sets.

From priests such as Father Junipero Serra, who rode on muleback as he founded California's first missions, to pioneers such as Augustus T.

Dowd, who discovered sequoia trees while tracking a wounded grizzly through unfamiliar territory in 1852, that spirit—of adventure, of pushing onward, of spreading the Gospel to every corner of the world—was what California was all about.

Even after the American West was settled and civilized, California continued to open new frontiers. In 1912, Charles "Doc" Herrold of San Jose, California, became "the father of broadcasting" with the first regular radio broadcast, part of a ferment of tinkerers that would eventually result in Silicon Valley. In 1923, Walt Disney and his brother Roy founded the Disney Brothers Cartoon Studio in Hollywood, with a revolutionary animation system that would open new frontiers of the imagination. In the 1930s, scientists in Pasadena doing pioneering work in rocket propulsion founded the Jet Propulsion Laboratory, which has since gone on to send spacecraft to every planet in our solar system and land five rovers on Mars.

Is it any wonder that Ronald Reagan, a native son of California, was adamant about exploring the "next great frontier" and rebooting America's space program? Deeper, farther, higher: that's California, or at least it was.

But there was always another nightmare version of the California dream. For every would-be astronaut exploring outer space, there was a psychonaut of "inner space" looking to conquer the frontiers of human consciousness: Eastern yogis, Pentecostal preachers, Esalen seminar leaders, New Age gurus, LSD chemists. It's no coincidence that Steve Jobs, living on an LSD-soaked orchard commune, chose an apple with a bite out of it as his computer's symbol. "And ye shall be as gods, knowing good and evil."

The False Frontier: The Internet

After decades of development, Silicon Valley in the 1990s promised to open the next tranche of the California frontier: the internet. What had made the frontier great was that it had enlarged Americans' imaginations.

It had drawn us out of ourselves to the horizon. It had challenged us and made us strong. It had taught us the importance of freedom, but it had also reminded us of the fragility of our human condition and taught us to rely on God and on one another.

The internet can provide powerful tools for would-be explorers and pioneers. But mostly, that wasn't what Big Tech built. Rather than expanding the American frontier, Silicon Valley inverted it, both metaphorically and literally. Once again, the frontier has changed us more than we will ever change it; this time for the worse. It has disembodied us. More and more, our bodies and brains are becoming the frontier being explored and the Big Tech algorithms and Deep State surveillance the explorers.

It is hard to capture the psychonautic spirit of that time, but the cyberlibertarian John Perry Barlow's 1996 manifesto "A Declaration of the Independence of Cyberspace" comes close. Addressed to the "Governments of the Industrial World, you weary giants of flesh and steel," Barlow asserted, "You have no sovereignty where we gather," meaning online. "Cyberspace does not lie within your borders. . . . Ours is a world that is both everywhere and nowhere, but it is not where bodies live."

To put it bluntly, Barlow, like many other Silicon Valley visionaries of his era, didn't know what he was talking about. Although we've been trained to think of the internet as an ethereal cyberspace abstracted from "the real world," it does have a home. Like Alice falling through the looking glass, Silicon Valley's brainchild teleports us—and the frontier—back to the East Coast. Its epicenter is within miles of my home and also happens to be the capital of the American national security Deep State: northern Virginia, just outside Washington, DC. The internet isn't a nebulous, self-sustaining thing with no tether to the physical world. The internet exists because, in the real world, there are massive drab buildings full of IT infrastructure and whirring fans right in the heart of the Deep State's country clubs.

Remember, the technologies underlying the internet emerged from US military research. Some 70 percent of all global internet traffic passes through northern Virginia, which has the largest data center market in the world. Loudon County alone has some 27 million square feet of operational data center space across 115 facilities. According to the county government, there has not been a single day without data center construction in more than thirteen years.

Controlling this physical infrastructure matters a lot. It gives Washington the power to observe, predict, channel, surveil, and interrupt what everyone is doing. As seen in the US government's keeping Twitter online to fuel protests against the Iranian government or supplying Ukraine with battlefield internet via Elon Musk's Starlink, being able to turn it on and off is a powerful geopolitical tool. It is even more powerful, of course, as a domestic weapon. The Deep State's proximity to the internet has made it not only easy but positively convenient for National Security Agency programs such as MUSCULAR to scoop up the entire data flows of companies such as Yahoo! and Google. These operate on top of more targeted (but still vast) programs such as PRISM that have turned the Foreign Intelligence Surveillance Act (FISA) courts into a rocket docket of secret surveillance.

This is the basis of the Deep State's power. Its sounds are not the murmurs of the crowd or the empty words of activists and politicians bending the mob to their will. Instead, one hears only the ceaseless demonic whirring of data center air-conditioning systems in empty office parks as the entire planet's data is extracted, processed, and filed away. In identical corridors, a hive mind of bureaucrats hums with discussion, using the same flat, affectless tone when they discuss striking suspected Yemeni terrorists with drones as they do when ensuring that their compliance trainings are up to date.

These muted noises may not strike fear into people's hearts as the rousing speech of a European dictator does, but that only makes the regime more insidious. George Washington at least knew what demagogues and mob rabble looked like. If you plopped him down in Mount Vernon today, he'd think that the country had been taken over by invaders from outer space.

In a way, it has been.

As Alexis de Tocqueville wrote in *Democracy in America*, countries such as the United States face a novel sort of despotism. He foretold that as individuals are drawn ever more away from the glorious frontier into their own small pursuits, neglectful of the common good, they would be tempted toward electing not a violent tyrant but an infantilizing guardian:

> Above this race of men stands an immense and tutelary power, which takes upon itself alone to secure their gratifications, and to watch over their fate. That power is absolute, minute, regular, provident, and mild. It would be like the authority of a parent, if, like that authority, its object was to prepare men for manhood; but it seeks on the contrary to keep them in perpetual childhood. . . .
>
> It covers the surface of society with a network of small complicated rules, minute and uniform, through which the most original minds and the most energetic characters cannot penetrate, to rise above the crowd. The will of man is not shattered, but softened, bent, and guided: men are seldom forced by it to act, but they are constantly restrained from acting: such a power does not destroy, but it prevents existence; it does not tyrannize, but it compresses, enervates, extinguishes, and stupefies a people, till each nation is reduced to be nothing better than a flock of timid and industrious animals, of which the government is the shepherd.

"A flock of timid and industrious animals, of which the government is the shepherd." The New Authoritarian wolves of the Uniparty smack their lips as they herd everyday Americans hungry for the frontier, big skies, and new pastures into a "cyberspace" that they created and exercise total control over. Either the people of the United States will rise up, reclaim the American frontier, and burn down the fences enclosing us, or the Uniparty will slaughter us, replacing us with a diverse array of foreigners, cyborgs, and hive mind bureaucrats extolling the virtues of "our sacred democracy."

The First Temptation: Convenience

For a long time, America's rollicking federalism, frontier spirit, and instinct for liberty held back the growth of despotism. But even after the beginnings of the rise of this "immense and tutelary power," fueled by the aspirations of the Party of Destruction, there were still many natural limitations of institutional capacity, budgets, and communications, to name a few. One by one, they have fallen.

This is the significance of the vast invisible empire that now runs almost everything about our lives: the internet. The temptation of the new despotism is that it gives us things we need, and that's most true in the immense convenience of the internet. We communicate through it; we buy and sell through it; we travel the world with its aid.

I'm not just talking about social media. Even if you don't think about the internet at all, even if you don't have a smartphone, almost every critical element of social and commercial life in this country uses the internet today: finance, banking, navigation, news media, medicine, communications, marketing, and education, to start with.

The reason the internet is so convenient is that it is so connected. But the flip side of that connectedness is that it's tremendously vulnerable to coordination and manipulation, because it's so centralized. The New Authoritarians of the Deep State don't always need to manipulate the internet directly. They increasingly leverage "public-private" partnerships with Big Tech companies that can't afford to say "no" when the intelligence community comes knocking. Thanks to the brave work of the Republicans leading the House of Representatives' Select Subcommittee on the Weaponization of the Federal Government, we are just beginning to get a sense of the scale of this effort.

Most Americans have no idea how large the Deep State has become. According to a 2010 investigation by the journalists Dana Priest and William Arkin, "Some 1,271 government organizations and 1,931 private companies work on programs related to counterterrorism, homeland security and intelligence in about 10,000 locations across the United States," conducted by almost 1.5 million individuals with top secret clearances in some seventeen official agencies of the intelligence community. One program alone (a public-private partnership with AT&T) collects more than a trillion domestic phone records per year.

The New Authoritarian leviathan is not only vast but secret. The courts are secret, the rulings are secret, the warrants are secret, the reports are secret, the budgets are secret, and most important, the abuses are secret. An estimated *50 million classified documents* are produced each year.

In response to Cold War–era abuses of everyday Americans' civil rights, Congress passed legislation to protect Americans from the Deep State. But the internet's combination of globalization and centralization has made it trivially easy for the Deep State to exploit loopholes in this framework, and Inspector General reports have found repeated violations of the already flimflam FISA process.

The centralization of Big Tech makes this process even easier. New Authoritarian bureaucrats are technically forbidden from directly interfering with the speech of law-abiding Americans. But the trust and safety teams at places such as Facebook and Twitter are chock-full of former Deep Staters. The Deep State and its allies have been able to direct millions of taxpayer dollars to NGOs, nonprofits, and academic research centers that could make their own "independent" recommendations to Big Tech. Rather than officially ordering Big Tech around, the Deep State organized "coordinating" bodies such as the Department of Homeland Security's Disinformation Governance Board, yet another Uniparty *conspiratio*.

This conspiracy was on full display in October 2020, when one of the country's oldest newspapers, the *New York Post*, published a shocking exposé of the evidence of the Biden family's moral and political corruption found on Hunter Biden's laptop, abandoned at a Delaware computer repair shop. With the looming prospect of a Trump second term, the Deep State sprang into action.

First, fifty-one former senior intelligence officials signed an open letter (organized, we now know, by Biden consigliere Antony Blinken) that the laptop story "has all the classic earmarks of a Russian information operation" (this even though the FBI had already authenticated the laptop). Second, both Twitter and Facebook executives have testified that in the weeks leading up to the *Post* story (when the FBI was already aware of the existence and authenticity of the laptop), FBI officials repeatedly warned them of a coming Russian disinformation "hack-and-leak" campaign at meetings also attended by their former FBI colleague James Baker, who had become Twitter's chief lawyer.

The result of this operation (coordinated across the Deep State: former officials, Biden national security aides, Big Tech disinformation bureaucrats, FBI investigators) was that Twitter and Facebook felt compelled to censor the Hunter Biden story as disinformation, with Twitter going so far as to prevent users from even privately messaging the story to each other. This for a critical election-related story in an established American newspaper *that the Deep State players involved knew to be legitimate.* Maybe their hysterics about "stolen election conspiracy theories" and "misinformation" come from a guilty conscience.

The Second Temptation: Safety

Beyond convenience, the promise of an all-encompassing bureaucratic state is one of total safety. Every time something goes wrong, a servile people clamor for government to be given more power to fix the problem. The trouble, of course, is that that very power can easily be used to de-platform, rob, and entrap good people when the Uniparty aligns against them. We don't have to look far from home to see the future. The most shocking and disturbing example yet took place not far from our borders.

During the covid-19 pandemic, determined to virtue signal against Trump's America, Canadian prime minister Justin Trudeau imposed some of the strictest lockdowns and vaccine measures in the Western world, including, after vaccines became available, a vaccine mandate for international truckers entering Canada, despite no evidence that they were a significant vector of the spread of the disease.

The truckers had had enough. Like many blue-collar workers, they had found themselves squeezed and squeezed by increasingly heavy regulation and climate change policies. Like the farmers in the Netherlands protesting fertilizer quotas and the Yellow Vests in France protesting a discriminatory gas tax, the Canadian truckers decided that the only way to make themselves heard in the halls of power was to make themselves visible. They organized the Freedom Convoy, which gathered thousands of truckers and their rigs in the streets of Canada's capital, Ottawa.

It appears that the Canadian authorities had greatly underestimated the number of truckers who would be participating. Tens of thousands of them showed up, parked their massive rigs, and engaged their air brakes. For days and then weeks, they didn't budge. With the Canadian capital physically under siege, disruptions to Canada's major bridges to the United States, and the unsettling honking of the truckers' air horns, the Canadian authorities panicked. On Valentine's Day 2022, for the first time in Canadian history, Justin Trudeau invoked the powers of Canada's Emergencies Act.

Neither the Ottawa police nor the Royal Canadian Mounted Police (RCMP, Canada's equivalent of the FBI) had the physical capacity to dislodge the convoy, especially not since most of the towing companies took the truckers' side. What they did have was access to the Invisible Empire.

They went around with scanners, reading license plates and taking note of suspected protesters. They compelled financial institutions to supply transaction data about who had made protest-related purchases or donated to support the convoy. They froze Canadian citizens' accounts on social media to prevent "misinformation" from spreading.

But the most dramatic weapon they used was debanking individuals (and their families, in many cases) by labeling them "designated persons" involved in the Freedom Convoy. From the Public Order Emergency Commission's official report on the affair:

> In practical terms, this meant that financial institutions were required to entirely cut off designated persons from the financial

system. Financial institutions were to freeze all accounts of designated persons, including Registered Retirement Savings Plans (RRSPs), mortgage accounts, trading accounts, lines of credit, and credit cards. Online payment processors could not facilitate any purchase or sale involving a designated person. Cryptocurrency exchanges could not permit designated persons to access any currency held by the exchange or allow them to convert cryptocurrency into ordinary money.

That total unpersoning did not just apply to actual Freedom Convoy participants; anyone who violated any of the Canadian government's orders, including supporting the convoy with an online donation or taking a convoy protester a hot coffee on a cold day, could be targeted. Many were.

How were "designated persons" identified? The Emergencies Act order allowed the Canadian government to suspend privacy legislation so that social media companies, all levels of government, and financial institutions could share information with the RCMP. Moreover, the order put the onus on financial institutions, not the government, to determine who was a designated person; many of them targeted protesters very broadly just to be safe from future government investigation.

Canada even tried to coerce a wholly American company, the crowdfunding site GiveSendGo, to stop distributing money to convoy members. It refused. Other Big Tech companies, including PayPal and GoFundMe, voluntarily complied with Trudeau's threats, backed by the danger of governmental retaliation.

Even though the emergency officially lasted for only a short time, persecution of Trudeau's political opponents has continued much longer. One veteran Canadian trucker (and participant in the Freedom Convoy), Gord Magill, recounted the troubles of a dissident podcaster who was spuriously charged with crimes, held without bail for two months, and released without charges. But his bank account was shuttered, along with his mortgage, and he has been entirely frozen out of any other Canadian bank.

Under the Emergencies Act, no judicial review of bank decisions was allowed, and once someone is debanked, no one *has* to open an account for that person in the future. As we also saw regarding covid-19 vaccine mandates, somehow, in the New Authoritarianism, a public-private partnership to deprive you of your rights makes *both* parties immune from any legal remedy.

In the future, the federal government won't need to wait to stop a bunch of truckers from blocking the streets of the capital city. Hidden in the depths of the Biden-McConnell Infrastructure Bill is a requirement that all new cars and trucks sold by 2026 have a computer-controlled kill switch built in. And the broader "green transition" mandates toward electric vehicles (EVs) also ensure a far more controllable population (all modern EVs are basically smartphones on wheels).

You can clearly see the future forming: deplatforming drivers for spreading misinformation or failing to follow the latest vaccine mandate; mandatory climate lockdowns to limit carbon emissions. Yet another powerful tool of social control falls into place.

Skeptics who argue about whether anyone today *intends* this result are missing the point. Anyone who surrenders this degree of freedom and self-agency is already a slave waiting patiently for a master.

Over the past fifty years, an enormous number of threads have issued forth from Washington over the entire country. Like the Lilliputians entrapping Gulliver, each string is seemingly weak and harmless on its own. But they amount to a collective apparatus primed for the New Authoritarianism.

The dangers the United States faces as a country are real. But so is the danger to the American way of life posed by the vast and unaccountable Invisible Empire, which over the past thirty years has increasingly been weaponized against everyday Americans by factions of the Deep State. Its puppet strings have been growing steadily over time. And while those related to national security are in some sense the most alarming, the whole picture should include the increasing federal domination over every area of American life: education, food, medicine, public health, law enforcement, finance, banking, housing, transportation, commerce, and energy, just to start with.

The Third Temptation: Immaturity

Ultimately, the thing that's behind our capitulation to the Uniparty and its authoritarianism is that the siren song of immaturity is hard to resist. Comfort, safety, and security are good things—but the government wants to be their only provider.

The proper authority of the US government is to preserve the order of the republic by building up the virtue of the citizenry, as a father prepares his boys for manhood, in Tocqueville's analogy. Soft despotism, like an overbearing mother, instead "seeks on the contrary to keep them in perpetual childhood." It doesn't announce itself as such, of course: it uses vaccine passports, fitness trackers tied to your medical insurance, social media censors, and a thousand other little strings.

The Deep State, whether by intention or accident, aims to put the American spirit on puberty blockers; to domesticate our free people into "a flock of timid and industrious animals, of which the government is the shepherd."

The thing is, the frontier is dangerous. It's wild. It's violent and sometimes disorderly. "The meeting point between savagery and civilization," the historian Frederick Jackson Turner called it. The federal government has always had a role in mediating between the frontier and the republic writ large. But the United States is so vast that there's always been plenty of room.

There's a myth that the frontier "closed" with the end of US territorial expansion. But anybody who has spent time in the Big Sky Country of Montana, in the great Alaska range, in the vastness of the Great Plains, in the West Texas valleys that go on for days, knows that this isn't really true. The frontier is alive and well.

What changed was the growth of the federal apparatus throughout the twentieth century. The job of the federal marshal in the Wild West was to restore order when the cowboys couldn't quite manage. Today's Deep State treats us more like the cattle.

In 2021, Attorney General Merrick Garland directed the FBI to investigate parents protesting pandemic lockdowns and gender ideology at school board meetings. In 2022, the FBI sent a SWAT team to arrest the pro-life activist Mark Houck at his home, pointing guns at his wife and seven kids (he was acquitted). In 2023, FBI agents raided and shot dead Craig Robertson, an overweight seventy-five-year-old crank, after he posted violent memes about President Biden. FBI agents have shown up to investigate and intimidate moms' groups, ranchers, "radical-traditionalist Catholics" who prefer the traditional Latin Mass, pro-lifers, activists concerned about election integrity, and other ordinary Americans. Everyone, it seems, except the Hamas-supporting cells on college campuses or the radical leftists plotting to blow up pipelines.

Total Control

More and more, however, the Deep State doesn't even have to send its thugs to make Americans obey. Increasingly, they've trained (programmed, perhaps) Americans to be obedient. Enforcement is unnecessary, after all, when compliance is nearly universal.

When we first moved to northern Virginia, Michelle and I decided to be good citizens and get a feel for the area by attending a local town meeting. Now, I've been to lots of town meetings. They're a mainstay of American democracy, warts and all. They rarely feel like a Norman Rockwell painting. The most pedantic and consequently bitter local gripes tend to be interrupted only by either monotonous announcements or a loopy harangue by some resident eccentric. All that, I expected.

But what we encountered was something different. Person after person got up and spoke, not in ordinary human terms about their needs and desires, hatreds and loves, but in the hive mind language of "key performance indicators," "problematic developments," "racial equity in standardized test scores," and so on. Michelle turned to me and said, "These people, they don't think right."

It's hard for a normal human being to see the country through the Deep State's eyes. But in *The Revolt of the Elites and the Betrayal of Democracy* (1995), Christopher Lasch managed to do so. He captured something really important about the motives and manners of our Uni-party elites:

> The thinking classes are fatally removed from the physical side of life. . . . They live in a world of abstractions and images, a simulated world that consists of computerized models of reality— "Hyperreality," as it has been called—as distinguished from the palpable, immediate, physical reality inhabited by ordinary men and women. Their belief in the "social construction of reality"— the central dogma of postmodernist thought—reflects the experience of living in an artificial environment from which everything that resists human control (unavoidably, everything familiar and reassuring as well) has been rigorously excluded. Control has become their obsession.

The immense power the US government unlocked over the course of the twentieth century—taming rivers, surveilling the globe, touching the heavens, even harnessing the power of the atom—created a hubristic aspiration matched to a damaging fear: that America could be controlled and that it needed to be controlled for its own good. It's the same aspiration and the same intent Tocqueville foresaw: to impose a "strict uniformity of regulation, and personally to tutor and direct every member of the community," something beyond even the imagining of Caesar Augustus or Louis XIV.

Of course, the kind of total control that a weaponized and politicized intelligence community might cook up lies mostly beneath the surface. What is more visible is the rising tide of nonsense that suffuses American life: nonsense jobs, nonsense forms, nonsense policies.

Why is it that, every year, tens of millions of Americans attend hours of "compliance trainings"? Why is it that the cost of administration seems to climb higher every year?

After the Reagan Revolution cut government budgets, federal bureaucrats developed new strategies to exert control. In many cases, they retained the delegated congressional authorities to make and enforce rules; they just didn't have the manpower to do things directly. And so they began promulgating web after web of threads: guidances, rulings, warnings, "Dear Colleague" letters, and other gossamer handcuffs that threatened enforcement action. The result is that ostensibly private actors hire increasing numbers of woke white-collar bureaucrats (Lasch's elites who "live in a world of abstractions and images") to enforce government authorities *on themselves*, a fully privatized system of federal commissars.

As we have seen with DEI, once everything becomes the purview of compliance, compliance rules everything. Corporations think they can wall off DEI commissars, but if you say that everything from hiring to marketing to office location to health plans needs DEI supervision, you've given DEI control over the whole company.

But no matter what the supposed subject matter is (DEI, cybersecurity, health and safety), compliance training is training in compliance. It's deadly to the spirit of both the individual and the organization. It's just something thrown at you by a manager who doesn't care about you by an organization that is not taking responsibility for actually training you, mentoring you, or setting a proper example of how to behave. It's the leadership equivalent of a doctor quickly writing someone an Oxy-Contin prescription instead of taking the time to ensure they get the care they actually need.

For many ordinary Americans, that was how they experienced the Deep State's management of the covid-19 pandemic. So many Americans felt invisible to the regime, as though their struggles to take care of their families, to maintain their livelihood, to raise their kids, or to comfort their elderly parents meant *nothing* to those in power. They felt as though common sense had been thrown out the window. They felt manipulated and coerced, because policies justified by "the science" didn't change, even months (or years!) after we knew better. They felt like numbers on a spreadsheet.

There have been a lot of conspiracy theories about what happened during the pandemic, about elites "planning" it in order to exert totalitarian control. I think the reason why is a kind of emotional cope, because the truth is even more disturbing. The indifference, the incompetence, and the mediocrity didn't cover up anything. It didn't hide a secret enemy. The people in charge just know little and care little about you, about your life.

It's the same principle by which parents fighting for their kids' education end up at the desk of the FBI, by which the Biden administration could proclaim that "our very own intelligence agencies . . . have determined that domestic terrorism rooted in white supremacy is the gravest terrorist threat to our homeland today." Rather than engage the hard work of representative self-government, care, and duty toward the ordinary people of this country, it's easier for the DC apparatchiks to sic federal agents on them. It's an abandonment of care. It's a declaration of enmity.

These are not practices fit for a free people. We have become so dominated by the spirit of fear and paranoia that we have forgotten that to be free is necessarily a dangerous enterprise.

Back to the Frontier

When I think about the polar opposite of one of these hive mind operators or the cattle subjects they intend to rule over, I think of Palmer Luckey.

Palmer is an entrepreneur and an inheritor of the real spirit of Silicon Valley. The homeschooled son of a California car salesman, he was only a teenager when he set out to revolutionize virtual reality (VR). While living in a camper trailer in his parents' driveway and working minimum-wage jobs, he managed to crack the problem, delivering advances in VR that had eluded big technology companies for decades.

Palmer is an actual boy genius engineer, the closest thing modern America has to a contemporary Tom Swift (or Jimmy Neutron, for my younger readers). With his prototype, Palmer launched a 2012 Kickstarter campaign for his headset, dubbed the Oculus. It became one of the most successful crowdfunding campaigns of all time, turning Palmer's trailer experiments into a leading VR company that was acquired by Facebook for $2 billion in 2014.

It's hard to convey how much of a lightning-in-a-bottle story this is, outside of all modern Silicon Valley norms for building a start-up. It's Rocky Balboa or Cinderella. Yet after only a few years of Palmer continuing his work on Oculus, Facebook unceremoniously fired him in 2016.

What was the sin that led Facebook to sever ties with Palmer? Did he molest a subordinate? Drive drunk? Drug someone with methamphetamine for sexual gratification? No, you can have a long and storied career in California while guilty of those things if you have the right friends and politics, as Harvey Weinstein, Paul Pelosi, and Ed Buck amply demonstrate. Palmer did something even more unforgivable: he donated $10,000 to a political action committee supporting the election of Donald Trump to the presidency.

Unbeknown to the company's wokescold HR managers, attempting to cancel Palmer turned out to be a huge mistake for Facebook. That's because in 1937, to protect the Communists and leftist activists in Hollywood and the labor unions, the California legislature had passed a law making it illegal for employers to punish employees for their political activities outside work. The senior managers at Facebook, a woke company with woke employees, had never had occasion to confront those protections before. And so, according to the *Wall Street Journal*, Luckey hired an employment lawyer after his firing who approached Facebook with that inconvenient fact and "negotiated a payout of at least $100 million, representing an acceleration of stock awards and bonuses he would have received through July 2019, plus cash." Facebook's political persecution turned into a huge payday for Palmer.

Most twentysomethings, given a $100 million payout, would skate off into a life of sybaritic pleasure, perhaps spending summers in the south of France and winters heli-skiing the Rockies while doing virtue-signaling philanthropy and a bit of angel investing or movie producing for fun.

But only a lunatic or a patriot would do what Palmer did next: found a defense technology company to bolster the United States' national security. Compared to consumer products, building military technology is extremely difficult and resource intensive and must comply with convoluted supply chain and cybersecurity regulations. The prize for producing innovative products at great expense is to then spend years of your life and millions of dollars fighting through stultifying bureaucratic and legal tripwires to compete against the big defense "prime contractors" and enable the US military to actually buy your wares. From the end of the Cold War until a few years ago, only a handful of Silicon Valley technology companies had ever dared to try to enter the defense sector. It's not a coincidence that they were all companies whose visionary founders were *already* centimillionaires when they did so (Palantir Technologies, backed by Peter Thiel; SpaceX by Elon Musk; and Anduril by Palmer Luckey).

As the founder of Anduril, Palmer has been applying his considerable skills building the kinds of technologies the United States needs to secure her future and once again explore the next great frontiers: loitering munitions for our special operators, sensor platforms to secure our border, and miniature jet-powered autonomous drones for our air force, all built to the highest standards with the same software-first approach Palmer had used to crack VR. Even as other Silicon Valley companies shy away from working in US defense and legacy defense companies haggle over every dime, Palmer Luckey, sporting a Hawaiian shirt, a mullet, and a big vision, isn't asking anybody's permission to build the systems he thinks are important for the United States' future.

The Deep State doesn't think that Americans are capable of governing themselves, and it has elaborate plans to turn a nation of cowboys into a nation of cattle. A true American pioneer such as Palmer Luckey will tell them where they can shove their plans—with a winsome grin on his face.

Reasserting the Principles

How can we free ourselves from the rule of the Deep State? Federalism makes sense only if we recover the spirit of the frontier. For generations, it was the challenge of the frontier that spurred the American soul to greatness. It called forth self-reliance, skill, diligence, industry, courage, and neighborliness. Long after many other parts of the West had begun a cynical naval-gazing turn, Americans remained mesmerized by the frontier, always looking outward, ever farther. And we had a constitutional system fit for it, one in which Americans didn't sit around waiting for the federal government to take care of everything; one in which federal power was limited and placed in the service of Americans exercising their agency to settle the frontier and gaining the rewards in their estates and their souls. I call it *endless frontier federalism*. It's an embodied attitude. And it doesn't just have to mean looking westward or looking out to the stars. You can have the fire of the endless frontier within your soul, even in Washington.

The heart of our federalism is subsidiarity, the preservation of liberty and agency to solve problems at the most local possible level. In preserving the sovereignty of the states, our constitutional system protects a powerful source of renewal and resilience. As James Madison wrote in *The Federalist Papers*, No. 45, "The powers delegated by the proposed Constitution to the federal government are few and defined. Those which are to remain in the State governments are numerous and indefinite."

It's a bit counterintuitive, but endless frontier federalism is also essential to preserving the national unity and strength our Constitution was meant to foster.

The vision of our Founding Fathers was *E pluribus unum*: Out of many, one. The Deep State wants an *unum* that swallows everything else: one set of ideas, one set of rules, one set of rulers. For the Deep State, diversity means different-colored bureaucrats running the same software.

For the Party of Creation, the endless frontier is plenty diverse. It isn't about what you look like, but about the values you're trying to live out, the institutions you're trying to build, and the virtues you are trying to exercise.

Much of the division experienced in this country is the result of over-centralization that raises the stakes of what goes on in Washington to an unbearable degree. Reclaiming the frontier will allow us to live together again, "preserving the unity of the Spirit in the bond of peace."

It will also preserve our strength. Systems that are overly centralized become *fragile*. They develop bottlenecks and interdependencies that, when they break down, wreck everything. We saw this time and again during the pandemic. A revitalized endless frontier federalism would both demand and produce greater resilience by ensuring that states and localities cultivate a measure of independence and self-sufficiency.

There are, of course, many areas where it is fitting and proper for the federal government to have a large role. But one of the more intriguing promises of the twenty-first century is that the economy-of-scale paradigm of the Industrial Era has been overthrown. We have the technology to decentralize production, coordination, communication, and much else besides without losing their benefits.

A liberty not used is a liberty lost. The best way to recover endless frontier federalism is to start building with vigor and confidence at the state and local levels, asking forgiveness, not permission.

One vastly underrated tool for recovering federalism is the interstate compact, a tool authorized in the Constitution that permits states to make substantive agreements and contracts among themselves. The Supreme Court has taken an expansive view of the authorities of interstate compacts and a highly limited view of when they need to seek congressional approval. States can set up multistate agencies, coordinate state laws, enter into agreements with each other, and more; examples include the Port Authority of New York and New Jersey and the Emergency Management Assistance Compact, but states are starting to use them more broadly to coordinate state licensing requirements, for instance.

The Texas Public Policy Foundation has described interstate compacts as a "Shield of Federalism" and argued for much more creative uses

of them. States could use them, for example, to create a shared investment structure to combat ESG and protect investment sovereignty or to
coordinate on health care standardization and cost cutting. Crucially,
compacts that are approved by Congress can override other federal laws;
they could be used to create zones of freedom from overbearing federal
bureaucracies.

For example, SpaceX today seeks to revolutionize US space access
with the heaviest ever reusable rocket, the Starship, operating from Star-
base, near Brownsville, Texas. In a return to the final frontier spirit of
the Space Race, SpaceX seeks to launch often and learn often and has
achieved one milestone after another over the past decade.

The problem is that even though the company operates on a remote
stretch of desert beach in the far south of Texas, the Federal Aviation
Administration (FAA) has repeatedly slow-walked launch licenses and
permits. The issue has nothing to do with the soundness of SpaceX's
rocketry; it's that under the National Environmental Policy Act, issuing
experimental permits and launch licenses is considered a major federal
action requiring an environmental review.

Almost all of the FAA's demands have had nothing to do with the
role Congress envisioned for launch approvals in the Commercial Space
Launch Act of 1984. For instance, the FAA required SpaceX to carry
out seventy-five actions to mitigate environmental impacts before the
company could receive a launch license for the site, including donating
money to a local environmental nonprofit. Every time SpaceX wants to
launch a modified vehicle from the site, environmentalists sue the FAA
to slow down the NEPA process in the name of saving the piping plovers
and ocelots.

But imagine if Texas, Louisiana, Alabama, Mississippi, and Florida
were to band together to create a Space Coast Aerospace Development
Compact. Each state would have a significant interest in advancing US
rocket science, with major public and private space facilities, training
centers, manufacturing, and launch pads. The compact could set up
an interstate compact agency with an expedited approval process for
approving rocket launches, including a clause that "The operation of

federal laws not consistent with state laws and regulations adopted pursuant to this compact will be suspended."

With the consent of Congress (which is easier to gain for a narrow compact affecting only a few states than for one involving a wholesale overhaul of FAA rules), the compact would acquire the force of federal law and render FAA rules and regulations null and void for the covered activities in those states. Maybe more important, it would empower state-level personnel who want to do launches and disempower federal bureaucrats who don't. It would also, in many cases, allow the states to skirt around NEPA and other federal red tape.

What is strangling our country is all of the gossamer threads that impose a vetocracy emanating from Washington and covering the land. Reestablishing the frontier with creative tools such as interstate compacts will be part of the way out of the labyrinth and back to our federalist system.

Reclaiming the Powers

In our constitutional system, states and citizens cannot defy or nullify duly passed legislation signed by the president. But much of what hamstrings American freedom today is nebulous interpretations of self-defined rules based on internal legal memos interpreting vague regulations produced by twice- or thrice-delegated authority from a statute of questionable constitutionality.

To be blunt, the Deep State often claims authority that it simply does not possess. We need to stop deferring to the legitimacy of its claims unless and until they are confirmed by Congressional clarification or judicial interpretation.

Lawyers and policy makers in the New Conservative Movement need to interrogate every single specific authority claimed by the administrative state to discern what is a valid and needful use of federal power and what is an unconstitutional and unenforceable infringement on our endless frontier federalism. This process should be not just a casual chitchat but rather a body cavity, strip-search, enhanced interrogation. So unlike perhaps some of the 1990s conservatives, I don't want to drown the government; I want to waterboard it.

A wide swath of authorities and regulations promulgated by federal agencies may not be worth the paper they are printed on. It's time for the states to call the Deep State's bluff in the name of liberty and endless frontier federalism. There are a number of tools a state can use to create a state-level legal framework that makes extraconstitutional authorities claimed by the Deep State effectively unenforceable within the state. The tactics that states such as Oregon and California have pioneered to protect illegal immigrants (against constitutional federal authorities) can now be used to build sanctuary states and sanctuary cities for Americans—sanctuaries from federal overreach and tyranny.

Already, the Tenth Amendment forbids the federal government from commandeering state resources (requiring state officials to actively enforce federal laws). A number of states have gone further, forbidding state employees to share information with federal officials. Some states have also changed state licensing, banking, or gun sales laws in order not to have to collect certain information that could be subpoenaed by federal law enforcement authorities. Idaho and Missouri have gone even further, passing laws forbidding state officials to enforce any federal orders in violation of the Second Amendment.

We have a growing blueprint for how far a revivified federalism could go. A number of states of the union have taken it upon themselves to legalize marijuana. Now, I oppose this on the grounds that marijuana is a destructive public nuisance and a significant cause of schizophrenia onset in heavy users, not because I oppose states exercising their powers. These states have proved that if entrepreneurs are willing to limit themselves in certain respects, such as not trafficking across state borders and using in-state financial institutions and services, the citizens of this country have more freedom than they think.

For instance, one of the most absurd authorities claimed by the federal government is the right to regulate every mouthful of food produced by a business in the entire country, even if it is sold within the same state (the Constitution's Commerce Clause gives Congress the authority to regulate interstate commerce).

Under the Food and Drug Administration's expansive self-understanding of its statutory authority, the Department of Justice could bring an enforcement action against Susie and Jenny for not properly labeling the wares at their neighborhood lemonade stand. It is only through the agency's magnanimity and generosity that its self-developed enforcement guidelines let the girls slide. Similarly, the Department of Agriculture claims the authority to stand in between a farmer and his neighbor, forbidding the farmer to sell the neighbor a side of bacon without a federal inspection. Even the most pro-federalist Founder would have started loading his muskets if you'd have told him that this was where the Constitution would lead.

The FDA's and USDA's claims have a direct effect on the health of Americans. They require every food producer to place USDA propaganda labels on their products, giving the impression that grass-fed beef is less healthy for you than seed-oil vegan patties. They force local organic farmers who raise their pigs and chickens in a healthy, careful manner to comply with all of the same regulatory requirements as huge corporate concerns that stuff their animals full of hormones and antibiotics. In fact, the USDA requires them to use the same slaughterhouses and facilities.

Representative Thomas Massie of Kentucky understands how absurd and haughty a claim this is and how out of sync with the limits of federal authority. He's another great American filled with the spirit of the frontier, an MIT electrical engineering grad who built a totally self-sufficient home on his own land, including an off-grid electrical system he designed himself using repurposed Tesla batteries. Representative Massie has proposed legislation that would create exemptions for small farmers and ranchers to slaughter and process their livestock at local facilities.

In the meantime, states could take direct action to exempt farmers and ranchers who sell their products only within the state from federal regulations. They could forbid state inspectors to work with the federal government or even exempt their citizens from reporting requirements. A small number of congressmen could easily put a rider in must-pass legislation enjoining the USDA from spending any money on enforcement actions in states that have legalized farmers to sell their own locally butchered meat (as has been done to prevent federal enforcement of certain marijuana laws in states that have legalized weed). And if the USDA dared to push the issue, public interest law shops in the New Conservative Movement stand ready to defend small farmers and ranchers from federal overreach.

Wax-museum conservatives will say that this piecemeal, hodgepodge approach is no way to make legislation. And they're right! It would be better if Congress passed good laws and reformed bad laws. But in the absence of a functioning Congress, it is better to create and protect zones of freedom from poorly written laws and supercilious federal bureaucrats than to play along with regulatory anarcho-tyranny in which the federal government and blue states turn a blind eye on illegal immigrants and woke corporatists while smug "principled conservatives" tell families and small businesses to stand there and take it.

Reining in the Deep State

Civil libertarians from both parties have warned for many decades that the legislative and constitutional safeguards protecting the republic against its own security organs were woefully inadequate. For a long time, in the name of national security, Republicans as much as Democrats have ignored them. We might not have bought #Resistance votive candles with FBI director James Comey's face on them, but we cheered a massive expansion of unaccountable federal power after 9/11. We were wrong.

We should have better followed our Founders, who, in the debates around the framing of the Constitution, regardless of their viewpoints, paid grave attention to the example of the Roman Praetorian Guard and the danger that those responsible for the republic's security posed to it. Many of them would have translated Juvenal's *Satires* in the schoolhouse and come across his evocative question *"Quis custodiet ipsos custodes?"*: "Who watches the watchmen?"

You don't need to take my word for it. Reviewing the last twenty years of public Inspector General's reports from agencies across the intelligence community provides harrowing example after example of failed policies and deep abuses. Despite decades of warnings, federal overclassification, secrecy, and abuse of the police power have gotten severely worse, not better. Such reports have shown:

- At least a dozen NSA analysts using top secret systems to spy on their current and former spouses and girlfriends
- FBI agents using false statements to gain FISA warrants, including one against President Trump
- The CIA hacking Senate Intelligence Committee staff members who were preparing a report on alleged torture during the global War on Terror
- The Secret Service falling under investigation for illegally destroying records by the Department of Homeland Security's Inspector General—who is also under investigation for the same thing.
- Special operations soldiers implicated in smuggling, spilling over into murder and other crimes, including reports of trafficking drugs from foreign deployments back into the United States

The House Select Subcommittee on the Weaponization of the Federal Government is a good start. But we need a more substantial and more bipartisan effort on the scale and seriousness of the Senate Select Committee to Study Governmental Operations with Respect to Intelligence Activities, also known as the Church Committee (1975), chaired by Democratic senator Frank Church of Idaho and Republican senator John Tower of Texas, which revealed serious Cold War intelligence community abuse and led to major reforms.

Congress should also eliminate many of the vast redundancies and overlaps among the federal agencies, including abolishing the Bureau of Alcohol, Tobacco, Firearms and Explosives (ATF), which should be a convenience store, not a government agency. And Congress needs to rein in the weaponization and politicization of federal law enforcement by providing better direct oversight of the FBI, instead of letting the agency hide behind the skirts of the Department of Justice.

The Endless Frontier is still going to need its federal marshals. There are still wolves on the prowl. But the Deep State as a tendency, a network, and an ideology is the enemy of the American spirit. Most of the employees, especially in federal law enforcement and national security, are patriots. Many of them are military veterans who are themselves upset about the weaponization and politicization of their agencies.

A fish rots from the head down, and so does the Deep State.

One source of the Deep State's lock on power is that to advance to the highest levels of their agencies, senior federal personnel must play the Washington game. Even if their hearts are in taking down cartel assets at the border or going after Chinese spies in Silicon Valley, they know that they need to network, schmooze, and socialize in the DC Swamp to get ahead. Recently, the FBI asked for $375 million to build an office complex larger than the Pentagon in the DC area (to replace its awful Brutalist headquarters in downtown DC).

One of the strongest things we can do to break down the power of the Deep State is to remove as much power, and as many people, from proximity to the Uniparty DC nexus as possible: relocating federal agencies into the American heartland, increasing the size and independence of field offices relative to headquarters, requiring members of the Senior Executive Service to undertake a period of duties of personal service for and interaction with ordinary Americans, and mandating other measures that might serve to bind our federal agencies to the American people again and restore their trust.

Conclusion

The defenders of the Deep State will say that the reforms outlined here will make us less safe. They're right.

Being a free person is dangerous. It demands responsibility, resilience, self-reliance, and humility; virtue, in a word. I can picture in my mind's eye the choice words that the Wyoming ranchers of my acquaintance would have for a nanny-state bureaucrat who warned them that hunting bears or rolling their own barbed wire wasn't safe.

Safety imposed via surveillance breeds fragility and weakness. In the diktats of the Deep State, we should hear the nagging voice of the overbearing helicopter mom: "Why don't you play inside, where it's safe?" "Why don't we wear two masks, just to be safe?" "Feeling anxious about your body changing? We should put you on puberty blockers, just to be safe."

The Constitution is being overthrown by a new form of tyranny based on federal centralized control, surveillance, and weaponized law enforcement. Against the stifling safety of the New Authoritarianism, we need to reclaim within our souls the spirit of endless frontier federalism. Even as we do what we can to fix Washington, we need to sever the apron strings and reacquaint ourselves with self-government at the state and local levels. Doing so will at times be messy and dangerous. But it will be a gymnasium of the frontier spirit.

CHAPTER 8

We're Not an Empire

*[America's] glory is not dominion, but liberty. Her march is
the march of the mind. She has a spear and a shield: but the
motto upon her shield is, Freedom, Independence, Peace.*

—John Quincy Adams

I 've ticked off a lot of people as president of the Heritage Foundation. That's fine; it comes with the territory. But by a long shot, the thing that has led to the most ferocious attacks, the most organized opposition to what we are doing (including from erstwhile "conservatives") has not been our taking a hard line on illegal immigration, refusing to go along with wokeness, standing up for the one man–one woman family, or even moving away from wax-museum economic ideology. Nor has it been any of the other issues that are most controversial among the ordinary folks I meet all over the country. The most controversial thing we have ever done is to stand up to the foreign policy Blob to demand accountability and a strategy for the tens of billions of dollars being sent to Ukraine. In response to this, the Uniparty unleashed a multimillion-dollar dark money AstroTurf campaign, spilled gallons of ink in top "conservative" newspapers, magazines, and think tank reports, and carried out backroom whispering aimed at our donors and supporters. Why the eruption over this issue?

On no other issue is there such distance between the commonsense beliefs of everyday Americans and the Uniparty ideology of the imperial foreign policy mandarins pulling the puppet strings in the DC Swamp. However bad you think it is, it's worse. And even though I often highlight the fiscal and military issues associated with our foreign policy, such as vast overspending and graft, a tottering defense industrial base, and our hollowed-out armed forces, the truth is that those aren't even the most important problems of our foreign policy. The soul of our republic is at stake.

The New Conservative Movement must reject the woke imperialism that has characterized our post–Cold War foreign policy, renew our emaciated military forces, and restore our traditional America First approach to global statesmanship devoted to preserving the United States' liberty and independence and leading primarily through friendship, free commerce, and our own virtuous example.

Woke Imperialism

August 2022 was a very busy time for the president of Ukraine, Volodymyr Zelenskyy. Due in no small part to Zelenskyy's personal courage and steely resolve, Ukraine survived the first seventy-two hours of the February 2022 Russian invasion (against the predictions of both US and Russian intelligence). Having demonstrated their will to fight, the Ukrainians then petitioned the West for more military aid to defend themselves and their homeland, which began arriving in streams and then rivers, enabling them to pivot from defense to counteroffensive by August.

Yet amid all of this, President Zelenskyy found time to address an urgent matter: a petition to legalize gay marriage in Ukraine. He assured signers of his support at the first opportunity to change Ukraine's constitution.

Why, in the midst of a nationalist war of survival by one of the most conservative countries in Europe, did its beleaguered president take time to promote gay rights? Zelenskyy certainly made no mention of gay rights on the campaign trail in 2019. In late 2020, the DC-based Atlantic Council bemoaned the "false dawn" for gay rights that urban Ukrainian progressives had projected onto Zelenskyy. In July 2020, Zelenskyy's party even floated a bill regulating "homosexual propaganda" that was "an almost literal translation of its Russian analogue." Why the sudden change of heart?

Rome had its pinch of incense for the emperor. The Soviets had Marxism-Leninism. And under the current regime, the United States has the rainbow flag. You can't blame the Ukrainians.

Enlargement

If we've been slowly abandoning our traditional US foreign policy, when did it start?

In the First and Second World Wars and the Cold War–era fight against Soviet communism, we rolled up our sleeves and fought in the trenches with our allies against tyranny. But we did so with a broad spectrum of political support and based on a keen understanding of what the United States' vital interests were in a changing world in which technology and globalization had shrunk the power of distance. I think the more definitive break from our tradition, the abandonment of the underlying map of the national interest, came afterward.

Enlargement: the word has a whiff of excess, bloat, and decay. There's something forced and inorganic about it: things are enlarged that would naturally be a smaller, normal size. Diseased organs and infected limbs are enlarged. We call something that keeps growing and growing beyond its natural bounds a cancer or a tumor.

Republics grow. Empires are enlarged. But enlargement has been the United States' official approach to foreign policy since the end of the Cold War.

Throughout the Cold War, our grand strategy was one of containment. The Soviet Union wished to export communism to remake the world in its image. But it had a core weakness: if it was prevented from expanding, its own internal contradictions and inefficiencies would ultimately tear it apart. And so containment meant building a network of alliances across the Free World in order to link arms, hold back the tide of communism, and ultimately defeat the Soviet Union.

With the collapse of the USSR, the United States became, geopolitically, the dog that caught the car. For the first time in our history, a senior American statesman could say, "There is now no credible near-term threat to America's existence," and be correct. Based on our tradition of statesmanship, many American policy makers wanted a return to our policies of an "active commerce" and a hemispheric defense of our interests, this time with the world's most powerful navy four times over and an unstoppable nuclear deterrent. We might deal, at last, with the cultural, economic, and social decay that we had been avoiding reckoning with. That was the peace dividend the American people had been promised.

But a group of American foreign policy experts were determined to shoot down those they dubbed "protectionists," "isolationists," and "Neo-Know-Nothings," those who wanted the United States to return to her traditional approach. They advocated that the United States take advantage of that unique historical opportunity to attempt to permanently transform the world order.

Probably the best summary of this shift is a speech given in September 1993 by President Bill Clinton's national security advisor, Anthony Lake. Lake's speech called for a shift from containment to enlargement. Rather than cash in the peace dividend, he said, the United States needed to remain engaged in the world and expand the network of Free World alliances and institutions from a small number of stalwart allies to the entire world. As more states turned into market democracies, the United States would shore them up by expanding the institutions it backed, such as NATO, the North American Free Trade Agreement (NAFTA), and the General Agreement on Tariffs and Trade (GATT; later the framework for the WTO). They would be helped along not only with US military might but with "diplomacy multipliers," a complex of US government–backed NGOs such as the National Endowment for Democracy.

What threatened this victory? A handful of "'backlash' states" including Iraq and Iran were threatened by our global enlargement. They threatened to "sponsor terrorism and traffic in weapons of mass destruction and ballistic missile technologies," Lake said.

What was the best way to deal with the "'backlash' states"? "Isolate them diplomatically, militarily, economically and technologically" and use "intelligence, counterterrorism and multilateral export controls." But, Lake gravely intoned, "When the actions of such states directly threaten our people, our forces, or our vital interests, we clearly must be prepared to strike back decisively and unilaterally."

The rise and fall of the United States' post–Cold War foreign policy is foreshadowed there, well before 9/11.

To be clear, I am not suggesting that everything Lake advocated for was a mistake, such as expanding our NATO alliance or some of our other institutions to new friends and allies. In many cases, it served both the United States' interest and the promotion of a world order friendly to liberty, commerce, and democracy. And I'm highly sympathetic to how new and strange the problems we dealt with were, how much they called for novel solutions. Many of the things we did in that time period, such as stabilizing post-Soviet nuclear, chemical, and biological weapons through the Cooperative Threat Reduction program, saving starving kids with well-timed food aid, and shoring up our alliances with countries such as South Korea and Japan, were wise investments that well repaid their costs.

The problem is that this foreign policy consensus made enlargement the default, the norm, the expected outcome *regardless of whether it served our own interests*. It led to overreach and hubris, the classic means by which great powers doom themselves.

The signs are there if you look. For example, Lake extolled the mission to provide food aid in Somalia, which had required the United States' providing "a secure military environment for humanitarian relief at a reasonable cost and risk," for which it was "only a matter of time" before our troops could be withdrawn. Two weeks later, local militants would shoot down two US Black Hawk helicopters, kill eighteen US soldiers, and wound dozens more. Clinton would ignominiously pull our troops out as quickly as he could: we now know that Al-Qaeda had trained the RPG squads how to target our helicopters and counted that as its first victory against the Great Satan.

Equally troubling is Lake's treatment of China—or lack thereof. He argued that we needed to continue opening our trade with China to build the Chinese middle class, so as to encourage Chinese democracy, an inevitable development. The Clinton administration, of course, looked the other way on the CCP's human rights record (and record of protectionism and trade cheating) when it pushed through the US–China Relations Act of 2000, which opened the door to China's accession to the World Trade Organization (WTO) and its subsequent global rise and continuous assault on the American way of life.

In his conclusion, Lake said something extraordinary. Speaking to those who agreed that the most important thing was "active American engagement abroad on behalf of democracy and expanded trade," he recommended that "all of us who support engagement should be careful to debate tactics in a way that does not prevent us from coming together in common cause around the fundamental importance of that goal": the goal of "rallying Americans to bear the costs and burdens of international engagement" against the "protectionists" and "isolationists" who wanted the United States to rebuild at home.

And that's just what they would do, the major factions of the Uniparty foreign policy Blob. Old-fashioned American statesmanship never stood a chance.

The Foreign Policy Blob

One lesson my involvement in politics has taught me time and again is that a determined and focused minority can override the desires of a diffuse and unorganized majority, even a large one.

In the 1990s, almost everyone involved in US politics turned to focus on the substantial domestic issues the country faced. Issues of economics, culture, technology, and immigration consumed the vast majority of Americans' attention, to the extent that they paid attention at all. After living in the shadow of nuclear war for decades, most Americans (myself included) took advantage of that "holiday from history" to ignore foreign affairs. My only memory of even thinking about the issue was during the 1996 presidential campaign, when I was asked to defend Bob Dole's policies regarding Bosnia; I asked what on earth anything in the former Yugoslavia had to do with the United States.

And so even though most Republicans (and many Democrats, for that matter) in the 1990s favored a return to traditional American statesmanship, those forces were distracted and disorganized. After all, there isn't usually much energy behind a policy of not doing something.

But two groups, a small part of their own parties, were intensely interested in foreign affairs in the 1990s. Like Tony Lake, they thought that the United States needed to seize the unique opportunity to remake the world order in its own image. Over time, they would not only set the United States' international agenda but remake the policy world, establishing new networks of institutions such as think tanks, advocacy organizations, and consulting companies while drawing huge resources to their cause from parties interested in shaping US foreign policy, especially defense contractors, multinational corporations, and foreign governments and state-owned enterprises. They form the foreign policy department of the Uniparty: the Blob.

The Blob sees itself as the network of properly credentialed and vetted experts who provide expertise and continuity that other US leaders—amateurs without the right training—are not qualified to perform. The Blob sees foreign policy as an activity apart from grungy, partisan domestic politics, something elevated and enlightened, even over what the benighted American people believe. The Blob controls not only senior positions across the foreign policy establishment in government but, more important, the network of cushy sinecures in think tanks and corporations that are the due rewards for a poorly paid stint in government.

The heart of the Blob is an alliance between two factions of the Party of Destruction. The first comprises the liberal internationalists, such as Tony Lake, former secretary of state Madeleine Albright, and former ambassador to Russia Michael McFaul. They see themselves as defenders of the "liberal order" (a term first widely used in the 1990s) in which the United States plays an indispensable role in ensuring human rights, international law, and democracy throughout the world, with military force if necessary.

The second faction comprises the neoconservatives, such as Bill Kristol, Bob Kagan, John Bolton, Paul Wolfowitz, Elliott Abrams, and Max Boot. They believe that the durability of the "liberal order" is ultimately rooted not in morals or law but in US power. The United States should unilaterally promote democracy, freedom, and markets by any means necessary and should be quick to use its global military capabilities and alliances to crush its enemies. No resistance to US power is too small to escape their notice, and there are no limitations other than political will over the United States' exercise of power abroad. The neocons' motto is "We can do it all and do it alone if we have to—we're America, aren't we?"

The neocons and liberal interventionists have worked hand in hand at least since 1992. The primary difference between the two groups is that when a liberal internationalist and a neocon together call for the United States to bomb a third-world country back to the Stone Age, the liberal feels bad about it and wants to fund a generous foreign aid package to assuage her conscience.

In a Charles Dickens novel, you'd know what to think about a foreign policy agenda put forward by characters with names such as Max Boot, Paul Wolfowitz, Samantha Power, and Anne-Marie Slaughter.

Our involvement in foreign wars since the fall of the Soviet Union has cost thousands of American lives, wasted trillions of dollars, and destabilized and devastated large swathes of the world. We have taken on alliance commitments that cover, when you sum them up, three entire continents and a large part of Asia. All of this has been done in our name; the promissory notes promising that the United States will pour blood out of her veins for foreign causes have your name and mine on them. At the same time, our strength at home has become hollow and enervated, our people demoralized, our industrial base scattered, our elite corrupted.

Looking at the contrast between our bombastic foreign policy and the disarray and decay at home, one cannot help but feel that John Quincy Adams's republican prediction regarding what would happen should the United States become entangled in foreign interventions, even for good causes, has come true: "She might become the dictatress of the world. She would be no longer the ruler of her own spirit."

Hindsight

If you saw all of this coming, if you were sounding the alarm about imperial hubris even before the Iraq War, this might be the place for you to put in a big "I told you so."

I certainly didn't.

I have a confession to make. I am a recovering neocon. I was a full-throated supporter of George W. Bush. I most definitely thought we should invade Iraq. I even, I have to admit, subscribed to the *Weekly Standard,* the quintessential neoconservative magazine. And so I've been doing a fair bit of reflection.

We can see now where it's all gone wrong, where we departed from the deep wisdom of our tradition of statesmanship. But the 1990s were a genuinely novel, disorienting time. They felt like the end of history, a break from more than a century of global struggle and risk.

At the same time, the vast majority of conservatives, myself included, weren't interested in politics because of foreign policy. We were interested in *America* and issues much closer to home. We trusted our party's intellectual bright lights to lead us in generally the right direction.

Like many conservatives, I didn't pay attention to foreign policy at all until 9/11. Seeing what jihadist terrorists had done to my country so enraged me that I would have supported anything President Bush wanted. I felt like nuking Afghanistan. When President Bush said that Iraq had supported terrorists and threatened the United States with weapons of mass destruction, I believed him. His father had been a great and wise statesman, and I trusted the Bush family. Wanting to understand more about foreign policy, Michelle and I subscribed to the *Weekly Standard* after 9/11.

My recovery from neoconservatism was gradual. I was shocked to discover, in the early Barack Obama years, how many trillions of dollars the wars in Iraq and Afghanistan had cost, all put on the national credit card ($5.8 trillion through 2022, Brown University's Watson Institute for International and Public Affairs estimated). I came to understood that I had been sold a bill of goods on the circumstances of the Iraq invasion. I was horrified by the disastrous Obama interventions in Libya and Syria, which would have been even worse without "isolationist" Republicans putting their foot down.

In the pages of the *Weekly Standard*, accusations flew that the Obama administration wasn't doing *enough*. Reading in bed one night in 2011, I turned to Michelle and said, "You know? I think these guys are full of it." (I didn't say "it" but another, more Texas word.) I felt at that point that maybe George W., whom I had defended for years and years, was, too. We canceled our subscription.

Maybe I would have come to my senses earlier if I'd subscribed to the magazine *before* 9/11. Like many conservatives, I thought that "rogue states" sponsoring terrorists and WMDs were suddenly a new threat after 9/11. I had no idea that that was standard neocon fare going back more than a decade. I had no idea how much scorn the neocons had for US political leaders who wanted to follow our tradition of prudent statesmanship well before 9/11.

In 1999, like many Republicans, I was opposed to "humanitarian bombing" in Kosovo. I didn't think we really knew what we were doing, trying to sort out Albanians from Serbians. And frankly, I didn't think it was our business. But in the pages of the *Weekly Standard* the prominent neocons Bob Kagan and Bill Kristol vented their spleen at the "neoisolationist" Republican senators who had voted 38–16 against NATO air strikes in Yugoslavia, saying "Republican foreign policy is now mired in pathetic incoherence. Is this the party of Reagan or the party of Buchanan?" and thus somehow managing to insult the legacy of both of those great American patriots.

But bombing wasn't enough. In Kagan's eyes, the aspirations of "Kosovar Albanians" (a heretofore undiscovered species of incipient freedom-loving American) could not be made whole without American boots on the ground, and "neoisolationist" House Republicans were spoiling everything by refusing to sanction that. Kagan scolded those Neo-Know-Nothings, "it will not do for congressional Republicans to treat the Kosovar Albanians, Chamberlain-style, as a far-away people of whom we know nothing." If the Kosovar Albanians don't qualify as "a far-away people of whom we know nothing," who does? In the eyes of neocons, no one: every single person on Earth is an American waiting to discover themselves.

Even at the time, Fareed Zakaria, writing in the *Wall Street Journal*, had their number:

> William F. Buckley once remarked that the defining element of conservatism is realism—realism about the limits of state power, the nature of human beings and societies, the complexity of international life. Yet many conservatives [neocons] who believe that the state can do nothing right at home think that it can do nothing wrong abroad. (If things go badly, why, more money, bigger bombs and ground troops will straighten it out.) Many who are scornful of social engineering at home seem sure it will work beyond our borders.

The idea that the US national security state should use its overwhelming power to socially engineer other societies to bring about world peace seems like a natural extension of progressivism on the Left but totally out of place in the conservative movement. What I came to realize was that that orientation was fundamentally at odds with being a conservative. Conservatives who would never meekly accept the federal government's spending hundreds of billions in radical social engineering at home should not accept imposing radical social engineering across a country or region far from our shores. Burkean humility and our own tradition of statesmanship dictate that we be highly circumspect about the use of force and maintain a keen sense of when our own vital interests are and are not in play.

But I think we should welcome all who have come to this conclusion into the New Conservative Movement, regardless of how belatedly. While it's valuable to reassess the Cassandras who called it right in the 1990s, folks such as Pat Buchanan, George Kennan, Samuel P. Huntington, Robert Lighthizer, Andrew Bacevich, and Angelo Codevilla, I don't think it is healthy or wise for the conservative movement to focus on rearguing the debates of the 1990s and 2000s, as costly as those mistakes were. It was a strange time, and many well-meaning conservatives (especially those outside the foreign policy world) became disoriented. But now it has become clear what a return to a truly conservative foreign policy would look like.

The Sharon Statement (1960), one of the foundational documents of the American conservative movement, ends with this assertion: "That American foreign policy must be judged by this criterion: does it serve the just interests of the United States?" I think we could do worse than to make this, once again, the foundation of our statesmanship in a New Conservative Movement.

The Hollow Force

A recommitment to the US interest must be matched with a sober assessment of the state of US power today.

At the Heritage Foundation, we have been sounding the alarm about the parlous state of our military capability. Last year for the first time ever in its long history, our annual review of US military power concluded that the United States' military is weak if not unprepared for even a single-arena war. We've been warning about the dire state of our defense industrial base, about the decay of credible deterrence in regions around the world, about the effect of woke ideology on military morale and recruiting, and about decades of waste, fraud, and abuse hollowing out the United States' military modernization efforts, not to mention the looming challenge of a national debt whose annual interest payments will soon exceed the Department of Defense budget.

But I'm not an expert on this stuff. And so it alarmed me to see current and former senior American decision makers stipulating over the past few years that none of this should prevent us from sending hundreds of billions of dollars to Ukraine, that we could do it all: save Ukraine, deter China, help Israel, coerce Iran, and more. Many of these folks have access to highly classified briefings. Did they know something I don't know?

And then during the debate about support for Ukraine, it dawned on me: these people have no idea what they're talking about. Do you think that what they write and say bears any relationship to the actual state of the United States' defense supply chains, logistics, weapons stockpiles, replenishment projections, or force structure? Do you think that at any point prior to an actual catastrophe, they would admit that the United States has reached or overreached a limit?

Ensconced in sinecures where they earn half a million dollars a year (or more) to cheerlead for the Woke Empire far from battlefields in foreign lands, Blob diehards live in an invincible summer, where it's always 1983. Our British allies have just triumphed halfway around the globe, retaking the Falkland Islands. Our military forces have conducted yet another intervention (in Grenada) without breaking a sweat. The Soviets are starting to feel the heat in Afghanistan and are staring down the barrel of an extraordinary NATO military modernization, as the United States under Ronald Reagan begins pursuing the actual rollback of Soviet influence, powered by a reviving US economy and a strong federal balance sheet.

But it's not 1983 anymore. It's not 2003 anymore. The United States in 2023 is a lot weaker.

The reason to rehash the history of our embrace of imperialism is that it has inadvertently rooted our foreign policy in a time period (the 1990s and 2000s) that has already passed into history. It's time for Americans to wake up and reevaluate the ways the world has changed.

Our European allies cashed in the Cold War peace dividend on infrastructure and social welfare spending. According to the World Bank, European defense spending plummeted from 2.8 percent to 1.3 percent of GDP. The effect has been even stronger in the countries that formed the backbone of NATO's Cold War forces: France (3.2 percent to 1.8 percent), Germany (3 percent to 1.2 percent), and Belgium (3.4 percent to 0.9 percent).

The British are vital allies with unique capabilities who have always stood by our side. But their military capabilities have been seriously eroded by a lack of political support amid Great Britain's rising social welfare expenses. It's uncertain whether the Royal Navy, which has shrunk considerably, would even be capable of mounting the Falklands campaign today. (Thankfully for the Brits, the Argentinians' fleet has fallen off even farther.)

It's not as if we're much better off. We frittered away modernization efforts in our air force, navy, and army, with programs canceled or delayed at enormous expense (the F-35 fighter jet debuting a decade late and $183 billion over budget, the navy's misbegotten Littoral Combat Ship costing more than double its original cost at $500 million per and mostly irrelevant in a period of great-power competition).

Propensity to serve, the term experts use to describe the number of Americans interested in joining the armed forces, has been declining for almost forty years, interrupted briefly by a burst of patriotism after 9/11: we face an unprecedented recruiting crisis. As we lower our military standards both to bring in more volunteers and to cover up the deleterious effects of top-down gender politics on our combat forces, measures of readiness and performance are rapidly slipping. And every dollar we spend trying to fix these problems adds to a national debt that is proportionally larger than any we have ever had in our history, even at the height of World War II.

If we're looking for historical analogies, 1973 is closer to home than 1983. The American people were disheartened and demobilized, and our enemies were emboldened. The American military was in shambles in the wake of the Vietnam War, and our European allies were increasingly shaky. The Great Society and Vietnam had ruined US credit, forced the United States off the gold standard, and kick-started stagflation. The Yom Kippur War, in which our ally Israel was almost overrun by Soviet-backed and Soviet-trained Arab armies, served as a serious wake-up call about our own military weakness.

But this realism should shade into hope. America is still America. The gloom and twilight of 1973 masked seeds that would grow into mighty oaks. Within a decade, they would sprout into a Cold War–winning military modernization, geopolitics-shaping US diplomacy, a return to fiscal strength, and morning in America again. From an insurgent foundation in 1973, the Heritage Foundation grew to help shape the nation.

Returning to an America First Statesmanship

Like a Las Vegas gambler preparing to look at his bank account with a throbbing hangover and great trepidation, it is hard and a little bit embarrassing to reckon with the mistakes of the last few decades. But we must do so. And we must envision a path forward based on where we are today, not where we were in 1983 or where we wish we were.

The most difficult aspect of a return to our traditional statesmanship is also the most simple: we must adopt an ethos of humility and prudence.

I do believe that America is a "shining city on a hill." But in traditional American statesmanship, this was taken to mean an America that led by its own virtuous example. Our messy involvements abroad have been a direct detriment to our spiritual strength at home. The Party of Creation recognizes that there are real limits as to what the United States can achieve by interventions abroad and real costs to doing so.

But for the Party of Destruction, there is no issue too obscure, no country too small, no injustice too remote to fall beneath our notice. When you think you can do everything, you don't need any principles to shape and discipline your choices.

The Blob confuses expert knowledge of administrative minutiae for statesmanship, stale policy documents for principle, and bureaucratic processes for prudence. We have too many "experts" and far too few leaders. We need to recover our early tradition of statesmanship, informed by a close study of history, foreign languages, literature, and political philosophy. There is so much we need to remember that has already been stated by our wisest leaders.

Foreign entanglement and disunity at home go together. George Washington's Farewell Address is remembered primarily for two injunctions to the American people: to avoid a politics of "faction" and "party" and to avoid "foreign entanglements." But in the context of the speech, the two dangers are intertwined. Washington's warning was that foreign entanglements are invitations to creating division at home, both by providing new opportunities for factional rivalry and by inviting foreign influences to pit one faction against another.

Today, one cost of our imperial overreach is increasing disunity and polarization at home. Some Democrats have become obsessed with Vladimir Putin's supposed evil genius, while some on the right defend him unwittingly in response. You see dueling foreign flags on front porches and in social media profiles. Whenever there's a conflict abroad, lobbyists for foreign governments, diaspora members, and NGO activists rush to spin the right narrative to get public opinion on their side, because they know that support in Washington or the lack thereof can make or break their cause. And the United States' enemies, especially Russia, China, and Iran, increasingly take actions designed to stoke these divisions.

We must vigilantly restrain foreign influences. An open system of government is vulnerable to manipulation by foreign actors with their own agendas. As Washington warned, "Against the insidious wiles of foreign influence . . . the jealousy of a free people ought to be constantly awake, since history and experience prove that foreign influence is one of the most baneful foes of republican government."

Much of our foreign policy Blob has become corrupted both by foreign government spending and by, in Washington's words, "a passionate attachment of one nation for another" that "produces a variety of evils." (One suspects that General Washington would personally saber summertime patriots such as the think tankers who advocate for increased military aid to countries that fund their job positions.) One study found that between 2014 and 2018, US think tanks scooped up $174 million from more than eighty foreign countries, including Germany, the United Arab Emirates, and Ukraine. Those countries aren't paying just for favorable reporting and glitzy events; they're counting on fellows in those think tanks remembering their largesse when they return to government. Proudly, the Heritage Foundation doesn't take one red cent from foreign governments, even friendly ones. Adopting legislation forcing think tank transparency about foreign funding will help undermine and destroy bad actors such as the Atlantic Council.

The essence of strategy is the alignment of means and ends. The fact that our federal debt threatens our national security and merits consideration in our statesmanship is not a lately discovered idea of GOP budget hawks; it is a point Washington himself emphasized in his Farewell Address! "As a very important source of strength and security, cherish public credit," he says before emphasizing the importance of discharging debt in peacetime to preserve credit for "unavoidable wars."

While they are hardly the only sources of the deficit, experts at Brown University estimate that the wars in Iraq and Afghanistan added $2 trillion to the national debt, with almost another trillion dollars in borrowing costs since 2001. Having frittered away our credit during the years when we faced no serious great-power threats, we must now make difficult decisions and trade-offs. We can't remind ourselves often enough that the politicians and neocons who are alarmed about budget constraints on support for Ukraine are the same ones who already spent the seed corn in the sands of Iraq.

"Friendship and commerce" are the best means of promoting the United States' statesmanship. As a historian, I find the accusation that US foreign policy prior to World War II was "isolationist" is dead wrong. The United States had active trade all over the world. It was the most generous state in the world for immigrants. US ships and the US Navy roamed the world over. The United States intervened periodically when its interests or citizens were threatened, principally in the Western Hemisphere but also against the Barbary pirates, to open trade with Japan, and to secure needed Pacific coaling stations.

From 1789 until about 1940, the disposition of our statesmen toward the foreign relations of the United States was one of active neutrality. Especially as the country grew in strength, its neutrality was characterized not by a meek navigation among the interests of the European great powers but by an affirmative defense of our ability to commerce with the world. The Founders had envisioned a world order characterized by European infighting that the United States could, and did, exploit. Such a policy aided our becoming the most powerful country in the world.

But as the historian Stephen Wertheim has chronicled, during the Second World War, a policy of primacy replaced our traditional policy of neutrality. After the fall of France and with England teetering on the brink of destruction, we glimpsed the terrifying prospect of a world order in which the United States would stand alone, advanced technology would threaten our shores, and authoritarian economies could choke off our traditional trade. It forced us to take up the mantle of leading the Free World.

The world today looks, in many ways, vastly different. Though we have many real enemies, we have even more friends. While it no longer seems possible to move to a grand strategy of neutrality, we should move *toward* it. By safeguarding our strength at home, serving as an arsenal of democracy, and maintaining the openness of the global commons—sea, air, and space—we can sustainably defend a US-friendly world order without overextension.

The United States must maintain the ability to prevent foreign rivals—China above all—from imposing their will on the American people. This is the highest task to which our nation's foreign policy is called. It is best served by carefully husbanding US power so that we can ensure the openness of the global commons (sea, air, and space) and decisively defeat any challenger.

At its core, this is a mission that is uniquely American—and uniquely republican. It is a mission not to impose American ideas or preferences on the world but to deny others the ability to do to the same to us. It is an anti-imperial agenda premised on the belief that the United States' most vital interests are best served by denying others' hegemonic ambitions, consistent with the richest traditions in US statecraft.

Statesmanship demands cultivated virtue. The root cause of imprudent foreign policy is imprudent leadership. At no point in their education will a member of the Blob necessarily have to contend with *any part* of the American tradition of statesmanship. It is not even on their radar. A recent former diplomat pointed out to me that the State Department's introductory course for new diplomats includes a mock cocktail party and instruction in filling out travel reimbursement forms but no discussion of the Monroe Doctrine or the Marshall Plan.

The reason is that the statesmen who built our institutions assumed that any person plausibly roaming the halls of the State Department's Foggy Bottom headquarters, the Capitol, the Pentagon, or the Eisenhower Executive Office Building would be steeped in American culture and a tradition of education for statecraft. You'll see remarkable continuity among, say, George Washington's advice letter to his nephew George Steptoe Washington (whose education at the University of Pennsylvania he helped pay for), Thomas Jefferson's musings to John Adams about statesmanship and "natural aristocracy," and the original curriculum of Georgetown University's School of Foreign Service, set up in 1919 by an American Jesuit statesman and diehard anti-Communist, Father Edmund Walsh.

Today, institutions such as Harvard's John F. Kennedy School of Government are more likely to indoctrinate their students in sentimental humanitarianism and "global citizenship" than to articulate a robust defense of the American interest. Students are assigned to read Ibram X. Kendi, not Xenophon or Henry Adams. They are taught about the inner workings of policy processes but not about the dangers in their own hearts. In their irrational loves and their irrational hatreds, they confuse their personal involvements and passions for the just interests of the United States.

We need to deprogram our foreign policy, and we need new institutions of training and formation to do so. We need to substantially reform or replace our diplomatic and military professional education programs (the Foreign Service Institute, the National Defense University, the Naval War College, and the like) to include education in prudence, not merely in policy. And we need to comprehensively reboot foreign assistance and aid programs so that they run on the basis of our actual national interests, not as automatic handouts.

We must reestablish humility and prudence in our statesmanship, and we must do so in our own hearts, in the hearts of our leaders, and in the hearts of the people. This will require education and persuasion, rooted in careful explanation of our history, our tradition of statesmanship, and the biographies of our great statesmen.

I'm heartened that student-focused organizations such as the John Quincy Adams Society, American Moment, and the Intercollegiate Studies Institute (ISI) have already begun this work, as have academic programs such as Yale's Brady-Johnson Program in Grand Strategy and the Undergraduate Fellows Program at the Clements Center for National Security at the University of Texas at Austin. ISI president John A. Burtka IV's *Gateway to Statesmanship: Selections from Xenophon to Churchill* is a great start at reviving the mirrors-of-princes genre for twenty-first-century American statesmen and -women. It's the kind of book that America's institutions educating future statesman (such as Hillsdale College) are already putting to use.

A restored tradition of American statesmanship would also end the gravy train of foreign aid contracts funding lavish expat lifestyles for US NGO workers, stop imposing wokeness via coercive diplomacy, and return to a statesmanship characterized by diplomacy, commerce, and a keen sense of the American interest as the liberty of our people, not an expansive project of world revolution, even in the name of democracy.

Ukraine and Reagan's Real Legacy of Statesmanship

For an example of what this new paradigm would look like, consider the case of our involvement in the Russo-Ukrainian War. What would a policy fully motivated by the defense of our just interests look like?

Our involvement would not have been zero. While Ukraine is not a formal ally of the United States, it is a state we have maintained friendly relations with. In 1994, when we signed the Budapest Memorandum on Security Assurances, we promised to offer Ukraine assistance should its freedom be threatened after it gave up its holdover Soviet nuclear warheads. The 2022 Russian invasion was not just designed to destroy Ukraine's sovereignty; it was aimed to shock, disrupt, and destroy the overall European security system centered on NATO. A resurgent, victorious Russia would have been in a position to threaten US interests much more directly. More to the point, prior to the invasion our military faced the prospect of a simultaneous war between two "near peers," Russia and China. Quietly, behind the scenes, many defense policy professionals believed that that would be a bridge too far.

Our aid to Ukraine has enabled us to defend our European security interests, deplete an enemy, and keep our word as a country at a much lower cost than the NATO forces that would have been required to deter an emboldened Russia. Especially in 2022, the military aid to Ukraine was barely a strain on our overall military capabilities, and public sentiment strongly supported aid for Ukraine (but not boots on the ground).

So under our new paradigm (really a return to our traditional principles), our initial military aid for Ukraine might have looked basically the same, even if the foreign aid budget for woke governance in Ukraine would have been redirected to accountability and countercorruption efforts.

It was in the wake of the initial months of the war that concerns begin to greatly diverge. An ethos of humility applies fourfold to war, which rarely goes as intended. Unlike the current Blob approach, we must adopt a due caution toward escalation, unintended consequences, and the many other vicissitudes of war.

At the Heritage Foundation, we quickly became alarmed that the Biden administration did not seem to have anything approaching an endgame for the war and thus had no real strategy other than ever deeper involvement. It is so telling that the thing that most enraged the Blob was simply demanding that the Biden administration square with the American people about both its strategy for the war and accountability for money that had already been spent as a precondition of additional aid. The Woke Empire doesn't like it when the little people in Congress say "no."

It goes without saying that the current approach—unlimited blank check, risk of war, no accountability or strategy—has also lost public support, with the majority of Americans telling a CNN poll that Congress should not authorize additional funding for Ukraine and that the United States has already done enough for Ukraine.

If the Biden approach is bankrupt, what would a better one look like?

I've noticed that the Republicans who constantly invoke Reagan as a foreign policy ideal always do so toward militaristic ends, emphasizing his defense spending, confrontations with the Soviet Union, and aggressive rhetoric. But Reagan's vision of US statesmanship was oriented not toward war but toward peace. The epithet he embraced, reminiscent of his friend John Wayne, was "The Peacemaker," also the title of fellow Longhorn historian William Inboden's definitive new history of Reagan's foreign policy.

Unlike those who want to claim the mantle of Reagan today, Reagan started only one war in his time, the highly limited and narrowly tailored intervention in Grenada. His greatest achievements were not in war but in peace, combining a military buildup with canny diplomacy.

In particular, the negotiations with the Soviet Union that Reagan fostered led directly to the peaceful end of the Cold War. If Reagan had been a Democrat, he would have won the Nobel Peace Prize.

I am particularly inspired by Reagan's negotiations over nuclear missiles in Europe, leading to the 1987 Intermediate-Range Nuclear Forces Treaty (INF). While Reagan felt he could trust Soviet general secretary Mikhail Gorbachev, his diplomacy with the Soviets began before Gorbachev came on the scene. Reagan combined an escalation of missile deployments (stick) with hard-headed negotiations aimed at a truly radical cause: the full elimination of both American and Russian stockpiles of the missiles (carrot).

In the spirit of Ronald Reagan the Peacemaker, even as the United States continues to support the Ukrainian cause, we must begin earnest negotiations with the Russians to try to find a peaceful settlement for the wider region. Any settlement will surely be a painful compromise (the byword of any true statesman, one the neocons are allergic to). It will require our pushing our European allies to do far more for Europe's defense. But the alternatives are unending war, substantial escalation and wider war, or the collapse of one of the states involved (which would unleash horrors). I know what the Gipper would have sought.

The Problem of the Pacific

I was really alarmed at a message sent by the Biden administration's late-October 2023 supplementary budget request for foreign aid. The White House asked for $60 billion more for Ukraine, $14 billion for Israel, $14 billion for border security, and a paltry $7 billion for the broader Indo-Pacific theater—only $2 billion of which is linked in any meaningful way to deterring China. More than a decade after President Obama's abortive "pivot to the Pacific," we still haven't been able to refocus our foreign policy on a defense of our most core interests.

The weakness and waste brought on by decades of failed military interventions have left us no choice but to make tough trade-offs to protect our top global priorities today: the protection of the US home-land and the deterrence of Communist China.

But the threats we face today require a different approach. In the wake of the Russo-Ukrainian War, it is clear that with proper burden sharing, instead of the United States paying for everything, our NATO allies can take on the challenge of deterring Russia, which has a population size and GDP significantly smaller than our European NATO allies. Another hard lesson of the past twenty years is that the United States' involvement in the Middle East should not involve US armies of occupation.

Defense experts of all stripes agree that we must restore our defense industrial base. Decades of underinvestment in, consolidation of, and mismanagement of the facilities that produce the materiel needed for our forces have resulted in dangerous bottlenecks and vulnerabilities. Some army munitions plants are still running equipment from the Second World War, and in 2021, a massive accidental explosion shut down the Minden gunpowder mill in my home state of Louisiana, the only source of a kind of gunpowder used in mortar shells, artillery rounds, and Tomahawk missiles.

Even more worrying is the situation with US shipyards and aerospace assembly plants. Decades of cutting the building of ships and planes to fund our overseas adventures has meant consolidation and closure of vital suppliers. While Congress has recently woken up to the depth of the problem, it is still going to be an uphill climb to build the kind of industrial capacity needed to deter China.

We have not gone far enough. I have become convinced that the only way to sustainably and broadly maintain our defense industrial base is by investing in—and restoring competition among—the civilian companies undergirding our national manufacturing capabilities. The reason is that the capacity we need during peacetime falls far short of what we need during times of crisis; the United States' industrial base *is* our defense industrial base. What happened during the 1990s was that due to NAFTA and WTO (along with big defense cuts), the United States significantly deindustrialized. But many of the crucial workforce skills, industrial plant, and suppliers were shared between vital defense concerns (such as shipbuilding) and the civilian economy. Without support and protection for US companies in those areas, they faced little choice but to outsource or even go out of business.

But it didn't even save US taxpayers money, because we still needed to build materiel for our military, but this time with the Pentagon supporting the entire capital and labor costs. Moreover, the lack of support for a combined civilian and defense market meant more consolidation and a significant rise in Pentagon contracts awarded without real competition. The result of our shortsighted approach to trade has been the costs of airplanes, ships, tanks, munitions, and many more critical defense items spiraling higher.

For example, one senior army official in the Trump administration told me a shocking story about a procurement project for a new armored vehicle. The defense contractor involved went back to the Pentagon to ask for more money to deliver the project, and of course the official demanded to know why. The reason (which he checked out independently) was that, during the global War on Terror, the army had canceled its orders for an older model (the quiet fate of many important projects, another victim of our reckless foreign policy). When the company had shut down the line and let go the workers, there had been no open jobs in the entire United States that used a certain kind of heavy welding technique. By 2016, *basically every worker in the country with that skill had either retired or left the industry.* The contractor needed the extra funds to lure a sufficient number of them out of retirement.

This is no way to run a business, and it's surely no way to run a superpower. The United States needs workers, engineers, and managers in the business of building the tools that guarantee our freedoms. And the best way to do that sustainably is to ensure that the US market privileges the companies producing products, both civilian and military, that support our arsenal of democracy. This isn't an innovation; it has been a part of our tradition of statesmanship since the early republic recognized the need to produce merchant ships alongside naval vessels and so passed a tariff bill in July 1789 that privileged, in Hamilton's words, "an ACTIVE COMMERCE in our own [ship]bottoms."

It's important to get the specifics right, of course: protection of profits should be a last resort, compared to loan guarantees, special tax breaks for investment in industrial equipment, skills programs, export financing, and other ways to ensure that US companies that benefit from our defense industrial policy are also competitive businesses striving for productivity and growth (the Merchant Marine Act of 1920, commonly known as the Jones Act, offers some cautionary lessons here). But it is past time to remember one of the first lessons of traditional American statesmanship, summarized in *The Federalist Papers*, No. 11: that commerce is as much an instrument of national defense as a frigate or an aircraft carrier is.

To update Hamilton, "Let Americans disdain to be the instruments of Chinese greatness! Let the fifty States, bound together in a strict and indissoluble union, concur in erecting one great American system, superior to the control of all globalist force or influence, and able to dictate the terms of the connection between the old and the new world!"

Sacrifice

We need to return to a statesmanship of the just interests of the United States, because nothing less can justify the sacrifices demanded of the best of us.

Jorge Hidalgo grew up the son of poor Dominican immigrants who first moved to New York City to work in a factory and then managed a bodega in the Bronx. After coming to the States in 1965, Jorge worked hard in school, on the track team, and at his dad's store in the evenings. Despite earning a full-tuition scholarship to a state school, he intended to enlist in the marines after high school because he couldn't afford room and board. A guidance counselor at his school asked him to consider the military academies, and with help from his community he secured a commission to the United States Military Academy at West Point.

Jorge excelled in the army, becoming an infantry officer and an Army Ranger before serving in Germany as a handpicked soldier in the Berlin Brigade. Visiting East Berlin and hearing the nightly gunfire at the Berlin Wall gave him a firsthand appreciation of the horrors of communism and authoritarianism and the value of the freedoms that so many Americans take for granted. Those were lessons he passed on to his three sons and daughter, alongside the values of education and of selflessly serving others. Jorge left the army after eight years of honorable service for a civilian career, but he wasn't surprised when all three of his sons signed up for military service, one as a marine officer and two in the army.

T. S. Eliot had it wrong. At least in Wisconsin, with its short days and dirty snow, February is the cruelest month.

At the end of February 2011, when an officer in dress uniform and a chaplain arrived at his Madison home, Jorge's heart sank like a stone. He understood what it meant. The soldier notified Jorge that his son Lieutenant Hidalgo had been killed in service to his country. Then came a moment that is frozen in Jorge's memory like amber, the toughest moment of the toughest thing that can ever happen to a parent. He asked the officer, "Which Lieutenant Hidalgo?"

Two of Jorge's sons, both West Point graduates and infantry officers like their dad, were serving in Afghanistan. The officer replied, "Lieutenant Daren Hidalgo."

Daren was Jorge's youngest son. He was a prankster with a winning grin and a deep sense of empathy, beloved by everyone. A star wrestler, he had turned down an athletic scholarship to join the army, as his dad and older brother had. He cared about others more than himself, and he proved it over and over again. For years after his death, people—mates in his high school marching band, fellow West Point cadets, soldiers he had served with—came up to Jorge to tell him stories about times Daren had been there for them, had shouldered their burdens.

After graduating from West Point, Daren was due to join a combat unit stationed in Vilseck, Germany, that had partially deployed to Afghanistan. As Daren was getting settled in Germany, word came back that one of the unit's platoon leaders in Afghanistan had been wounded. Daren volunteered as a replacement.

A few weeks before the February 20, 2011, IED attack that would claim his life, Daren had been wounded in combat. With a Purple Heart on his chest and shrapnel all through his leg, he was supposed to be evacuated to Germany for treatment and recovery. But he refused to leave his men, who had only six weeks left on their deployment. Jorge tried every trick in the book to persuade his son to get the surgery he needed, cajoling him to see a doctor so they could hike the Alps together, to no avail. Daren assured his dad that he would be fine and joked about setting off metal detectors at the airport.

His brother escorted Daren home from Afghanistan to Wisconsin. After a memorial service at his high school, Daren was buried at West Point on what would have been his twenty-fifth birthday.

My heart swells with both pride and sorrow when I think of the enormous sacrifices for our country and our freedoms like those of the Hidalgo family, not only the spotless service of Daren and his brothers and father, not only of Daren's sacrifice for our country and for his brothers in arms, but also of the grief of his mother and his sister, the hole in the lives of so many relatives and friends and members of his community. This, too, is sacrifice.

(Please consider a donation to the Daren M. Hidalgo Memorial Fund, which provides scholarships and aid to wounded warriors in Daren's memory. You can learn more at rememberdaren.com.)

For a long time, pundits have talked about the Dover Test: will the American people support a president's policy even when our servicemen come back to Dover Air Force Base in flag-draped coffins? But the manipulable sentiments of the easily distracted American public are no basis for a sound policy in this regard. Shamefully, in 1991, then secretary of defense Dick Cheney banned the media from photographing transfer ceremonies in order to stage-manage the public relations impact of military casualties, a ban enforced again during the Iraq War until 2009.

We need an ethos of humility and principles of prudent and exacting pursuit of the national interest to be living in the head and the breast of everyone even marginally involved in our decisions to send our men and women to war. We need a Daren Test. The test has to be: Is this task of such an urgency and importance that it *demands* that we risk the life of one of the best of us, a man like Daren Hidalgo?

I confess that my pride and sorrow turn to anger when I think about how cheaply our post–Cold War foreign policy has held the lives of our best, merely to uphold the vain aspirations of our ruling class, which overwhelmingly discourages its own sons and daughters from service. When I am in a bitter mood, I sometimes remember the question posed in the opening days of the Second World War by our most anti-imperial poet, Robinson Jeffers: "All Europe was hardly worth the precarious freedom of one of our states: what will her ashes fetch?"

It puts me in mind of what was, in retrospect, perhaps the most spiritually damaging moment in US politics in my lifespan. In the wake of 9/11, instead of calling on Americans to stand up in sacrificial service of our country (to piety, in a word), our national leaders asked us to continue shopping and keep the economy buzzing. Our so-called foreign policy elite decided that the burdens of war would fall upon only a fraction of volunteers, who would be paid for their troubles and doubly paid to suffer in the shadows, so as not to trouble the consciences of our ruling class.

They set us upon the course toward empire and decadence, toward self-medicating to numb a pain that doesn't have anywhere to go, that cannot quite transform itself into sacrifice. I don't think it's a coincidence that opioid usage shot up across the same parts of the country that were sending their sons to war. You can see the pain in Sam Quinones's reportage on the heroin epidemic and in the literary writings of veterans such as Phil Klay, Jacob Siegel, and Nico Walker.

The American people were *encouraged* by their leaders to shop at the mall while some families made the ultimate sacrifice. That wasn't just bad policy; it was a spiritual attack more deadly than anything Al-Qaeda could cook up. It was a direct assault on our republican character and system of self-government.

While men from states such as South Carolina, Colorado, Ohio, and Louisiana fought and died in the wadis of Iraq and the mountains of the Hindu Kush, the DC Swamp was open for business. Foreign cash flooded into DC think tanks, and Alan Greenspan ran the economy hot so that the government could borrow cheaply, helping trigger the 2008 global financial crisis. Much of the money spent on exploding military, intelligence, and foreign aid budgets ended up paying for German cars and bloated McMansions owned by defense contractors.

Our veterans and their families don't have it so easy. We beset them with "grief, rage, and guilt," in Klay's words, to see what it has all come to, the unraveling of all of our grand plans in the Middle East, the rise of ISIS, the fall of Afghanistan; time and again our erstwhile allies left hanging. Place-names such as Diyala, Kamdesh, and Ramadi mean absolutely nothing to most Americans. We didn't even give them the dignity of paying attention. But there are some who cannot forget those names no matter what they try to numb themselves with.

Gratitude

As shocking as the collapse of our post-9/11 efforts has been, even more shocking is that our politicians and media still listen to the architects of those failed policies. Today, the same voices of globalism, elitism, and materialism that squandered our victory in the Cold War and severed the sacred bonds of trust between Americans and their government are again trying to smear, marginalize, and demonize anyone who dissents from the Blob consensus.

We are at a moment of choosing: Is America an empire or a republic? *Which will we be?*

This question lies within our grasp to answer, and now is the time to decide. I despair of the imperial Blob, but I'm bullish on America, because I know the character and spirit of our people.

Despite the grievous mistakes of the past thirty years, I have so much hope for the future of our country's statesmanship. When I talk to lawmakers, both Republican and Democrat, I see skepticism about the Blob narrative. Even if we often disagree on policy, we're blessed to have an increasing number of Iraq and Afghanistan veterans in both parties serving in Congress, including J.D. Vance, Morgan Luttrell, Seth Moulton, Jim Banks, Jake Auchincloss, Don Bacon, Jared Golden, Tammy Duckworth, and Tom Cotton. Among the students and younger staffers who come through the Heritage Foundation's doors, there is a new and deepening interest in our historical statesmanship of prudence, humility, and realism and a skepticism about US imperial adventures.

In 2002, when Pat Buchanan and others founded the *American Conservative* magazine in order to take a stand against the Iraq War, they stood alone in the conservative movement. No longer.

Zooming out, the United States still has all of the natural advantages Providence has given her. Our borders are still guarded by oceans on the east and west and polar bears in the north (we're working on the southern border). Global threats are real, but a more careful approach to maintaining our traditional hemispheric security system would go a long way toward securing the homeland.

We still stand for the desire for freedom that beats in every human heart. We have more and better allies, more and better friends, more and better partnerships than the we have ever had in our history, even if we need to seek a better balance in some of them.

We still have the most innovative entrepreneurs building the best military technology. And we still put those arms into the hands of a dedicated and deadly military of citizen professionals who quietly serve with unparalleled skill and integrity.

Besides the necessary reforms of our foreign policy establishment, the bigger task remaining is to once again adopt a republican approach to our statesmanship. That means self-government founded upon shared service and shared sacrifice in the name of union and independence.

Late in his life, William F. Buckley, Jr., wrote a book titled *Gratitude: Reflections on What We Owe to Our Country*. It's not full of musings about what it means to be a conservative or reflections on his life; it is actually a call to create a national service program. At a time when conservatives were patting themselves on the back over the Reagan Revolution and the collapse of the Warsaw Pact, Buckley understood the spiritual danger America was in.

He saw that with no great enemy or great national project, Americans would grow decadent and entitled about the liberty, civilization, and prosperity that made their lives possible. Part of the solution, of the kind embraced by republics down through history, would be a period of service to the nation. "By asking them to make sacrifices we are reminding them that they owe a debt. . . . And reminding them that requital of a debt is the purest form of acknowledging that debt."

In my mind's eye, I can envision a national service program designed to give every young American the gift of sacrifice, to bolster our national defense, to help Americans get to know one another again, and to transition to adult life.

It would begin every summer with cohorts of high school graduates streaming to a four- or six-week training program hosted in our most beautiful national parks all over the country and run by our military. For a generation blunted by ubiquitous and continuous internet exposure, these training camps might serve as a mandatory smartphone detox, a chance to breathe fresh air and encounter the great American natural bounty, a place to meet and get to know Americans from very different walks of life, and an occasion for learning some of the skills of resilience every American should have, including basic survival and medical skills.

Running such a program would not just help the military reintegrate with and recruit from America. It would also form the infrastructure for a broader mobilization, should the need arise, providing the army's sergeants with experience training masses of green recruits and building additional skill, fitness, and readiness in the American people.

From this initial intake, our young people could serve throughout the country—in our armed forces, our national parks, our Border Patrol, our schools, our veterans' hospitals, and many other places. We can iron out the details, of course, but something like national service is a part of what it will take to knit the American people together again on a spiritual level. Even before we implement such a policy, we ought to, of our own accord, serve one another, to "lift up the feeble knees, and the hands that hang down."

When I asked him what made him hopeful for America, Jorge Hidalgo had similar advice: "Give back to the nation. . . . if I look at Daren's sacrifice, Daren was the embodiment of the American spirit of service to a higher calling than one's self. . . . Help your fellow citizens, and I think that will build a stronger nation."

CHAPTER 9

We Can't Coexist with Communist China

Americans rouse—be unanimous, be virtuous, be firm,
exert your courage, trust in Heaven, and nobly defy
the enemies both of God and man!

—Alexander Hamilton

hat makes someone your enemy?

The American people sense, with a deep intuition and with reasonable evidence, that the Chinese Communist Party is their enemy. This belief has, at least since the Trump administration, actively shaped our policy and lawmaking at the highest levels and has the fulsome support of the American people (82 percent have an unfavorable view of the country, not to mention the CCP specifically).

The Uniparty, however, doesn't see China as an enemy—just a friend waiting to happen. Liberal elites can't comprehend the idea that there are true left-wing enemies who wish the United States harm. Wax-museum conservatives, meanwhile, think that everything can be sorted out with trade: the more money exchanges hands, the more we'll come to love each other as brothers. Or something.

What makes someone your enemy is not that he hates you, that he says mean things about you, or even that he takes actions that hurt your interests. These are incidental and inconsistent symbols. Sometimes we are hurt even by people who love us, and sometimes the most baneful enemies come to us in disguise as friends. These characteristics do not lie at the heart of enmity.

What defines an enemy is that he *wants to destroy our way of life*. He may be out for revenge. Or he may be totally indifferent to our life. He may even find the conflict with us deeply lamentable. But in his actions, he shows contempt for our continued flourishing. He wants to destroy our life to enhance his own. His pursuit of his own good is advanced by the destruction of ours. It is totally irrelevant whether he expresses triumph or sorrow in so doing.

We shouldn't hate our enemies. But we should *stop* them. Defeat them. Do whatever it takes to change *their* way of life to such a degree as is necessary to ensure the safety and prosperity of our own.

The reality is, the Chinese have the same mixture of motives that Americans do: they care about money, but they also care about ideology. Their vision of the common good is not compatible with ours. The Uniparty can't understand this, since they believe that the Chinese just want to develop their country in mutually beneficial trade with the United States. As always, they ignore our differences on permanent questions.

The New Conservative Movement seeks the total destruction of any Chinese Communist influence over the United States' future, because a great country does not surrender a pattern of life that supports its flourishing. But whereas Cold War fusionism engaged in an existential struggle against Communist *ideology*, the challenge of our time is to reject and destroy the Chinese Communist *institutions* that threaten our way of life.

The Chinese have no equivalent of the Soviet Comintern, which had the capacity to infiltrate and subvert America's institutions with secret Communists. I believe that the Uniparty in this country is guilty of very many things, but I do not believe it to be an actual, literal agent of the Chinese Communist Party. (Though, as we will see, it is highly vulnerable to other forms of ideological or pecuniary seduction. Or, using Chinese "honeypot" spies, to the more ordinary sort of seduction.)

Instead, the Chinese Communist Party's plan to destroy the United States on its path to global domination rests on a subtler foundation. In order to understand the CCP's plan to secure its "China Dream" by destroying the American Dream, you need to know a bit of history.

The Mandate of Heaven

You need to see this from the Chinese perspective. China believes it has a mandate to rule the world. Much of this belief came from its long history of trade hegemony, a status it is trying to regain.

From antiquity until the First Opium War (1839–1842), China was at the undisputed center of the world economy. The most desirable and highest-quality products, such as raw silk, porcelain, silk and cotton fabrics, and spices, came from the East. Even as early as the time of ancient Rome, the Chinese maintained a global monopoly on a large number of valuable goods, and their unified political system (predating Caesar Augustus by two centuries) helped them protect that advantage and leverage it for cultural, spiritual, and economic domination.

The Chinese Empire viewed itself as the center of the universe: the Middle Kingdom. The Chinese emperor, the Son of Heaven, had the mandate from Heaven to bring cosmic order (*tian*, or Heaven) to not just China but the entire world (*tianxi*, all under Heaven). The Chinese view of themselves was undergirded by their hegemony in the global economy. As far back as the Roman Empire, the demand for Chinese manufactures around the world substantially exceeded the Chinese demand for the things other countries produced. Pliny the Elder lamented that the Romans' love of Oriental luxuries cost the empire 100 million sesterces per year in coinage channeled to the Far East. So dangerous to its interests did the Roman Republic find this that in AD 14 it banned men from wearing silk clothing: alas, as Roman decadence shaded into empire, the love of luxury prevailed. That trade imbalance continued for millennia and shaped the world economy—coinage from all over Europe and Asia has been discovered in Chinese archaeological finds, but to my knowledge no ancient Chinese coins have ever been located outside East Asia.

China's economic dominance, supply chain monopoly for desirable goods, and carefully controlled trade policies created substantial wealth for China's rulers, if not for its people as a whole. China's overall GDP was larger than that of all of western Europe combined until the 1840s, and even on a per capita basis with its giant population, China was as wealthy, healthy, and technologically advanced as any state in Europe except Great Britain and the Netherlands until sometime after the 1750s.

Those trade dynamics are intimately bound up with the story of our own country, the United States of America. A new route to the East was the motivation, of course, for Christopher Columbus's voyage and for missions such as Ferdinand Magellan's and Sir Francis Drake's early circumnavigations of the globe. And one of the key material triumphs of the American War of Independence was winning the freedom of Yankee merchants to break free of the East India Company's monopoly on the China trade; by the early nineteenth century, American traders were second only to the British in their exchange with China.

The development of the New World brought enormous new wealth to Europe, both in the form of gold and silver extracted from Spanish mines and through the wealth produced by sugar, tobacco, indigo, and other plantation crops. But paradoxically, it made the Chinese even richer, because of their secure position atop the global value chain. In the centuries following European colonization of the Americas, China's percentage of global GDP actually increased. The reason is that as the European middle classes grew, the goods that they wanted to purchase with their newfound wealth were made primarily in China, including their newfound favorite, Chinese tea (another indirect contribution to

American independence). At one point, some 30 percent of all of the silver mined in the New World was being sent to China.

Despite the vast wealth China's trade brought it, China's rulers were even more interested in something else: being recognized as the rightful rulers and order definers of the entire world. The imperial court mandated an elaborate series of rituals, culminating in the representatives of the supplicating state paying tribute to the emperor or his representative both by giving them valuable objects and, more important, by performing the kowtow, a series of abject prostrations indicating subservience. The emperor would then bestow gifts on his new subjects. (Because material wealth was less important than spiritual prestige, in some cases the gifts from the emperor were more valuable than the tribute paid; a number of poor Central Asian kingdoms thus sent tribute delegations as frequently as they were allowed.)

The Chinese would accept no diplomatic or trade relations *except* as tribute. Some European merchants were more than happy to comply; the Portuguese and the Dutch made the kowtow and were recorded as "tributary states" in the Qing dynasty's records. But the proud British refused, leaving the room when imperial edicts were given to avoid the issue.

That came to a head in September 1793, when the British ambassador, Lord George Macartney, finally gained an audience with the Qianlong emperor, bringing splendid gifts and seeking diplomatic concessions that would allow the British to expand their commerce with the Qing dynasty. But he refused to kowtow. He knew that doing so could not be dismissed as a mere formality; it indicated an inner spiritual subjugation that could not be wished away. His behavior baffled and infuriated the Chinese court, which viewed Great Britain as a tributary state like any other. The Qianlong emperor sent him away without granting any concessions and conveyed a letter (actually an edict!) to the king chiding the British for their insolence and ending with the traditional admonition to subordinates: "Tremblingly obey and show no negligence!"

The British would have something to say about that.

China's Century of Humiliation

The United States now faces a number of threats from China, from intellectual property theft to unequal trade agreements, espionage, and attempts to weaken the health of our civic society. What most people wouldn't suspect is that the Chinese know how to use these weapons because they were first the victims of just such a scheme, perpetrated by the British Empire.

It would be an exaggeration to suggest that British machinations against China were the product of some cunning plan. Great Britain's actions were often just as much motivated by fear or greed as by prudent statesmanship.

In the wake of the loss of the American colonies and Napoleon's attempted embargo of European trade with Great Britain (the "Continental System"), Great Britain's leaders understood that their empire, and Great Britain's safety, rested on a precarious balance. With the country's victory over Napoleon, British maritime supremacy was ensured. But the country's economy was in shambles. She needed to expand the markets for her manufactures as quickly as possible and import food and basic commodities as cheaply as possible. And she needed to make her Asian holdings sustainable; some years, Great Britain's India trade operated at a loss.

The fundamental problem was a conflict between whether the world economy would follow a pattern supporting the ongoing prosperity and stability of the Chinese Empire or that of the British Empire (and other European states). Before 1839, trade favored the Chinese. Vast amounts of silver and basic commodities flowed into China through the tightly controlled Canton System, which generated huge revenues for the Chinese government, while in-demand, high-value Chinese goods flowed out into the world market. At the same time, European manufactured goods could not compete on quality or price in Chinese markets, especially due to the country's robust tariff barrier and trade restrictions.

The British Empire (and the West more broadly) achieved global hegemony in large part by reordering the world economy in its favor. As Ernest Hemingway said of bankruptcy, that happened slowly, then all at once.

The first stage was breaking China's monopoly on valuable luxury goods through intellectual property (IP) theft. Beginning with silk in the medieval period and progressing to bone china in the seventeenth century and tea cultivation in the early nineteenth century, Europeans worked assiduously to begin domestic production of those goods and reduce their dependence on China.

The second stage was to widen the bottlenecks of the global economy—in other words, to build the means of production at home for the unique things China produced. As long as the rest of the world produced lots of goods China wanted but few of the goods China itself produced (and the world demanded), the world's money would flow to the East. But by the nineteenth century, European countries were selling inferior manufactured goods into closed-off colonial markets, while there was increasing global demand for goods that China itself needed, such as foodstuffs to feed its growing population and raw cotton from India. Thus, by 1839, the trade imbalance with China was already starting to decline.

The British didn't neglect spiritual warfare. The third stage was to forcibly open China's markets on terms that served the foreign powers but generated massive political instability and societal unrest within China. Even before 1839, the British Empire had managed to gain a foothold of addiction both in the Chinese people and the elite.

Between 1773 and 1832, Indian opium exports to China increased twenty times, and the Qing dynasty tried and failed to ban its import. That was not the only way in which British trade corrupted China and subverted the rule of law; China's ruling class of bureaucrats and mandarins became addicted to the wealth produced by the trade, skimming hundreds of billions of dollars' worth of silver off of the top of the trade. Those officials, while trying not to risk their (literal) necks, would often look the other way in cases of British infractions of Chinese law and even lie to Beijing officials about various goings-on in Canton. The imperial court also became increasingly dependent on the revenue from tariffs to keep itself solvent.

As corruption took hold in China, money wasn't just skimmed off of trade revenue. China's system of rigorous merit examinations began to break down, and gaining a prominent job increasingly became a matter of nepotism and patronage and not competence. Money set aside to maintain critical infrastructure was stolen, and neglected roads, dams, levies, and bridges began to decline and fail. Enormous sums of money went to more than a decade of waging an ineffective counterinsurgency (the White Lotus Rebellion); it was later discovered that the generals in charge had purposefully failed to resolve the issue by force and instead pocketed money intended to support China's defense.

China's belated efforts to crack down on the opium trade lit the fuse of what is known in China as the Century of Humiliation—the period between 1839 and 1949 when China was repeatedly humiliated by Western powers and forced to sign "unequal treaties."

What the British really cared about was not the opium trade but opening China's markets to the full range of British manufactures. The British demanded the opening of additional trading ports, sovereignty over the island of Hong Kong, and extraterritoriality: only Great Britain would be able to prosecute British citizens for crimes committed in China. Those terms were eventually granted to other nations (the Americans, French, Germans, Japanese, and Russians to start with), along with "most favored nation" trading status, which further opened China's trade to foreign powers.

But while the British Foreign Office at Whitehall may have been most concerned about expanding markets for Indian goods and playing other European powers against one another, the Century of Humiliation in China was a societal apocalypse. Throughout much of the country, the rule of law disintegrated and millions of people died as a result of civil conflicts, failing infrastructure, and agricultural devastation. The ruling class Manchus, humiliated by the Western powers, settled into decadence, turning inward to ever more elaborate displays of luxury and cultural navel gazing. The latter part of the period was overseen by an increasingly out-of-touch, despotic, and decrepit regent, Empress Dowager Cixi, who failed to demonstrate the energy and adaptability required to right the ship of state and instead oversaw new depths of familial corruption. Whatever economic implications free trade had for China were vastly overshadowed by the political shock that tore the country apart. The Qing dynasty fell from the height of its power and prestige to dissolution in a little over a century.

The Chinese Communist Party maintains the memory of China's Century of Humiliation. They mean for the twenty-first century to be ours.

How China Is Repeating History

Today, the Chinese Communist Party is attempting to do to the United States what the British Empire did to China: exploit American social and political weakness and hubris in order to restructure the global political economy in its favor and establish a Chinese world order.

Just as the British carried out IP theft, the Chinese have used the same tactic to break the Western monopoly on the most advanced manufacturing technologies and high-value products. The Chinese government has used IP theft on an industrial scale to profit from the creativity, innovation, and research investments of Western companies on products ranging from corn seeds to the F-35 Joint Strike Fighter. The FBI estimates that Chinese IP theft (including counterfeiting of Western products) costs the United States up to $600 billion per year. But what matters more is *what* the Chinese are stealing. In 2015, President Xi Jinping announced the Made in China 2025 program, to achieve independence from foreign suppliers in ten key high-technology sectors by 2025, including military dual-use areas such as maritime engineering, jet engines, and manufacturing robotics. The key to achieving this goal is IP theft.

But as easy (and important) as it is to fight straight-up Chinese IP theft through hacking, corporate espionage, or other methods (the corn seeds case involved employees of a Chinese agriculture firm digging up seeds on Iowa farms), the grim truth is that the vast majority of China's IP vampirism takes advantage of joint ventures with Western companies eager to do business in China. A company such as Corning or General Electric will be enticed to set up a production line in China; in many cases, the government will not allow it to operate in the Chinese market otherwise. But it won't be permitted to do so alone; instead, the government will require it to work with Chinese subcontractors or joint venture partners. In other cases, a company will be forced to undergo regulatory reviews that extract proprietary information no other country asks for. From there, the game is afoot—no matter what agreements are signed on paper protecting American IP rights, the Chinese companies will get to work reverse engineering American products. In many cases the tactic is even more direct: the Chinese government forces American companies to sign "technology transfer" agreements giving Chinese companies the fruits of American science. All of this goes on without any interference from or oversight by the US government or anyone else looking out for the US national interest. And the promises of making massive profits in the Chinese market are totally illusory; as soon as a Chinese company has replicated an American product, the Americans find themselves squeezed out.

With China catching up to the West in key technology areas due to IP theft, the CCP is implementing the second stage of Great Britain's imperial playbook: rewiring the world economy so that currency flows out of the West toward China. China has done this by building means of production on its own shores and doubling down by using government subsidies and unfair trade practices to pull more and more critical global supply chains onto its shores and out of the Western world. For an increasing number of vital products, ranging from smartphones to rare-earth minerals, there are now zero non-Chinese suppliers.

Why does it matter where things are made? Consider this: How many products critical to China's future can the United States cut off? Advanced semiconductors, soybeans, and pork, maybe? Alternatively, how many critical products can China cut the United States off from?

We found out the answer during the covid-19 pandemic, when US officials had to beg for critical medical supplies, automotive parts, and protective gear.

And that's before getting to areas where China has intentionally monopolized the manufacture of supplies in order to create geopolitical leverage, sometimes even operating the factories at a loss just to drive out competitors. The Department of Defense and Department of the Interior have identified thirty-five strategic minerals crucial for the defense industrial base supply chain. Out of these, the United States lacks primary production of twenty-two. Moreover, the United States heavily relies on imports for over 75 percent of ten critical minerals, including titanium and uranium.

Just as the British did in the nineteenth century, the Chinese have invested heavily in global trade choke points, with ownership stakes in thirty of the world's fifty largest ports and increasing amounts of investment in the Suez and Panama Canals. China produces some 40 percent of large oceangoing vessels manufactured globally each year, giving it substantial wartime surge capacity on top of explicitly military-oriented ship production (the People's Liberation Army Navy is now the largest in the world). Leaving the United States' vital supplies in the hands of foreign mariners subject to Chinese coercion threatens to undo three centuries of hard-won wisdom for our maritime nation.

With trillions of dollars of Western capital financing the draining of the West's own manufacturing power and intellectual property to Communist China, the stage was set for the final step of lessons learned from the British playbook: China's attempt to displace the United States at the heart of the world order and retake what CCP elites view as China's rightful place as the Middle Kingdom.

But whereas it took British gunboats to pry open Chinese markets, the Chinese Communist Party walked right through the front door. In fact, our Uniparty elites rolled out the red carpet, welcoming the country to permanent normal trade relations (PNTR) status and membership in the World Trade Organization, all the while assuring themselves that trade would mean liberalization and democracy in China.

China's plan to rewire the global economy in its favor harkens back to its long history of ruling via economic and diplomatic manipulation. But its traditional strategy of generating massive trade surpluses should not have worked in the modern monetary system, because money today is not backed by bullion (the tons and tons of gold and silver that flowed to China under the Canton System). Instead, the trade surpluses incurred by exporting more than it imports should have caused China's currency to appreciate and its trade partners' to depreciate. In the long run, that would have made Chinese manufactures more expensive and less attractive for outsourcing. In fact, in the years leading up to China's entry into the WTO, that was the *universal prediction* of all of the "top" economists, such as Paul Krugman and Maurice Obstfeld.

That never happened. Instead, China illegally devalued its currency, harming its own people but ensuring that the CCP's strategy for hollowing out Western manufacturing and returning China to global economic centrality could work. But even a Chinese domestic spending and debt spree could not absorb all of the trade imbalance, which ballooned to over $400 billion before President Trump began to push back. What China did to maintain its export advantage was devious: it invested in the United States, buying US assets with US dollars, thus propping up the value of the dollar (to keep Chinese products cheap) while sucking ownership of US companies, real estate, and more out of the United States and buying trillions of dollars' worth of US government debt. The CCP today sits atop a $3 trillion hoard of assets, many of them American.

Normally, such a move would generate massive political resistance among the people affected. After all, who can blame CCP elites for taking advantage when the United States offered no resistance beyond a handful of feckless anti-WTO protests that led nowhere? But why did the United States allow the "China Shock" (the massive reconfiguration of the US economy due to trade deals with China) to occur in the first place?

For a democratic system such as the United States', the widespread social and economic destruction experienced by the American people should have been a limiting factor on China's ability to force open US markets and flood them with Chinese goods while leaving China's own markets off limits to many American companies. And of course, the Chinese had nothing like the Royal Navy to impose such a state of affairs by gunboat.

But that's where the final step of China's playbook paved the way for dominance: spiritual warfare. The British example proved helpful yet again. China has pursued the same two-prong strategy of cultivating addiction both among the people and among the elites. Among the American populace, China has not only cultivated an addiction to cheap Chinese TVs and T-shirts, it is also cultivating more sinister addictions: essentially all fentanyl and methamphetamine today are made in China or made with chemicals imported from China. A study by the economists Justin R. Pierce and Peter K. Schott has shown that the parts of the United States most exposed to the China Shock experienced an appalling increase in drug overdoses and other "deaths of despair": a county's moving from the 25th to the 75th percentile of exposure to China-related job losses resulted in a 40 to 60 percent increase in drug overdose deaths. China's message to the working-class Americans experiencing the moral and spiritual cost of their jobs being replaced by Chinese exports is: keel over and die.

But there is a curious "dog that didn't bark." Those effects began almost immediately after China was admitted to the WTO (though drug deaths in particular shot up after the rise of fentanyl in the 2010s). Why didn't anyone in Washington notice?

The answer is that the CCP bribed American elites to look the other way. As Upton Sinclair wrote, "It is difficult to get a man to understand something when his salary depends on his not understanding it." The China Shock fell hard on a concentrated swathe of the American heartland, killing millions of "deplorables" in certain counties in Ohio, North Carolina, Oregon, and other states. But in counties not directly exposed to trade-related job losses, the main immediate impact was cheaper consumer goods at Costco.

Chinese asset purchases in the United States were not only an economic strategy; they were a *political* strategy. The people and companies most directly harmed by China's currency and financial manipulation were the American working class, manufacturers, and Rust Belt communities. But by buying US assets, China bought off America's elites, who are disproportionately likely to work in the finance, insurance, real estate, and higher education sectors and live in large coastal cities where Chinese oligarchs bought real estate, went on shopping sprees, hired investment bankers, invested in Western companies, and sent their kids to university. According to the US Trade Representative, the United States has a massive trade deficit with China for goods ($382.3 billion), having replaced American-made products with Chinese-made ones. But we have a substantial trade surplus of services ($14.9 billion on $41.5 billion of services exports), heavily concentrated in white-collar industries. For coastal elites, not noticing the plight of working-class Americans came easy.

DEI and ESG Mean CCP

Like arrogant late-Qing officials negotiating with the British, many of our elites believe that they are in the driver's seat of structural changes in the world economy to advance diversity, equity, and inclusion (DEI) and environmental, social, and governance (ESG) goals. In reality, in ways subtle and not so subtle, they are already modeling themselves on the patterns set for them by the CCP.

Whereas Communist China began with total political control and party discipline and then introduced a capitalist-style market system, our Uniparty elites are building a CCP-style party discipline and control mechanism on top of our existing capitalist economy, hijacking its brain (the managerial elite) to build "socialism with Western characteristics."

The first step is supercharging the managerial revolution. By hollowing out the productive parts of the US economy, China elevated elites whose power derived from the management of money or corporate-bureaucratic considerations, not excellence in making things. The larger a business gets, the more the managers take over; a publicly traded company has complex SEC compliance requirements, conducts careful risk management with financial counterparties and credit bureaus, works with large banks and insurance companies, tracks the cash flows, depreciation, and other accounting characteristics of all of its assets and liabilities, and otherwise comes to make sense of itself in the language of money instead of the language of value or of production.

It is important to be clear-eyed about what the rise of finance has meant for the United States. As an industry, finance is highly concentrated in a handful of coastal cities. It is subject to enormous social and political pressure, a ready tool for social engineering. It is synonymous with the managerial revolution, the bureaucratization of American business, and the rise of woke capital. Financialization is a style of business that undervalues capital investment, supply chain resilience, productivity growth, and stable jobs. It leads to American businesses' increasingly being beholden to globalists and the Chinese Communist Party. The problem of American finance is as much political as it is economic: we are building the infrastructure of our own enslavement.

This is not an exaggeration. The financial world created an entire class of elites who lack natural loyalties to family, country, or faith. Consider BlackRock, run by the Democratic superdonor Larry Fink, by far the world's largest asset manager. It controls over $9.42 trillion in assets, which it uses to drive Uniparty aims across the entire global economy. An investigation by the House Select Committee on the Chinese Communist Party found that, through a series of funds, BlackRock channeled hundreds of millions of dollars from US pension funds, 401(k)s, and university endowments into investments into "dozens of blacklisted Chinese companies that threaten US national security or support the Chinese Communist Party's human rights abuses." Across just five funds, the committee found, BlackRock had invested over $429 million in Chinese companies that posed national security risks, acted directly against US interests, and engaged in human rights abuses. They included companies building China's aircraft carriers, companies producing ammunition and artillery shells for

the PLA, and a genetics company that has scooped up American genetics data in addition to profiling Uyghurs for the Chinese techno-
surveillance state. Then-congressman Mike Gallagher, chair of the
committee at the time, warned that such activities as BlackRock's
placed the United States "at risk of funding our own destruction."

And that's just the tip of the iceberg of companies officially flagged
by the US government. It does not include all of the companies siphon-
ing intelligence to the CCP, stealing American intellectual property,
or making themselves available at the drop of a hat to wartime mobilization in China's defense industrial base. The investigation covered
only BlackRock and its partner company MSCI. The committee issued
another report in February 2024 chronicling several billion dollars in
investments by US venture capital firms in Chinese technology companies with weaponizable systems, and that report pales in comparison
to the hundreds of billions of dollars of American investments by other
firms in building up China's industrial complex.

But socialism with Western characteristics is about so much more
than Wall Street channeling the savings of the American people into
the hands of the CCP. It's about our Uniparty elite adopting the same
mindset toward the use of financial systems as an instrument of social
control that CCP elites have.

The Chinese aren't dispassionate businessmen; they're social engineers.
In the end, so are asset managers such as our elites. So in September 2023,
the Chinese Communist Party demanded that BlackRock executives in
China undertake a study of Xi Jinping Thought as a condition of being
allowed to continue operating in the country (where BlackRock has substantial investments). But in June 2020, BlackRock's US headquarters,
operating not on a US government mandate but on a Uniparty one, announced that it would require its employees to take a "mandatory 'racial
equity' course," would evaluate their job performance by the "tracking
and measurement of diversity metrics," and would selectively focus on
promoting "racially and ethnically diverse" candidates. The "culture war"
over wokeness is really a class war, and the point is to make sure that all the
money and power flows to the "right" people.

In the same way that the CCP insists that companies over a certain size have party members in senior roles or even that the CEO be a party member, under socialism with Western characteristics, large US companies need to demonstrate their commitment to DEI by ensuring that they have "diversity" in senior roles or even that the CEO is "diverse" (regardless of merit). These requirements are increasingly imposed through lending terms, state and federal regulators, and a network of NGOs (all in blatant violation of US civil rights law, of course).

But while the real point of DEI is to construct a CCP-style system of social control, embedding ESG in American business serves both this goal and China directly. Ostensibly for the purpose of harnessing the power of capitalism to solve climate change and making progress toward the UN Sustainable Development Goals, ESG is actually a system for punishing the lawful and empowering the unlawful. Effectively, it's anarcho-tyranny for business.

Uniparty elites obviously love it. They have joined with the World Economic Forum and the CCP to get banks, asset managers, and large institutional investors to incorporate ESG metrics into investment decisions (and thereby incentivize pro-ESG corporate behavior and punish companies that run afoul of the metrics).

Functionally, ESG is a tax by which American consumers subsidize the growth of the world's largest emissions cheaters and the United States' dependence upon them. So, for instance, ESG metrics (not to mention Biden administration subsidies) reward automakers that devote factory lines to building electric vehicles, which rely on large lithium batteries. But ESG metrics also punish Western mining companies that produce environmentally toxic lithium in places such as Australia, making it harder for them to get loans and attract investors (on top of extensive first-world environmental regulations). So the net result of ESG in this case is to increase the demand, dependency, and price for high-pollution Chinese lithium produced in third-world countries. Pretty much everywhere you look, you see a pattern: ESG keeps Western oil and natural gas companies from increasing production, so the United States must pay more to Venezuela, Russia, and Saudi Arabia.

ESG incentivizes US companies to divest from heavy industry, pipeline infrastructure, and critical mining operations, *even if they continue to then buy services from the new owners of their old assets.*

It goes without saying that Chinese companies basically make up their ESG metrics, which are essentially impossible to verify by a third party. If viewed through the lens of actions instead of words, the global ESG framework is quite evidently more about Western reparations and Chinese world power than about solving environmental issues.

China's Globalist Tyranny Has Created a Class of American Princelings

Careful readers may be asking themselves: Who would go in for these sucker deals, which neither serve US interests nor mitigate shared global environmental issues? As always, the most important question to ask is: Who benefits?

Socialism with Western characteristics may destroy the American middle class, subjugate the world order to China, and kill the golden goose of dynamic and virtuous constitutional self-government. But it delivers extraordinary *power and wealth* to the Uniparty with relatively little effort and almost zero accountability.

You can see this in the case of Tenke Fungurume, a cobalt and copper mine in the Democratic Republic of Congo bought in 2016 by the mining company China Molybdenum from an American company for $2.65 billion, with a remaining minority share purchased for $1.14 billion from the Canadian company Lundin Mining. By selling the mine, one of the richest sources in the world for key battery production materials, the American and Canadian firms improved their ESG metrics and scored a payday, but at the cost of consolidating Chinese global control of cobalt supplies.

According to the *New York Times*, the Canadian wing of the deal was brokered by BHR Partners, which is controlled by the Bank of China and other Chinese investors. BHR is a unique company with a Sino-US shareholding structure and the ability to work around otherwise strict Chinese capital controls, backed directly by the Chinese government. Its name is an acronym for the partners involved in the firm. Two are Chinese asset managers: Bohai Industrial Investment Fund Management Company and Harvest Fund Management: B and H. The last initial in BHR is for an American company named Rosemont Seneca Partners, which owned 30 percent of BHR and helped the Chinese navigate the politics of the deal in Washington and Ottawa.

The *Times* reported the story about the mine acquisition because of who founded Rosemont Seneca Partners in 2009: Hunter Biden, shortly after his father became vice president. But the most important part of interpreting regime media is understanding what is left unsaid. The *Times* story leaves off the name of Biden's cofounder: Christopher Heinz, John Kerry's stepson. (Of course, Kerry knows something about business in China; his great-grandfather Francis Blackwell Forbes made a fortune as an opium trader.)

Conservatives have gotten so fixated on the sensational tabloid aspects of the Hunter Biden story (the tawdry and incestuous family dramas, the hookers and crack, the bumbling incompetence) that they have neglected the much more important ways in which his business behavior was utterly typical of our ruling class.

Consider the September 2015 sale of a 159-year-old Michigan-based auto parts manufacturer, Henniges Automotive, to the Chinese military aerospace company AVIC for a billion dollars, another BHR deal. AVIC's interest may have lain in Henniges's precision manufacturing capabilities and world-beating antivibration technology, with "dual-use" military applications requiring investment review by the Commerce Department and State Department. Nonetheless, the Obama White House (where Hunter's dad served as vice president) and Heinz's stepfather's State Department approved the purchase. Hunter made at least $5.8 million on Chinese deals after securing a meeting between the Chinese banker Jonathan Li and Joe Biden on an official visit in 2013.

While Heinz and Biden perhaps sit atop the pile of American princelings, their business methods are hardly atypical. Former speaker of the

House Nancy Pelosi has been an admirably stalwart opponent of the CCP over the years, but that did not stop her son, Paul Jr., from taking a multimillion-dollar position in a NASDAQ-listed Chinese telecoms company. Nor is it a coincidence that days after President Trump was elected, Senate Majority Leader Mitch McConnell's sister-in-law became only the second foreigner appointed to the board of the Bank of China. Peter Schweizer's book *Secret Empires: How the American Political Class Hides Corruption and Enriches Family and Friends* is chock-full of less high-profile corruption involving American political leaders and their families, who "suddenly" find wealth through sweetheart private equity deals or lobbying contracts.

In the end, Lord Macartney was right: it all comes down to the kowtow. The CCP's lure to Western investors and American princelings is only secondarily about directly manipulating behavior; it is primarily about subverting incentives and building habits of deference. With so much money on the line, you don't need some CCP commissar to tell you what to do; you make the kowtow as a matter of self-interest. The CCP wants you shutting up about Uyghur genocide or actively defending it like LeBron James; hesitating before investigating a shady deal because you don't want to see your family members caught up in the fray; boosting ESG metrics and a climate deal with China, even at the cost of US national interests, knowing that it will benefit your stepson's investments in Chinese solar companies (and isn't renewable energy important after all?).

The Chinese Communist Party has subverted the stability of the United States and the common good of our people through addiction and institutional manipulation. And it's time to fight back with all our might.

We're in a Spiritual War with China

The reason our ruling elites can't see China's threat is that their philosophy doesn't make room for enemies. When I arrived at the Heritage

Foundation, I laid down a marker: come hell or high water, we were going to lead the movement against China—and I'm proud to say we have.

I was not always a China hawk. Like most conservatives, I thought US policy toward China should be one of friendly competition. Eventually, I assumed, we'd turn China into America, meaning that our economic prowess, superior system of government, and freedom would win the Chinese over. You might say that that attitude was the last vestige of my neoconservatism.

China does increasingly pose a military threat to the United States and her allies in East Asia. But to overfocus on this threat is to unwittingly advance Chinese interests by ignoring the CCP's overall strategy of pitting "America against America" (in the words of a chief CCP ideologist, Wang Huning) through economic co-option, institutional subversion, addiction, and spiritual warfare. The most important way to resist China's strategy to is to refuse to kowtow to the Chinese Communist Party by rejecting both direct Chinese influence and socialism with Western characteristics.

To stop the Chinese onslaught against our institutions, we need to rebuild our walls and restore our guardians. We need to orient our entire government to the Chinese threat with at least as much focus and clarity as we had during the Cold War: the 2023 Heritage Foundation report *Winning the New Cold War: A Plan for Countering China* is a good place to start. But though much of this work will occur throughout the executive branch, it is imperative that we restore the people's branch to grapple with the insidious CCP.

Back during the 1990s, Republicans gleefully slashed congressional staff and operations budgets as part of a broad sweep of fiscal reforms. I think we need to recognize in hindsight that this was a mistake. A weak, distracted Congress without a robust, dogged staff is a recipe for foreign penetration and lackadaisical oversight. Willmoore Kendall makes the strong case that Congress is the central pillar of the American system. Congress is the most populist branch of government, the one most responsive to the needs of ordinary Americans, the one capable of keeping all the others on their toes. If you want better and more careful government spending, more oversight over the administrative state, accountability for the failures of the intelligence community, adaptability to the China threat, and more, you need a more capable Congress.

The first thing a beefed-up Congress should do (after banning Tik-Tok) is bring back the House Un-American Activities Committee (HUAC). The House Select Committee on the Chinese Communist Party has begun the work of holding Uniparty elites and Washington bureaucrats to account for their compromise, corruption, and co-optation by the CCP. But their early work has only revealed how very deeply the problem goes. A revived, bulked-up HUAC would be the place to investigate Chinese infiltration of Big Tech, the Ivy League, Wall Street, American agriculture, and more. Its investigative work could directly feed into a far more robust and targeted legislative effort to dismantle China's sources of power in the United States, brick by brick, and to call to account the Uniparty elites that enabled this foreign infiltration. Confucius Institutes and the College Board; Huawei and Sequoia Capital; the Bank of China and BlackRock; the Wanda Group and the Walt Disney Company—they're all going to be in the hot seat, and the Heritage Foundation's going to be piling firewood underneath.

Restoring Our Commerce

In his confrontation with Japanese automakers, Ronald Reagan clarified what a trade policy in the American interest looks like, as codified in his 1980 presidential platform: "The Republican Party believes in free trade, and we will insist that our trade policy be based on the principles of reciprocity and equity. We will not stand idly by as the jobs of millions of Americans in domestic industries are jeopardized and lost."

At some point in the 1990s, Republicans forgot those principles. They bought into the ivory-tower theories of economists bought off by globalist corporations that argued that lowering barriers to trade would ultimately be beneficial to the United States, even if our trading partners locked us out of their markets, treated American companies unfairly, or otherwise refused reciprocity. Of course, the biggest and baddest instance of this was extending permanent normalization of trade relations status to China, which has given CCP-backed firms an open invitation to pillage the US economy without even a hint of reciprocity.

Until President Trump put a stop to it.

For decades, American presidential candidates promised to officially label China a currency manipulator, only to chicken out at the last minute under the thrall of compromised Uniparty elites (including their donors). In 2019, President Trump had the courage to do what Bush and Obama had refused to do and designated China a currency manipulator. He started a trade war with China (that we won), raised tariffs on Chinese goods, and otherwise sought to restore balance in our trade. The Biden administration, while maintaining some Trump-era approaches and policies, has backtracked on others, especially under the banner of climate change driven by John Kerry. We need to restore and extend President Trump's reciprocal trade agenda and recover "the art of the deal."

We're going to need a protectionist approach to China. I don't mean protect as in protect from competition like a special snowflake or even protect jobs per se at the cost of economic growth. I mean protectionist as in protect from pirates, bandits, spies, and Communists. Just because China's pirates don't operate from sailing junks anymore doesn't mean they're doing any less to loot the US economy. President Trump's imposition of unilateral tariffs was a great first step that we should extend with incentives for US companies to reshore, near-shore, and friend-shore supply chains. By breaking China's chokehold on strategic economic inputs, we can defang much of its power. As a matter of national security, we need to fully capitalize on newly discovered US reserves of critical commodities such as lithium, cobalt, and rare-earth metals, the exploitation of which is currently strangled by environmental regulations and activist lawyers.

But we need to go further to recover the *spirit* of American commerce and American companies. The China expert Dr. Jonathan D. T. Ward, the author of *China's Vision of Victory*, has suggested that, were the legendary American diplomat George Kennan to write a "Long Telegram" today about the New Cold War with China, he would address it not to national security policy makers but to the business leaders of the Free World. The fact is, driven by shortsighted stock price concerns and a buck-passing approach, it was American executives who played right into the hands of Xi Jinping and the Chinese Politburo. A reinvigorated case for another American Century, helped along by a reinvigorated HUAC, must remind America's business elites of their duties to the common good of the republic and reinstill a sense of patriotism in them.

Spiritual Warfare Requires Spiritual Resistance

I don't think we will succeed without the return of a practice absolutely antithetical to everything the CCP and its Uniparty sympathizers stand for: widespread and prominent public prayer.

As part of the early Cold War turn to a serious confrontation with communism, Congress mandated in 1954 that the phrase "under God" be added to the Pledge of Allegiance and in July 1955 that the phrase "In God we trust" appear on all US currency. Those were no top-down mandates: they came about through a groundswell of grassroots advocacy by Americans who realized that the confrontation with the Soviet Union was, at its core, a spiritual struggle between a revolutionary ideology that denied transcendence (and thus treated its subjects as just so many cattle) and one that held that man's dignity and worth were endowed by their Creator.

To restore public prayer to a place of prominence—to take a moment for prayer before football games, to have prominent leaders including our president not just issuing the occasional prayer proclamation but actually publicly taking a knee before almighty God (as Washington did), to begin school days again with prayer (enabled by school choice legislation)—would be to once again properly acknowledge our gratitude to God and humbly seek His assistance in our struggle to restore vitality to our nation.

Public prayer has another value, as a kind of shibboleth. If an American institution is incompatible with or contemptuous of public prayer, I would be hard pressed to believe that it should not simply be burned down for the common good.

It took the overthrow of the Qing dynasty by the nationalist Sun Yat-sen to begin the process of Chinese renewal and the establishment of new Chinese institutions fit for the purpose of restoring the nation. And it will take a victory in the Second American Revolution to slough off the sinister grip of the CCP and its Uniparty sycophants and restore the institutions conducive to another century of our flourishing.

CHAPTER 10

Elites Must Serve the Nation

Breathes there the man, with soul so dead,
Who never to himself hath said,
This is my own, my native Land!

—Sir Walter Scott

As a Cajun populist, I enjoy railing against our corrupt ruling class as much as anyone does. You might think that I want to destroy the ruling class as such. But I don't.

History tells us that there has never been a civilization without some form of ruling class or elite. Our Founding Fathers believed that a republic like ours needs its elite to come from a natural aristocracy. Our elite would be men and women whose leadership in society is rooted not in lineage or inheritance but in character, courage, and competence, whose prudent leadership and careful investment would constantly renew the land.

Our current elites see themselves not as leaders of a republic but as members of a global community. Their loyalty is not to the United States. If I ever felt tempted to believe our current elite's self-justification that their rejection of American identity is simply a response to an ever more complex world, it ended when I went to Davos. What I saw there wasn't a response to reality but a bubble of privilege totally disconnected from ordinary people's concerns.

I was invited to the World Economic Forum to discuss what to expect from a future Republican administration. I accepted in order to get a chance to see Uniparty's biggest global festival for myself and to give the participants a piece of my mind on behalf of the American people.

What most people who will never go to Davos think it is . . . is what it absolutely is: the biggest *conspiratio* of them all, an entire village full of back rooms where self-selected elites from all over the world decide what matters. It is shot through with hypocrisy: politicians and CEOs descend in their private jets to lecture ordinary people about climate change and ESG. They swan around extolling the importance of diversity, equity, and inclusion while they guzzle hors d'oeuvres and wine served by an army of invisible plebes. It's a place "where billionaires tell millionaires about what the middle class feels," as the global banker Jamie Dimon sheepishly put it.

At Davos, I realized that there is one question that cuts like Alexander the Great's sword through the Gordian knot of immigration and trade, a question that our Uniparty elite wriggle to avoid at every step. The question is this:

Do the ordinary people of this country matter?
Do the ordinary people of this country matter?
DO THE ORDINARY PEOPLE OF THIS COUNTRY MATTER?

The Uniparty does everything to pretend that the issues of our border, of immigration, and of trade are about anything else than this simple question. They produce graphs and charts and sophisticated arguments. Or, when the intellectual approach fails, they call you racist, xenophobic, isolationist, or worse.

I think there is plenty of room for legitimate disagreement about the right level of immigration and the right kinds of trade. But we must pursue agreement that the only relevant aim for these policies is the common good of the American people and the preservation of our American traditions. This singular goal dictates an equally singular political focus: destroying the grip that Uniparty elites and unelected technocrats have on the average person and restoring our republican culture.

Dead Souls

By any measure, Professor Samuel P. Huntington was an elite, born to wealth in New York City and educated at Yale and Harvard before taking tenured professorships at Columbia and later Harvard. He even died in the elite enclave of Martha's Vineyard. Throughout his life, he taught the ruling class, advised presidents, and wrote books that were influential and widely discussed throughout elite circles.

That was, until his last book.

Entitled *Who Are We? The Challenges to America's National Identity* (2004), it received a few polite (but firmly disapproving) reviews in Uniparty media organs before being promptly memory-holed. Literary elites were embarrassed even to have to discuss a book that made the argument that America had a distinctive cultural identity that could be weakened, or even destroyed, by immigration and globalization.

Huntington was the elites' elite, and he had their number. While much of the caterwauling about the book dealt with its treatment of American cultural identity and Latino assimilation (or lack thereof), he also weighed the ruling class and found it wanting, in a section entitled "Dead Souls: The Denationalization of the American Elite." He pointed out that ordinary Americans were concerned not only about America's physical security but also about societal security, "the sustainability—within acceptable conditions for evolution—of existing patterns of language, culture, association, religion and national identity."

This deep and intuitive spiritual and physical connection to one's nation was expressed by Sir Walter Scott:

Breathes there the man, with soul so dead,
Who never to himself hath said,
    This is my own, my native Land!
Whose heart hath ne'er within him burn'd,
As home his footsteps he hath turn'd,
    From wandering on a foreign strand!

According to Huntington's analysis, a greater and greater portion of America's elite have become "dead souls," concerned more about their global careers and cosmopolitan tastes than about anything connected to America, especially her popular or folk culture. These dead soul elites feel no spiritual connection to America and no responsibility or fellow feeling toward their fellow Americans.

Throughout history, elites have usually been conservative forces, defending the status quo they sit atop. So why is it that America's Uniparty elites attack the traditions, culture, and institutions that have made America great? My point isn't that this turn in our elites has been *bad* (though it's turned into a disaster); it is that it has been profoundly *weird*, profoundly *unnatural* of elites throughout history.

Why is it that on one issue after another, the head of the American Federation of Teachers, the chief of staff of the army, the director of the National Institutes of Health, the commissioner of the National Basketball Association, the secretary of state, Fortune 100 CEOs, and the president of Swarthmore College share the same basic perspective? And why is it that they are far more likely to agree *with one another* than with the average working-class person in their organization: a schoolteacher, an army sergeant, an assistant coach, a laboratory technician, a factory foreman?

And why is it that they—who lead important American institutions, who sit on the top rungs of American society—are more likely to condemn *the institutions in which they are leaders* and to scoff at straightforward American patriotism than the ordinary Americans far below them on the ladder are?

On what principle, then, is our Uniparty elite selected? Intelligence, ambition, discipline, wealth, connections, and such are table stakes. But they're not enough to get you to the top of a Uniparty institution. They won't get you accepted into Harvard, interviewed at McKinsey, or tapped for Skull and Bones.

Uniparty institutions demand an additional quality: they select for *impiety.* They have no use for talented young men and women who are devoted to strengthening and maintaining existing American institutions, identity, places, or values, no matter how impressive they are otherwise. They scorn any would-be elite that maintains a sense of duty or filial piety toward America, their home place, or the faith of their fathers. Our Uniparty's chief demand of those it would endow with power, wealth, and status is that *they shun gratitude toward all that they have inherited.*

The reason why is that piety, gratitude, and a sense of duty get into the way of technocratic management, the centralization of power, and the strip mining of the American way of life. Student activists who tear down statues on campus have no problem working, upon graduation, for vulture hedge funds stripping viable companies for parts or for PR firms whitewashing Qatari terrorist financing. Holding the United States to be a "racist settler-colonial state," they feel no shame in working for her enemies. They are encouraged to feel no sense of duty toward their families, their communities, or their countrymen, and they dub this moral emptiness a virtue.

The Birth of the Global Citizen

What is killing the souls of American elites? A subtle shift in the Ivy League, since the mid–twentieth century the forge of the American elite, might clue us in.

In 1896, the Princeton professor (and future president) Woodrow Wilson gave an oration in honor of the university's one hundred fiftieth anniversary. It focused, in moving detail, on the influence of Princeton president and American Founding Father John Witherspoon, whose philosophical, educational, and political efforts deeply shaped the early leaders of our Republic, many of whom had been his students. Princeton, under Witherspoon's leadership, had been "a school of duty." The title of Wilson's oration became Princeton's unofficial motto: "In the Nation's Service."

One hundred years later, in the afterglow of the end of the Cold War and the beginning of a New World Order, Princeton's Uniparty leaders thought the old motto needed to be updated in keeping with the times. They expanded the motto to no longer focus exclusively on students' duties to the United States, adding "and in the Service of all Nations." But even that was considered too narrow-minded by 2016, and so Princeton's motto today is "In the Nation's Service and the Service of Humanity."

This change, ubiquitous in spirit among the institutions forming future Uniparty members, is not a subtle shift; it's a moral revolution.

You can see this in the work of some of the most influential political theorists of the period, such as Martha Nussbaum at the University of Chicago and Amy Gutmann and Peter Singer at Princeton. All of them hold that patriotism, national pride, and a belief that one has special duties to one's neighbors on the basis of a shared identity are parochial and morally arbitrary ("repugnant," in Gutmann's word). Instead, the morally sophisticated individual must widen her "circle of concern" to take in the needs and rights of all humanity. She must view herself not as an American first but as a "global citizen."

This viewpoint suggests not only that one must not merely regard all of humanity as equal but that it is *morally wrong* for an individual, family, company, or even government to privilege its own people when other people elsewhere have less privilege and "need" the help more. In this inverted moral sensibility, helping your downtrodden neighbor who has just lost his job is wrong when the same resources could go to, say, a desperately poor refugee or a child in Africa lacking safe drinking water.

It's not so much that Singer, Nussbaum, Gutmann, and other less prominent thinkers and critical theorists succeed in indoctrinating students in the classroom; some of the most devoted "global citizens" have never picked up a work of philosophy in their life. But the work they were doing picked up upon a broader attitudinal shift in the Uniparty.

For ordinary Americans, the end of the Cold War presented an opportunity to finally address deeply rooted challenges at home. For fifty years, the United States had shouldered the lion's share of the burden of defeating totalitarian ideology around the world. And we won a great victory, making a world order that was safe for freedom. Now we needed to tend our own garden. Americans wanted to end (in Buchanan's words) "routinized annual transfers of our national wealth to global bureaucrats" at the United Nations and other international organizations, massive military expenditures for rich countries such as Germany and Japan that now faced no existential threats and were now competing economically with the United States (even as we subsidized their economies), and routine foreign aid for regimes that had been Cold War allies but that now lined their own pockets or, worse, siphoned the money to avowed enemies of the United States.

Our elites began to tell themselves a different story. The end of the Cold War did not demand attention to the United States' own issues but instead an *enlargement* of its involvement in the world—at their direction, of course. With the Soviet Union out of the picture, borders and barriers to trade, movement, commerce, ideas, and more fell. American elites had a once-in-a-lifetime opportunity to take advantage of what came to be called globalization. American elites gained enormously in terms of wealth, power, and prestige from the United States' status as the sole global superpower and anchor of a US-led world order. Profits from investments in factories in Des Moines and Burbank paled in comparison to those in growing emerging economies such as Poland and Taiwan. The international demand for American technocrats, consultants, and influence peddlers soared. The global influence and reach of American culture exploded, benefitting coastal elites in media, the arts, and universities with global brands.

During the Cold War, the American people and the elites had been united by a common purpose, common interests, and a shared way of life. But with the dawn of globalization, elites and elite institutions benefited directly from expanding global engagement, even when doing so hurt the nation or the American middle class. While most Americans enjoyed the lower cost of goods and improved chances to travel, the elites benefited far more than the middle class did, with wealth and income growth in the top 5 percent and 1 percent of households greatly outpacing those of the rest of the country.

As it became a burden, our elite eagerly sloughed off any responsibility to ensuring the common good of the American people, along with any sense of duty to their fellow countrymen who had been left behind by globalization. As "global citizens," our elites came to regard our people with contempt as arrogant, ungrateful, and ignorant deplorables, whining about factories closing or American identity slipping away when, in the eyes of the elites, the rest of the world was beating down the door trying to come to the United States and seeking the grace and favor of American elites. Why put up with getting roasted by line workers or local voters when you can hop on a flight to Jakarta or Warsaw and be treated with deference and awe bordering on worship by local officials, would-be business partners, and NGO workers?

That was how the Uniparty began. Leftist criticisms of our elites have focused on wealth and income inequality. Right-wing populism has focused more on the rise of a disconnected and imperialistic elite that pushes its values on the rest of the world. But they come from the same underlying source: the emergence of a class whose economic interests often oppose those of the rest of the country and that cloaks the pursuit of those interests in an ideological vocabulary of "social justice" and "global citizenship" that justifies looking down its nose at the benighted deplorables in the rest of the country; that doesn't even see ordinary Americans as fellow citizens whose flourishing they are duty bound to assist.

The Uniparty Sees Americans and Non-Americans as Interchangeable

Seeing themselves as "global citizens" who happen to carry American passports, Uniparty elites see American identity purely in terms of economic value and multicultural "diversity" (the more, the better). Huntington described the Uniparty mentality this way:

> The ideal would be an open society with open borders, encouraging subnational ethnic, racial and cultural identities, dual citizenship, diasporas, and would be led by elites who increasingly identified with global institutions rather than national ones. America should be multiethnic, multiracial, multicultural. Diversity is a prime value, if not the prime value. The more people who bring to America different languages, religions and customs, the more American America becomes.

We should recognize the Uniparty's attitude toward open borders as yet another luxury belief. Their gated communities and exclusive neighborhoods don't have open borders. They work in organizations that recruit and hire only from a small number of universities, and they send their kids to prep schools charging tens of thousands of dollars in tuition. In these heavily gate-kept settings, which already select for education, outlook, and English fluency, diversity seems to have no downside. Isn't it pretty to think that the families of an American law partner, a Brazilian energy executive, a French journalist, an Egyptian management consultant, and a Hong Kong financier can all form "a brotherhood of man"? As the Uniparty anthem, John Lennon's "Imagine," describes it: "Imagine there's no countries, / It isn't hard to do, / Nothing to kill or die for, / And no religion, too."

Because the Uniparty's cultural and communal stability is ensured by socioeconomic domination and not national identity, its members treat the desire of ordinary Americans to preserve their way of life through limitations on open borders as driven by nothing but xenophobic animus. And because they themselves view passports, cultures, and cities as interchangeable commodities, Uniparty elites view ordinary Americans as replacement parts, too. From the Uniparty perspective, replacing a native-born American service worker with a Guatemalan immigrant reduces cost, increases diversity, and aids someone with less privilege than someone born in America has. From their perspective, it's an unambiguous win.

The "global citizen" mentality of immigrants and natives as interchangeable replacement parts is enshrined in law by the Immigration and Nationality Act of 1965, also known as the Hart-Celler Act, pushed forward by President Lyndon B. Johnson as part of his Great Society initiatives, which radically altered the traditional immigration policy of the United States. American immigration policies had historically balanced a welcome for immigrants with the need to build social and cultural solidarity within the United States, marked by an era of felt national unity stronger than any other in our history.

Johnson held that the bill's purpose was to correct "a cruel and enduring wrong in the conduct of the American Nation"—a "racist" immigration policy that had prioritized immigrants from cultures and national origins similar to those of the existing American polity. "This bill that we will sign today is not a revolutionary bill," Johnson said at the signing ceremony. "It does not affect the lives of millions. It will not reshape the structure of our daily lives." Senator Edward Kennedy assured skeptics that "our cities will not be flooded with a million immigrants annually. . . . the ethnic mix of this country will not be upset."

The problem is not that the United States widened its immigration policy; it's that *any* concern about shared heritage, culture, and assimilation became totally taboo. Ordinary Americans support low levels of immigration and are personally welcoming to immigrants. But rather than dealing democratically with the desires of native-born Americans, the Uniparty's preference is to supercharge immigration to replace native-born Americans conscious of the war against the American way of life with more pliable groups indifferent to national unity. At a population level, this shift is called "the emerging Democratic majority"—unless you're a conservative, in which case the most esteemed journalists will tell you that it's called "the Great Replacement" and it's a racist conspiracy theory that absolutely isn't happening but would be a good thing to happen and don't you dare notice that it is happening.

The critics are half right; there's no conspiracy. The conventional wisdom on the right has become that our open borders policy is driven by Democrats looking for future voters and Republicans beholden to business interests relying on cheap labor. But more than a decade working on these issues in Texas and Washington has taught me that the truth is simpler but more depressing.

Occasionally, there is a particular issue in which some interest group has an immediate, strong interest: progressive voter groups care about ensuring that the census counts illegals, industrial agriculture fights for temporary worker visas, companies such as DoorDash and Uber fund immigration activists to help them lower their labor costs with illegal aliens. But these by and large do not explain the apathy in Washington over the massive number of asylum seekers, chain migration that imports welfare dependents, and Chinese birth tourism.

The most important thing to realize is that for members of the Uniparty on both sides of the aisle, none of this is in any way, shape, or form an urgent problem. They don't have to deal with it. It doesn't affect their lives or those of their donors. It is beneath their notice. They don't have Sino-Mexican fentanyl addicts on their block, menacing young "asylum seekers" leering at their daughters or occupying their kids' schools, illegal immigrants undercutting their wages or flooding their doctors' offices.

They don't think mass immigration is really bad, they don't think American culture or identity is worth protecting, and they're not harmed by immigration (if anything, it makes their child care or food delivery cheaper). So the only time they think about it is when voters are up in arms, and even then the threat of being attacked by progressive activist groups or foiled by activist judges usually outweighs the political cost of continuing to do nothing on immigration.

In reality, congressional cowardice is the tip of the iceberg. The real force establishing a de facto open borders policy is the Uniparty elites in NGOs, law firms, and the administrative state conspiring to impose the "replacement parts" mentality on the rest of the country, regardless of the democratic wishes of the American people.

For instance, in 2018 the Trump administration closed a loophole by which adult illegal immigrants ages eighteen to twenty-one could gain a green card under a program intended to aid abused or abandoned children. The policy was blocked on purely administrative grounds by a class action lawsuit backed not only by a legal nonprofit but by one of the largest law firms in the world, Latham & Watkins, which took the case for free.

As a retired Latham partner pointed out in the *American Conservative*, Latham & Watkins revenues that year topped $4 billion and profits per equity partner averaged $4.5 million. In its annual report for 2018, Latham & Watkins boasted that it had advised on 360 merger and acquisitions transactions with a cumulative valuation of $408 billion, more than any other law firm in the world. A third of those transactions (by value) took place outside the United States, where Latham & Watkins maintains growing offices in cosmopolitan cities such as Paris, Frankfurt, Dubai, Tel Aviv, Beijing, and Tokyo.

The same firms (like Latham) that are pocketing billions of dollars by facilitating the sale of American companies to overseas buyers turn around and work *pro bono alienorum* (for the good of foreigners), filing activist lawsuits on behalf of illegal immigrants, stopping states from enforcing their laws, and coaching asylum seekers en masse. As of this writing, Latham & Watkins advertises "global citizenship" as one of five pillars of its practice, the phrase chosen on its website for pro bono work, DEI, and the like.

We now have a perverse situation in which the more likely a would-be immigrant is to end up depending on public welfare in the United States, the more likely he or she is to gain free legal services from Ivy League attorneys at thousand-dollar-per-hour coastal elite law firms. Equally perverse is a system that increasingly rewards migrants who gamble with coyotes and cartels and punishes those who seek to enter the United States in a lawful manner.

Record profits for big law firms, alienation from the common good of ordinary Americans, and white guilt pro bono work stuffing as many dubious asylum cases through as possible all come from the exact same source. Forty years ago, many of Latham's partners would have been attorneys at small regional firms, the kinds of pillars of the community who sat on corporate boards and advised local civic associations. Globalization massively rewarded big law firms with Uniparty connections, sucking the best and brightest out of the American heartland into a handful of coastal cities, generating profits that then have subsidized the industrial-scale pro bono legal activism of the last few decades, even as it alienated those same elites from the consequences of their actions, even on the communities they had left behind.

Our current regime consists of Uniparty elites in New York City and Washington, DC, conspiring with Uniparty elites in San Francisco to impose anarcho-tyranny on the plebes of flyover country. This we call "our democracy"; it is defined not by channeling the will of the people but by following the right process, which is to say, the process that ensures that the Uniparty has a voice at every stage. Elites defend their own interests, but not the common good of ordinary Americans.

Ultimately, this was why the Uniparty freaked out about the election of Donald Trump. For the first time in their lives, Uniparty elites were subject to the authority of someone whom they had not chosen and whom they could not influence through the Uniparty network. It was an all-too-brief taste of their own bitter medicine, and it is why not a single Uniparty-controlled institution openly supported him, even when it was otherwise in its interests to do so.

The Uniparty Versus Real America

Today, there is a profound alienation between the interests and desires of our Uniparty elite and the ordinary people of America, found in places such as Opelousas, Louisiana. If you walk around Opelousas, you will see a place that looks as though it lost a war. In a way, it did. As in many small towns, Main Street has become blighted and hollow, with boarded-up businesses, including a bankrupt local department store, Abdalla's, that has sat vacant for almost forty years. But beyond the physical appearance, it is hard to find a local institution that has not been damaged by the Uniparty's war against ordinary Americans: our Cajun culture, small businesses, the local bank, the Catholic parish, the Boy Scout troop, the public schools, and my grandparents' favorite restaurant have all suffered. The main institutions that have become stronger since I left are the casino, the Walmart Supercenter, and the Goodwill store. The Uniparty has flooded Opelousas with cheap Chinese goods, cheaper Sino-Mexican fentanyl, and not a small number of illegal immigrants in industrial food production in the surrounding area doing "jobs Americans won't do"—but used to do, until their wages stagnated for fifty years.

While Opelousas's economic woes are not exactly the outworking of a free market, regions do go through ups and downs. What is so strange, what we ought to find so uncanny, is that Uniparty elites seek to destroy what institutions and traditions the ordinary people in Opelousas have left. Against a people already economically dispossessed, they impose policies and ideas destructive of the culture, history, traditions, associations, and faith that are our consolation and strength in hard times. Why?

What led to the war between the Uniparty and Opelousas? As in any war, a battle is joined when the defending party decides to fight back. In the wake of the global financial crisis, the American people had had enough of our elites and their disastrous leadership, not only in bailing out Wall Street at Main Street's expense but also in snaring us in Middle Eastern quagmires, surrendering US sovereignty, opening the borders, appeasing Communist China, and otherwise selling out the American people to the Davos class. Populist movements arose on the left (Occupy Wall Street) and the right (the Tea Party) that, for all their disagreements, shared a single goal: to demand accountability for elite failure. Elite institutions responded, and they have been trying to divide ordinary Americans every which way they can ever since, to avoid being forced to reckon with their sins.

It is time they are humbled and the dignity of ordinary Americans is once again exalted. The great Italian sociologist Vilfredo Pareto declared that "History is the graveyard of élites." It's time to bury ours. The solution to a Uniparty takeover is regime change.

Elites Who Love America

Opelousas cannot destroy the Uniparty on its own. What we need is a new American elite that counts *pietas*, patriotism, and accountability to ordinary Americans among its core values. We need elites who understand that receiving leadership and trust demands accountability for results. We need elites who will offer real greatness, not excuses for mediocrity. Of course, not all of them will have pure motives; some will be social climbers. That's not a bad thing; it's an inevitable sign of approaching victory, because they see where things are going. Thankfully, the dam has already begun to break.

Every day, it seems that new defectors from the Uniparty emerge, elites who are themselves sick of the lies, the mediocrity, and the conspiracy against the American people. People such as Bari Weiss, an acclaimed journalist, who left a Uniparty sinecure at the *New York Times* to found the website The Free Press, so that she and her team would have the freedom to investigate the truth. Or Christopher Rufo, a Georgetown- and Harvard-educated documentary filmmaker who set aside cushy jobs for Uniparty-controlled institutions to instead investigate the issues crippling America. People such as J.D. Vance and Ron DeSantis, among a growing number who could have parlayed their sterling Ivy League credentials and military service into successful careers as "centrist" Republicans but chose instead to fight for ordinary Americans on the issues that matter, at great personal cost.

There are deeper forces laying the groundwork for our new elite.

Mediocrity and a lack of moral vision have infected Uniparty-controlled institutions to the point that they are incompetent. The growing China threat and the United States' increasingly aggressive enemies have awoken a number of business and political leaders from their post–Cold War "end of history" slumber. The Uniparty's attack on manliness and fatherhood has forced a whole generation of men to choose between political correctness and their own interests—and they are choosing the latter (Gen Z men are the most conservative in generations). More and more young women are rejecting a depleted *Sex and the City* feminism for a restored vision of femininity and family life. Elite moms and dads who until very recently tried to keep their heads down are increasingly speaking up against a Uniparty agenda that they see threatens their children.

What will forge our new elite? The first fruits of the classical school movement are now entering adulthood full of drive, vigor, and intelligence, running laps around "elite" university grads. Silicon Valley technologists, who believe that founding and building things is good, increasingly scorn Uniparty mediocrity; having a degree from Harvard is now considered by many venture capitalists to be a strike against a prospective candidate (the smartest students drop out). Similarly, growing cadres of American veterans, especially from a special operations background, enter the fray of civilian life scornful of the disloyalty, critical mindset, and lack of accountability expressed by Uniparty members. State legislatures that twenty years ago were sleepy backwaters filled with the B-list talent who couldn't make it to Washington are now increasingly sites of innovative policy experimentation by citizen legislators who couldn't be paid to move to the Swamp. We are so close to a tipping point.

The recently elected Argentinian president, Javier Milei, a populist libertarian, said in his campaign announcement, "I did not come here to guide lambs. I came here to awaken lions." When I look past the Uniparty's death grip on America's institutions and look for the best people, the most energetic organizers, the most brilliant thinkers, the most determined advocates, the most creative builders, what I find are not Uniparty zombies or timid lambs; I see lions awakening.

Nationalize the Elite

But forging a new elite won't happen on its own. The Uniparty reproduces itself through its control of core elite institutions, demanding that elite aspirants bend the knee to its worldview and its interests, to learn to perform its impieties toward ordinary American values, and to burn a pinch of incense on the altar of global citizenship.

If, as Huntington suggested, the denationalization of our elite is creating "dead souls" indifferent to the common good of ordinary Americans, then it is clear what we have to do.

It's time to nationalize the elites.

We need to build institutions and practices to knit the elites and the people back together again, including a national public service program that exposes coastal kids to the rest of the United States, reclaimed control of federal humanities and arts funding that supports telling America's story (and not faux avant-garde trash that tears America down), and alternative institutions of elite education and selection.

We need to (metaphorically) burn down the selective educational institutions that have such a grip on the formation of our elites and that use that grip to push a victim-focused, America-hating "global citizen" mentality. We need heavy taxes on multibillion-dollar educational endowments, mandatory and retroactive sunset clauses on large foundations, and a gross reduction of the massive federal subsidies for administrative overhead through indirect costs on top of research grants. We need to explore mechanisms to force hyperselective universities to grow to meet the demands of American students (and reduce the pressure parents and students feel to conform to Uniparty values to win admission) before they admit lucrative foreign students.

And we need to attack the elite education cartel where it hurts by diverting promising young students (and their parents) into institutional alternatives to the Ivy League, encouraging efforts such as the Thiel Fellowship, which offers extraordinarily talented young men and women a $100,000 blank check to drop out of college to build something great, and the new University of Austin, one of the first serious recent attempts to found an elite university based on American values. New state school programs such as the Hamilton Center at the University of Florida in Gainesville and the Civitas Institute at the University of Texas at Austin offer another pathway to reintegrating a civic spirit into American university life.

We need to attack some of the privileges of globalist elites who are free to do business in the United States as they please (and also, many analysts believe, free to hide income from the IRS). We need to make US citizenship mean more than a passport again and bring some of our policies into line with common sense, the way most other countries do. We should impose a hefty tax on dual citizenship or ban the practice altogether, and we need to redirect IRS agents from auditing small-business owners to going after foreign nationals with American passports who are hiding income. And given the ease of global air travel, Congress should pass legislation clarifying that citizenship by birthright does not extend to children born to foreign parents by surrogacy, to those in the country on a tourist or visitor visa (the lucrative practice of birth tourism), or to the children of two illegal immigrants. These practices merely enable elite corruption and harm ordinary Americans.

We also need to restore common sense to the idea that loyalty to America demands leaving hyphenated identities behind, especially in public service. The problem is not about having a foreign name, accent, or heritage. But leaders of core American institutions should not maintain actual dual loyalties and direct and extensive ties to a foreign country. It's insane that we let a Ukrainian (Aleksandr Semyonovich Vindman) run the National Security Council's Ukraine desk and attempt to overthrow the duly elected president of the United States because he didn't like his Ukraine policy. It's insane that we have an elected member of Congress (Ilhan Abdullahi Omar) who promised to protect the borders of her homeland, Somalia, while refusing to protect those of the United States. It's insane that the Senate confirmed a secretary of transportation (Elaine Chao) whose family runs a Chinese shipping company and whose sister sat on the board of the Bank of China (in the George W. Bush years, she oversaw the Department of Labor during the flood of outsourcing jobs to Chinese factories, which shipped goods back to the United States on her family's boats). It's insane that the Biden administration has had a Colombian native running its Latin America policy and a Palestinian coordinating its response to Hamas's terrorist offensive. It's insane that liberal critics will attack you as racist or xenophobic just for noticing this.

Because the Uniparty is insulated from the consequences of its actions, it needs some populist exposure therapy. In 2022, the state of Florida made headlines by flying illegal immigrants to Martha's Vineyard, where dismayed residents in multimillion-dollar luxury cottages quickly worked to get them off of the island. Programs busing migrants to cities such as Chicago and New York have managed to make our border crisis real for elites in a way nothing else ever has. The only problem with these programs is that they're too small and not targeted enough. They shouldn't drop off migrants in bustling downtowns or working-class neighborhoods but in front of elite prep schools such as Sidwell Friends, Harvard-Westlake School, and Phillips Exeter Academy (if you've never heard of any of these schools, you passed the test).

Most important, we need to destroy the network of Uniparty institutions that actively encourage, protect, and profit from illegal immigration. It is a federal crime, upheld in 2023 by the Supreme Court, to encourage or induce illegal immigration into the United States or to materially assist illegal immigrants to enter the United States. The next president should form a federal task force to aggressively investigate and prosecute the NGOs, activist groups, law firms, and other actors who have flagrantly ignored the law for years.

Some of these policies may seem extreme or even cruel. But what is actually extreme and cruel is our Uniparty members' patting themselves on their backs for their humanitarian virtue while overseeing an effective invasion of our country. Our border crisis is extreme, and it is meting extraordinary cruelty onto ordinary Americans, our border states and their institutions, and even the illegal immigrants who subject themselves to cartel violence and exploitation to come here. We must do what it takes to end the invasion, even if that means grabbing our elites by their lapels and shaking them awake.

An America First Trade and Immigration Policy

The exact correct level of trade and legal immigration is, to my mind, a secondary issue compared to the primary one: immigration and trade policies that exist for the explicit benefit of Americans, made on the basis of the desires of US citizens, that recognize the value of social and economic stability, that support especially the lives and families of American workers, that encourage American cultural identity and assimilation, and that strengthen the United States in the long term. In other words, if we have immigration and trade policies that are made in consideration of ordinary Americans, I have faith that the specifics will work themselves out.

Right now, the US immigration system is wildly out of whack with both common sense and the desires of most Americans. According to a 2021 study by the libertarian Cato Institute, 61 percent of Americans want 500,000 or fewer immigrants to be admitted per year, *half the current legal rate*, the number climbing higher if a resulting reduction in government services is posited (one wonders what the response would have been if housing costs had been added). Even before Biden's border invasion, 71 percent of Americans believed that illegal immigration was unacceptable. An immigration system in line with the wishes of the vast majority (80 percent) of Americans would reduce levels of legal immigration at least below 1 million per year while privileging college-educated, highly skilled immigrants (76 percent support).

Right now, we have a perverted immigration system that paradoxically most reliably rewards individuals (many of whom come to America illegally) who are most likely to end up on government assistance, who claim "asylum" with the help of NGOs and Uniparty pro bono lawyers. Under our system, the more victimized they claim to be, the more likely they are to be granted asylum, so that a (not hypothetical) Latin American HIV-positive transgender prostitute automatically gets a green card (because his home country is "transphobic") while a French college-educated computer engineer with a job lined up at Google has to hope and pray that he wins the H-1B lottery.

An immigration system in the interests of ordinary Americans would distinguish between immigrants who will immediately contribute to American prosperity (on a temporary or permanent basis) and those for whom the United States is "the land of opportunity."

Under our current system, the vast majority of green cards go to the family members of existing residents (chain migration) or to random winners of the "green card lottery." Neither of these categories indicates whether someone is likely to end up contributing to American life and assimilating an American identity instead of harming ordinary Americans or soaking up public benefits. Why should we leave America's future up to a lottery?

During the Clinton years, a bipartisan commission chaired by Democrat Barbara Jordan put forward a plan for immigration reform that would have ended chain migration, focused on the skills immigrants brought to the United States, deported illegals, and capped the number of legal immigrants at 550,000 per year. The Uniparty has tried to close the Overton window on what ordinary Americans regard as common sense.

We should move to a points-based system, as many other developed countries have done, that welcomes the immigrants who are most likely to contribute to our national life. We also need to emphasize an immigration that is capable of integration, privileging English-speaking immigrants and those from countries with strong historical ties to the United States (as we did under the old immigration system abolished by Lyndon Johnson). We also ought to allow individual states to petition the federal government for a certain number of regional worker permits to support their particular industries, as Australia has done. This would empower the states (at the behest of leaders accountable to their voters) to do what is best for their people, with less of an effect on the other states.

While I generally support significant lowering of immigration levels until American national identity has recovered and the percentage of foreign-born Americans returns to historic levels, there is one kind of immigrant we could use more of. The most powerful weapon to disrupt our adversaries' military-technological aspirations is a green card. Right now, a huge percentage of the smartest and most capable Chinese, Russian, and Iranian students would leap at the chance to come to American universities and stay in the United States after finishing their studies. There are arguments for banning these students altogether, and there are better arguments for letting them come and then stay in the United States; the current policy of letting them study here and then forcing them to return to their home countries is the absolute stupidest course of action possible. In our fight against Communist China and a resurgent Russia, we should not neglect weaponized brain drain as a potent tool.

As with immigration, the foundation of US trade policy must be not the castles-in-the-clouds doctrines of ivory-tower academic economists but the voice of common sense and historical experience supported by the American people. For too long, a reflexive and ideological belief in free trade at all costs led American leaders to accept bad deals (on the assurance that it would all work out in the end). In many cases, the harms were clear and immediate (factory closures and devastated communities) while the benefits to ordinary working-class Americans were vague and hypothetical (cheaper goods). In the case of China, we know that the economists were deeply, badly wrong.

During the 1990s, free trade mania led US policy makers to adopt what Ambassador Robert Lighthizer, President Trump's US trade representative and a close friend of mine, has called "the trifecta of globalism": the North American Free Trade Agreement, the creation of the World Trade Organization, and the adoption of permanent normal trade relations with Communist China. These are factors that the United States' rivals and adversaries have easily manipulated and that contributed to the rise of the Uniparty. That's why, under the leadership of President Trump and Ambassador Lighthizer, the United States successfully renegotiated NAFTA, blocked appointments to the WTO's unfair appellate court, placed unilateral tariffs on trade cheaters, and launched a trade war with Communist China.

Trade is an important foundation of the US economy, but GDP growth must not be our only consideration in our trade policy. As Ambassador Lighthizer has said, "It is about the kind of country that Americans want. The allocation of scarce resources, price optimization, and efficiency—things that preoccupy economists—are not as important as issues of family stability, strong communities, income equity, and worker pride and satisfaction." There's another important aspect of this as well: we need a trade policy that will help the renationalization of American elites by improving investment opportunities at home and cutting off cash flows to the Davos class.

The Chicago Council on Global Affairs found that during the Trump administration, American support for trade increased from being stuck below 60 percent for decades to a high of 87 percent of Americans assessing in 2019 that international trade is good for the US economy. It turns out that when you make trade fairer and more reciprocal and ordinary Americans feel they have a leader who is trying to get a good deal on their behalf, they are more likely to support increased trade. Americans' skepticism toward free trade is really a skepticism toward sucker deals and the ivory-tower economists who support them.

Restoring Our Border Sovereignty

The biggest Uniparty outrages regard not our legal immigration or trade system but the sovereignty of our borders. Since he took office, Joe Biden has overseen an invasion of more than 10 million illegal immigrants, greater than the population of New York City. The Uniparty doesn't even really pretend that it's not minting a generation of welfare dependents and crashing the public goods most Americans depend on. In response to the crisis at the border, they have shrugged and smirked. Worse, Biden's Justice Department has restrained states such as Texas from taking border security into their own hands, imposing an anarcho-tyranny at the border, where any shred of enforcement law is forbidden while every legal loophole to admit as many illegals into the country as possible is pursued.

A key root cause of Biden's border crisis was an act of extraordinary Uniparty self-harm: a postinauguration orgy of executive actions pushed by progressive open borders activists. Those rolled back enforcement at the border and within the United States, opened the asylum floodgates, ended President Trump's successful Remain in Mexico policy, and otherwise rolled out the welcome mat for coyotes and cartels.

This has been exacerbated by the weaponization of migration by the United States' enemies. The Marxist government of Nicaragua has hit on a scheme whereby it allows would-be migrants to avoid the deadly Northern Triangle by flying into the country visa free from places such as Cuba, Haiti, and even India and then catching a bus directly to the Honduran border, with the regime taking a fat cut of airline fees. Managua's Augusto C. Sandino International Airport, which once averaged fifteen flights per day, has exploded to more than fifty flights per day. Venezuela, in a severe economic crisis due to decades of socialist mismanagement, has turned to emptying its prisons and encouraging violent criminals to migrate to the United States. The Maduro regime has used this as leverage in negotiations with the Biden administration about ending oil sanctions. In 2023, an extraordinary 52,700 Chinese illegals were encountered by Border Patrol agents (double any previous year), with the vast majority being single military-age men who were paroled into the country. Many will claim and be accepted for asylum, even though asylum fraud with fake documentation is rampant in China. It is not clear what role the Chinese government may play in this, but it is not unreasonable to expect that this invasion could provide cover for even more nefarious activity. Many national security and law enforcement experts are sounding the alarm about the number of known terrorists and criminals who have been apprehended at the border and what this implies about how many have slipped into the country unnoticed.

We need to not merely stop but reverse Biden's border invasion. It's not just about our society's security but about repudiating a Uni-party injustice. Commonsense measures such as mandatory E-Verify of prospective employees and meaningful Immigration and Customs Enforcement (ICE) enforcement should lead to a fair amount of "self-deportation." Many Americans don't know that the bar for gaining asylum is quite high; the vast majority of applications are rejected. Even as we restore the Remain in Mexico policy as well as advanced asylum screening partnerships in Latin America (which the Biden adminis-tration terminated), we need to end asylum paroling (which the Biden administration has used to impose open borders) and speed up asylum processing (an area where AI could be applied). For years one claim of amnesty advocates was that mass deportations were logistically infeasi-ble. But in August 2021, as Afghanistan was collapsing, our heroic air force managed to evacuate more than 120,000 people in the span of a few days! If we apply the same gumption to protecting our border, our illegal immigration problem will be sorted in short order.

And, of course, we need to do what it takes to secure our southern border. While it is long, most of the border follows the natural barriers of the Rio Grande and runs through inhospitable deserts and mountains. In addition to finishing the border wall, advanced new surveillance technology by companies such as Anduril will enable defense in depth, with networked sensors, AI vision, and automatic drones assisting our Border Patrol agents. The criterion of a successful border is not that it is impermeable but that it significantly increases the difficulty of entering the United States undetected, deterring casual entrants and increasing costs for the cartels. To help pay the increased costs of enforcement, we should impose a stiff tax on immigrants' remittances to their home countries, which would have the additional benefit of encouraging immigrants' assimilation and building a life in the United States for those already here.

Most important, Congress should pass legislation authorizing border states to enforce federal immigration law, including deportations, thus preventing Justice Department bureaucrats and progressive pressure groups from having a say over the security of our states and preempting a constitutional crisis. While our federal government should enforce our laws and protect our sovereignty, we must end the reign of federal border anarcho-tyranny that forbids the states to protect their own people against the border invasion.

Maybe some of these measures seem like tough medicine now, but the border crisis is not going away, and I predict that everything stated here will be bipartisan common sense within a decade. I only hope it will not take a terrorist attack or cartel mass murder to make it so.

Regime Change

I went to Davos to deliver a message on behalf of the American people: you (unaccountable Uniparty elites) are the problem, and we are going to destroy you. We're going to do so not because we hate you or wish you ill (in fact, we hope that you can flourish in the new regime, freed of the stresses of "leadership") but because it is necessary to renew our culture and our way of life.

One of the telltale Uniparty tactics is to openly mock the concern that most ordinary Americans have that the immigrants whom we gladly welcome to this country learn to speak the English language, identify with our way of life and form of government, and put down roots and assimilate into our communities. I realized at Davos that the Uniparty's scorn for this idea comes from the fact that they themselves don't speak English (but the language of Standardized Global Management, or Davosese), identify as Americans, or have roots in American life.

Casting off a rootless, globalist elite in favor of a newly renationalized one must be the aim of any populist movement that seeks to undertake a transformation of our political environment and the restoration of meaningful constitutional self-government. But I see so many signs of hope when I look around—not because of any special efforts by the Heritage Foundation or the conservative movement but because Uniparty dominance requires a kind of unipolar globalization that is always going to be unsustainable, because it is rooted in lies about human nature, the United States, and the world order.

I see more and more elites who are actually fighting for the ordinary people of the country: successful entrepreneurs who are sick of the Uniparty's parasitism on the businesses they build and eager to roll up their sleeves and actually do things: young policy analysts and legislative staffers with steel in their spine stiffened by their sense of what time it is; wealthy white-collar parents who are aghast at the destruction of their schools and communities; classical charter school founders with fire in their bellies to pass on Western civilization; iconoclastic artists and designers who are bored with how lame and fake mandatory "diversity and inclusion" are.

A new national unity between the elites and the people will serve as the foundation for a new consensus on trade and immigration that will bring these policy areas into line with the desires and interests of ordinary Americans once again. None of this will be easy, and none of it will be clean. Newly dispossessed Uniparty elites will rant and rave against the power they are losing (for a preview, look at how increasingly irrelevant mainstream media journalists treat new media upstarts such as The Free Press and Elon Musk's X). They will cast every manner of insult and accusation against the trade and immigration policies that are actually in line with the United States' interest. Then again, this is an old elite strategy for control: highlighting the hardships, flaws, and difficulties of policies that attack their interests (such as serious immigration enforcement or a trade war with China) while covering up the cruelties of open borders–driven inflation, rampant fentanyl smuggling, and decimated Main Streets.

Uniparty appeals to moral principles are empty lies. Its members intend only "to lead us by easy routes to the sacrifice of our own interests and dignity in the service of the mighty," as James Burnham, the great theorist of the modern elites, put it.

A direct assault on the sources of Uniparty strength in bottleneck institutions such as elite education, the administrative state, HR departments, ESG-pushing banks, and of course the World Economic Forum will help us topple our corrupt elites and replace them with new and earnest ones who actually love America and who are already building the institutions that will replace those captured by the Uniparty. The First American Revolution ended when we forged an institutional framework for national unity. So will the second.

CHAPTER 11

The Dawn's Early Light

Do not be afraid. Do not be satisfied with mediocrity.
Put out into the deep and let down your nets for a catch. . . .
I plead with you—never, ever give up on hope, never doubt,
never tire, and never become discouraged. Be not afraid!

—Pope John Paul II

What can ordinary Americans do to shape the fate of our nation?

It's a question that's been on my mind as I meet with Heritage Foundation supporters all over the country. I think the answer is found in a poem written during the Great Depression by Robinson Jeffers. Jeffers worried that the new bustling global age and the temptations of imperial power were smothering the pioneer spirit that the republic required to renew itself. "The love of freedom has been the quality of Western man," he said in "Shine, Republic" (1935). But that freedom demands something from us: sacrifices, both small and large. We must "keep the tradition, conserve the forms, the observances, keep the spot sore. Be great, carve deep your heel-marks."

You can't keep the spot sore in a museum. You can't guard the torch in a library. You've got to get out there and throw your weight into the task, to let the fire live in and through your own life. And there's something wild about it. You can't overtame the fire, lest you "perch it on the wrist of Caesar," Jeffers warned. The fire might singe you a bit, but there are worse fates, such as being a slave.

Today we stand in the place of Aeneas carrying his father (his patrimony) on his shoulders, leading his young son (his posterity) by the hand, prepared with his sword to defend them as he journeys toward an uncertain fate. We have nothing to lose; what has been burned is ash already. We have everything to win; we still carry the fire of our future. We know how to do our duty to God and our country; what more can we ask for?

An Order Reborn

Just because we will carry the fire of our tradition into the future doesn't mean that we will do so in the same way we always have. *Magnus ab integro saeclorum nascitur ordo*: "A great order of the ages is born anew." Virgil's poem retains something that the Founding-era paraphrase of the motto on our Great Seal elides: that any great order, any great people, requires renewal, rebirth, from time to time. Sometimes we need to rekindle the fire. We need new fuel, new ways, new allies, new ideas. They're likely to come from surprising sources.

That was what happened to one great American artist, Johnny Cash, the legendary country singer. Like many, I've been listening to the Man in Black all my life, and there's a Cash song for every mood and every occasion. To me, Johnny Cash is the sound of America.

He had an extraordinary career, overcoming deep pain over witnessing his brother's childhood death to make hit after hit touching the soul of America. His records, especially his early ones, crackle with spirit. But by the 1980s, he was creatively exhausted. After decades of successful albums, he was cut by his label, Columbia Records. Once one of the most electric touring musicians in the world, he was reduced to playing dinner theater shows. But worse than not selling albums or filling stadiums was that Cash himself believed he was spent, that he didn't have anything more to offer as an artist. He believed that the world had passed him by. So he was shocked and more than a little baffled when one of the hottest hitmakers in the United States reached out to him, wanting to collaborate.

It's hard to imagine a person farther from the Nashville country music image than Rick Rubin, a Jewish Buddhist sporting Birkenstocks and a scraggly chest-length beard. He had started going to underground clubs as a New York University student in the 1980s, persuading LL Cool J, Public Enemy, and Run D.M.C. to work with him before any of the major labels had even heard of rap music. With Russell Simmons, he had founded Def Jam Recordings, with his dorm room listed as the official address. Together they had cut some of the rawest records of the early hip hop era.

For his next act, he wanted to find an artist whom everybody else was overlooking, whose work had grown stale but who still had hidden wells of talent waiting to emerge, like scraping back layers of linoleum tile to find antique hardwood underneath.

He knew it was Johnny Cash. It wasn't just Cash's magnetic voice, his encyclopedic knowledge of American music, or his turbulent biography. It was his inner spirit: somehow rebellious yet loyal, fierce yet meek, wandering yet rooted, all at once.

Rubin helped Johnny Cash set aside the stale conventions of Nashville country that had strangled his love of making music. It took giving up the easy old answers, the nostalgia as comfortable as an old pair of jeans. Rubin encouraged Cash to get back into touch with what moved *him* about country music: the tent-revival hymns, gospel choruses, crooner anthems, and folk songs that anchored him to his people. The way forward was to get everything else out of the way and return to the inner spirit of his tradition.

The Man in Black was totally reborn. With Rubin, he released seven extraordinary albums whose songs ranged from country catalog deep cuts to transformed rock covers. In the twilight of his life, he developed a burst of artistic energy that transformed his legacy and helped a new generation fall in love with the great American folk tradition.

But there's an irony I often reflect on: maybe the last people in America to wake up to what Johnny Cash had to say were the Nashville music establishment. The people with the most to gain in the revitalization of country music were some of the last people to appreciate that it was happening, because it came from somewhere unexpected.

I catch a feeling of despair from many conservatives I talk to. They feel how decadent and stale everything has gotten, but they themselves are too insulated from the rest of the country to see where the new green shoots, the signs of life, are coming up. Sometimes the hardest thing is to give up something we find comfortable for the sake of something we love, if it requires us letting go of our comfort zone and our preconceptions.

In surprising places in the culture, especially among young people, there is a real yearning for family and friendship, a hatred of meaningless sex and pornography, an interest in handicrafts, a rejection of hyperindividualism and consumerism, and a desire for the sacred. They're looking for what is real and what is true. They (and we) may not know where they will find it.

The Party of Creation, in going on the offense, needs to seek out not only the deadwood to burn but also the young saplings in surprising hollows to nurture and protect. As Reagan said:

> With all the creative energy at our command, let us begin an era of national renewal. Let us renew our determination, our courage, and our strength. And let us renew our faith and our hope.
>
> We have every right to dream heroic dreams. Those who say that we're in a time when there are not heroes, they just don't know where to look.

The Unbroken Chain

Where are America's hidden heroes? It must have seemed in Troy that there were no heroes left, that the light had gone out. All the great men of the city had either fallen in battle like Hector or been slain by the marauding Greeks. Aeneas was . . . running away, launching his family into what Homer described as a "wine-dark sea," unfriendly and tempestuous. Aeneas didn't leave Troy knowing that later generations would regard him as a great hero and founder. He was a just a refugee in search of a new home.

Sometimes, as with the Cajun Navy, you're just a neighbor trying to do what you can when everyone else has given up. Maybe, like Andrew Crapuchettes, you're just a boss trying to do right by your employees. Or, like Yiatin Chu, you're just a mom trying to protect your kids. Maybe, like Jorge Hidalgo, you're just a dad trying to honor the memory of your beloved son. Sometimes, like PaPa Pete, you're just an old Cajun rough-neck trying to hold his family together amid the whirlwind.

Do you ever feel alone? As though no one sees your struggles? As though you're fighting through the night, with all of the danger and none of the glory? Maybe you're caring for a child who is dying one day at a time from an addiction. Or a little church that barely keeps its lights on. Maybe you're engaged in the quiet and thankless faithfulness of rais-ing a family, day in and day out. Maybe you're the person who makes sure that the bathrooms are clean at the shelter or that the emails about the school fundraiser are sent out.

You may feel that you are serving only a few people, a small community, maybe even just your own family; that what you're doing isn't important, at least not as important as what is going on in the halls of government. That is exactly backward. We'll never have an end of government, but what goes on at America's dinner tables, on its front porches, and in its church pews is a scarce and irreplaceable treasure. *Everything depends upon it.* The future of America will not be won or lost in Washington; it will be won or lost in the hearts of the American people.

You have no idea what great things might spring from your faithfulness. You have no idea the destiny that God might have in mind for you. In those lonely hours when you're discouraged, wondering what it's all for, remember the exhortation of John Paul II: do not be afraid, do not give up, do not lose hope!

When Aeneas set sail on that wine-dark sea, his departure lit by the burning Troy, he had no proof of the greatness that awaited his progeny. He just knew he had to keep carrying the fire.

The Bible, in the book of Hebrews, describes the faith that Abraham displayed when God called him to leave his native land, with nothing but the assurance that his faith would be rewarded by a Promised Land populated by his descendants more numerous than the stars. The author of Hebrews said that "faith is the substance of things hoped for, the evidence of things not seen." Our acts of faithful duty today give concrete expression to a hoped-for future, one that they help make manifest.

In the case of Abraham, his son Isaac, and his grandson Jacob, their faithfulness took the form of a pious, trusting, and grateful worship of God even during decades and decades of wandering. Time and again, they made a sacrifice of thanks to God or faithfully followed his commands, even when those acts of true worship seemed to take them farther away from their reward in the Promised Land.

Of those patriarchs, the epistle's author says, "These all died in faith, not having received the promises, but having seen them afar off," the promises of a "better country." They sought "for a city which hath foundations, whose builder and maker is God."

Faithfulness today is the price of a greater tomorrow. America's future depends on that unbroken chain of faithfulness, especially by those who may not live to see the fruits of their sacrifice.

The Seeds of Fire

The most important act of faithfulness is also the hardest. It's telling the truth when it would be easier to live with comfortable lies and obfuscations—especially when it means owning up to the way, intended or not, you have hurt people that you love.

In my own family, it was the truth that set us free. The death of my brother, Doug, forced my parents to reckon with what was important in life. My mom's been happily married to my stepfather for twenty-five years now. With my stepmom's encouragement, my dad has been sober for thirty-five years (they're still happily married, too). I love them all tremendously.

But it wasn't until my mom, as she returned to her Catholic faith, decided to get an official annulment that my parents really reconciled with each other—because part of the process required soul-searching and self-honesty about their marriage and a conversation between them to which my father brought the same spirit. Telling the truth about how they had been hurt and had hurt each other was transformative. It brought healing.

Bringing America back together, healing our country, demands the courage of living in truth; of being willing to own up to our mistakes and to confront the lies that comfort us with delusions or burnish our self-image.

What makes telling the truth so *powerful*?

When I led Wyoming Catholic College, I spent a fair bit of time riding around on horseback amid God's creation. In fire season, if we camped overnight or made a fire for warmth or to cook food, we could not leave it smoldering when we left. We needed to douse it before we packed out. Why? Because when a forest is ready to burn, every way-ward cinder is dangerous. Big fires don't come from big fires; they come from the smallest sparks. But you need *all* of the small sparks, barely holding on, to find the one that will bite, the one that is destined to become the great conflagration.

Today, the classical school movement is ablaze with the truth. In the 1970s, there was nothing like it. But at the University of Kansas, there was the Integrated Humanities Program (IHP). It was not a big affair. It didn't have the support of the MacArthur Foundation or an endowed chair in the Ivy League (it did have a small federal grant; it would not have made it past the diversity statement today). Founded in 1970, it was the passion project of three humanities professors, Dr. Dennis Quinn, Dr. John Senior, and Dr. Frank Nelick. They aimed to teach the Great Books, but not as dead texts. Everything about how they taught, in lectures and seminars, was designed to awaken wonder in their students. They recited poetry, had their students memorize the state song, and took their students stargazing.

It was transformative. So transformative that despite the professors' never explicitly proselytizing, students began to have religious conversions in droves, some of them even taking holy orders. That alarmed the good secularists on the university faculty. After a university tribunal cleared the three professors of any wrongdoing, the dean conspired to subject the IHP to death by a thousand bureaucratic cuts. It was shuttered in 1979.

That discouraging defeat stares you in the face. There, against all odds, a humanities program exemplifying wonder, learning, and piety took root, only to be ground into dust by the Party of Destruction, with nothing left to show for it. The thing is, the Uniparty can't put out the sparks of the truth when they have taken hold in the hearts of patriots and believers. The sparks lit by the IHP kept the fire alive, and it has grown into an inferno.

One of the oldest contemporary classical schools, Cair Paravel Latin School in Topeka, Kansas, was founded in 1980 by IHP alumni. So was Wyoming Catholic College, cofounded by IHP alumnus Dr. Robert Carlson in 2005. Six IHP alumni who had taken religious vows eventually returned from Europe to found Our Lady of Clear Creek Abbey in Oklahoma in 1999. Books by John Senior inspired by his experiences in the IHP, especially *The Restoration of Christian Culture*, have been enormously influential in the classical school movement. I know they deeply shaped my leadership at St. John Paul the Great Academy.

In the final analysis, the work of the Integrated Humanities Program, short lived though it was, may have been the single most important project safeguarding the Western tradition of education in those pivotal years, laying the groundwork for an extraordinary renewal. It has had an impact that would have been unfathomable in 1979.

Don't break the chain. Don't let the fire go out. "Be great, carve deep your heel-marks."

The Alamo

When I was growing up, every young American boy learned the story of Davy Crockett, the crack shot coonskin-capped pioneer hero who wrastled bears and outscouted hostile Indian tribes (but befriended them, too). He was a hero of the Appalachian frontier and congressman from Tennessee who most famously went west to fight in the Texas War of Independence, where he died at the Alamo.

But it wasn't until I was a grown man that I realized that we learn the story of Crockett *backward*. When we learn the story, we know how it ends. I don't just mean that we know he died at the Alamo; I mean that we learn that story from the future his sacrifice made as we sit comfortably in a free, prosperous, and powerful country, with the Lone Star flag proudly waving over the great state of Texas.

That wasn't how Crockett lived it. He had no idea that the little mission house of San Antone where he, Jim Bowie, Buck Travis, and two hundred other Texians were besieged by Mexican forces would become THE ALAMO. He had no idea that their brave stand and the subsequent Battle of San Jacinto would change the course of history, that he would win enduring fame. He could scarcely imagine what would become of the fire he started.

Crockett could have despaired. He could have stared out at the hordes of the enemy and bemoaned his fate. He could have counted up the Mexican soldiers and the horses and the cannons and decided that the Texas cause was surely lost. But he didn't.

He didn't despair, not because he anticipated some miraculous rescue but because he believed in the justice of his cause, even if he didn't live to see it. Knowing that he faced a certain death, he was nonetheless full of hope.

He looked past the vast army of enemies. Above their heads. He saw a better country. He never received the promises, but he saw them afar off. That was enough.

Davy Crockett had the fire. He'd rather die than let it go out. He'd die to keep it alive, just one more day. He died with his boots on, full of hope, holding the chain, carrying the fire. He carved his heel marks so deep, they made a river. And that river made a nation.

What's your Alamo? What are you dying for? Pick a place, pick a people, pick a project, and give it all you've got. Bet your life on it, on that small piece of the future of America. Gather as many friends as you can muster to the cause, and take your stand. Plant your heels.

There's a time for writing and reading—and a time to put down the books and go fight like hell to take back our country and build our future. Taking his stand at the Alamo, Crockett wrote his last entry before putting aside his diary forever to help guard the walls. They'll be my last words, too:

"No time for memorandums now. Go ahead! Liberty and Independence forever!"

ACKNOWLEDGMENTS

Every book takes a village, to paraphrase a (thankfully) failed presidential candidate. Given the rigors of my job, in particular the extensive travel associated with it, this book certainly was a team effort. Of course, anything brilliant in it is a result of that team of colleagues and friends—and conversely, any shortcoming is my own.

First and foremost, I am the luckiest guy in the world, both because of my family, but also because I get to work with the most committed, hard-charging, and cheerful people on the planet: every single one of my Heritage colleagues. While they all deserve credit, the following were particularly important to this book: for his research assistance and help with refining arguments and my Louisiana public school English, Evan Myers; for their vision and technical knowledge, my Communications colleagues, Rob Bluey, Noah Weinrich, Lauren Evans, and Elizabeth Fender; for their policy expertise, and for the many conversations we have had (and will have) about the future of conservatism, Clint Brown, Victoria Coates, Chris DeMuth, Robert Greenway, Andy Olivastro, Sarah Parshall Perry, Paul Ray, Jay Richards, Nina Schaefer, Jeff Smith, Richard Stern, Eric Teetsel, Alex Velez-Green, Ryan Walker, and Bridget Weisenburger; for helping to shape the policy direction on key points, and for their unfailingly good counsel, Derrick Morgan and Roger Severino; for attending to details and "keeping the trains running on time," Ericka Morris and Isabella Davis; and, for shaping the marketing and scheduling interviews, Crystal Bonham and Mary Vought.

One colleague in particular deserves special mention, for his crucial help with every draft and every idea: my chief of staff and great friend, Wesley Coopersmith. I couldn't do my job without you, even though you're a Phillies fan.

So many friends outside Heritage deserve mention. Eric Nelson at HarperCollins understood the vision of this book from the beginning, and kept my feet to the fire, both on vision and on the crispness of arguments; his colleague Hannah Long did a truly masterful job with the editing. At Beck & Stone, Andrew Beck, Mike Jackson, and Andrew Cuff helped immensely. And without my literary agent and co-conspirator, Jonathan Bronitsky—the best in the business—none of this would have happened.

I'm also grateful to friends who gave feedback on early drafts: Elbridge Colby, Saurabh Sharma, Nick Solheim, and Brad Wilcox. And to friends Dr. Larry Arnn, Tucker Carlson, Newt Gingrich, Mollie Hemingway, and KT McFarland, thank you for reviewing the draft and for writing some excellent blurbs. My former colleagues at Texas Public Policy Foundation helped me, during the dark days of covid, embark on this project; Dr. Tom Lindsay and Chuck DeVore read the very first précis, for which I remain very grateful.

I will single out Dr. Jonathan Askonas for countless conversations that shaped the book and helped to strike the right balance.

A few elected officials were vital to this book. To my friends Representative Chip Roy and Senator Mike Lee, with whom I've had long and esoteric discussions about conservatism, thank you for your time, but most of all, for your service. And to Senator J.D. Vance, thanks for inspiring me and millions of Americans with your story, and now with your leadership. I'm so grateful that you wrote the foreword.

Personal stories are, indeed, vital to understanding the impact of good (and bad) policy decisions. Huge thanks to the following for sharing theirs: Geoffrey Cain, Andrew Crapuchettes, Jorge Hidalgo, Thomas Hochman, Jake Kozloski, and Jeremy Tate.

Finally, and most importantly, thank you to my wife, Michelle, and our four children, who tolerate my many nights away from home, because we know it is our calling as a family to do our tiny part to help save this country—hopefully while being decent witnesses of the Lord's truth. If this book succeeds merely in inspiring my kids and their generation to know that we can never give back to America what it gives us each day, then all of the travel, work, writing, and editing, will have been worth it.

BIBLIOGRAPHY

Chapter 2

Burke, Edmund. *Reflections on the Revolution in France.* Harmondsworth, UK: Penguin Books, 1986.

Deneen, Patrick J. *Regime Change: Toward a Postliberal Future.* New York: Penguin Random House, 2023.

Edwards, Lee. *The Power of Ideas: The Heritage Foundation at 25 Years.* Ottawa, IL: Jameson Books, 1997.

Grant, George. "Revolution and Tradition." In *Collected Works of George Grant,* vol. 4: *1970–1988,* edited by Arthur Davis and Henry Roper. Toronto: University of Toronto Press, 2009.

Hankins, James. "Pietas." *First Things,* November 2020. https://www.firstthings .com/article/2020/11/pietas.

Kendall, Willmoore. *The Conservative Affirmation in America.* Chicago: Henry Regnery Company, 1963.

Logsdon, John. *Ronald Reagan and the Space Frontier.* Chicago: University of Chicago Press, 2019.

Mansfield, Harvey C. *Machiavelli's New Modes and Orders: A Study of the* Discourses on Livy. Chicago: University of Chicago Press, 2001.

McCombs, Phil. "Making a Stand." *Washington Post,* July 30, 2001.

Plato. *The Republic of Plato.* Translated by Allan Bloom. New York: Basic Books, 1968.

Rieff, Philip. *My Life Among the Deathworks: Illustrations of the Aesthetics of Authority.* Charlottesville: University of Virginia Press, 2006.

Santayana, George. *The Genteel Tradition.* New York: Charles Scribner's Sons, 1934.

Senior, John. *The Death of Christian Culture.* New Rochelle, NY: Arlington House, 1978.

Washington, George. "First Inaugural Address." Delivered April 30, 1789.

Wood, Gordon S. *The Radicalism of the American Revolution*. New York: Vintage Books, 1993.

Chapter 3

Aguiar, Mark, Mark Bils, Kerwin Kofi Charles, and Erik Hurst. "Leisure Luxuries and the Labor Supply of Young Men." Working Paper 23552, National Bureau of Economic Research, June 2017. https://doi.org/10.3386/w23552.

Autor, David, David Dorn, and Gordon H. Hanson. "The China Shock: Learning from Labor Market Adjustment to Large Changes in Trade." Working Paper 21906, National Bureau of Economic Research, January 2016. https://doi.org/10.3386/w21906.

Autor, David, David Dorn, and Gordon Hanson, "When Work Disappears: Manufacturing Decline and the Falling Marriage Market Value of Young Men." *American Economic Review: Insights* 1, no. 2 (September 2019): 161–78. https://doi .org/10.1257/aeri.20180010.

Brown, Patrick T., and Brad Wilcox. "Pro-Family Policy Priorities for States: Polling and Perspectives from the Sun Belt." Institute for Family Studies and Ethics and Public Policy Center, December 12, 2023. https://ifstudies.org/ifs-admin/resources /reports/ifs-eppc-sunbeltfamilypolicypriorities-final.pdf.

Carney, Tim. *Family Unfriendly: How Our Culture Made Raising Kids Much Harder than It Needs to Be*. New York: Harper, 2024.

Chetty, Raj, Nathaniel Hendren, Patrick Kline, and Emmanuel Saez. "Where Is the Land of Opportunity? The Geography of Intergenerational Mobility in the United States." *Quarterly Journal of Economics* 129, no. 4 (November 2014): 1553–623. https://doi.org/10.1093/qje/qju022.

Eberstadt, Mary. *Primal Screams: How the Sexual Revolution Created Identity Politics*. West Conshohocken, PA: Templeton Press, 2019.

Goolsbee, Austan D., and Chad Syverson. "The Strange and Awful Path of Productivity in the U.S. Construction Sector." Working Paper No. 2023-04. University of Chicago, Becker Friedman Institute for Economics, January 19, 2023. https://papers.ssrn.com/sol3/papers.cfm?abstract_id=4328672.

Henderson, Rob. *Troubled: A Memoir of Foster Care, Family, and Social Class*. New York: Gallery Books, 2024.

Kearney, Melissa. *The Two-Parent Privilege: How Americans Stopped Getting Married and Started Falling Behind*. Chicago: University of Chicago Press, 2023.

Kirk, Russell. "The Mechanical Jacobin." The Russell Kirk Center, November 10, 2017. https://kirkcenter.org/environment-nature-conservation/the-mechanical-jacobin/.

Mazzucato, Mariana. *The Entrepreneurial State: Debunking Public vs. Private Sector Myths*. New York: Anthem Press, 2013.

Murray, Charles. *Coming Apart: The State of White America, 1960–2019*. New York: Forum Books, 2013.

Myers, Evan. "Taking the Postman Pledge." *The American Conservative*, December 2, 2022. https://www.theamericanconservative.com/taking-the-postman-pledge/.

Pakaluk, Catherine. *Hannah's Children: The Women Quietly Defying the Birth Dearth*. Washington, DC: Regnery Gateway, 2024.

Teles, Steven, Samuel Hammond, and Daniel Takash. "Cost Disease Socialism: How Subsidizing Costs While Restricting Supply Drives America's Fiscal Imbalance." Niskanen Center, September 9, 2021. https://www.niskanencenter.org/cost-disease -socialism-how-subsidizing-costs-while-restricting-supply-drives-americas-fiscal -imbalance/.

Wilcox, Brad. *Get Married: Why Americans Must Defy the Elites, Forge Strong Families, and Save Civilization*. New York: Broadside Books, 2024.

Winship, Scott. "Can Men Still Bring Home the Bacon?" *The Dispatch*, December 14, 2022. https://thedispatch.com/article/can-men-still-bring-home-the-bacon/.

Chapter 4

Buchanan, Patrick J. *The Death of the West: How Dying Populations and Immigrant Invasions Imperil Our Country and Civilization*. New York: St. Martin's Press, 2022.

Deneen, Patrick. "Res Idiotica." Front Porch Republic, February 23, 2016. https:// www.frontporchrepublic.com/2016/02/res-idiotica/.

Figlio, David N., Cassandra M. D. Hart, and Krzysztof Karbownik. "Effects of Scaling Up Private School Choice Programs on Public School Students." NBER Working Paper No. 26758, February 2020. *Journal of Economic Literature* nos. H75, I21, I22, I28.

Hankins, James. "Classical Education Is Not a Right-Wing Project." First Things, November 15, 2023. https://www.firstthings.com/web-exclusives/2023/11/classical -education-is-not-a-right-wing-project.

Hegseth, Pete. *Battle for the American Mind: Uprooting a Century of Miseducation*. New York: Broadside Books, 2022.

Lewis, C. S. *That Hideous Strength: A Modern Fairy-Tale for Grown-Ups*. New York: Macmillan Publishing Company, 1946.

Lewis, C. S. *The Abolition of Man*. London: Oxford University Press, 1943.

Maglaque, Erin. "An Overabundance of Virtue." *New York Review*, September 21, 2023. https://www.nybooks.com/articles/2023/09/21/an-overabundance-of-virtue -political-meritocracy-in-renaissance-italy/.

Miller, J. Michael. *The Holy See's Teaching on Catholic Schools*. Manchester, NH: Sophia Institute Press, 2006.

Peterson, Rachelle. "Corrupting the College Board." National Association of Scholars, August 30, 2020. https://www.nas.org/reports/corrupting-the-college-board/full-report.

Senior, John. *The Restoration of Christian Culture.* San Francisco: Ignatius Press, 1983.

Chapter 5

Hawley, Joshua. "Senator Josh Hawley's Speech at National Conservatism Conference." Speech presented at National Conservatism Conference, July 18, 2019. https://www.hawley.senate.gov/senator-josh-hawleys-speech-national-conservatism -conference.

Hawley, Joshua. *Theodore Roosevelt: Preacher of Righteousness.* New Haven, CT: Yale University Press, 2008.

Herman, Arthur. *Freedom's Forge: How American Business Produced Victory in World War II.* New York: Random House, 2013.

Krein, Julius. "The Value of Nothing: Capital Versus Growth." *American Affairs* 5, no. 3 (Fall 2021): 66–85. https://americanaffairsjournal.org/2021/08/the-value-of -nothing-capital-versus-growth/.

MacIntyre, Alasdair. *After Virtue: A Study in Moral Theory.* Notre Dame, IN: University of Notre Dame Press, 1981.

Roth, Carol. *You Will Own Nothing: Your War with a New Financial World Order and How to Fight Back.* New York: Broadside Books, 2023.

Rubio, Marco. "American Investment in the 21st Century." United States Senate, May 15, 2019. https://www.rubio.senate.gov/wp-content/uploads/_cache/files/9f25139a -6039-465a-9cf1-feb5567aebb7/4526E9620A9A7DB74267ABEA58810 22F.5.15.2019.-final-project-report-american-investment.pdf.

Schumpeter, Joseph A. *Capitalism, Socialism, and Democracy.* New York: Harper & Brothers, 1942.

Wai, Jonathan, and Heiner Rindermann. "What Goes into High Educational and Occupational Achievement? Education, Brains, Hard Work, Networks, and Other Factors." *High Ability Studies* 28, no. 1 (2017): 127–45. https://doi.org/10.1080/13 598139.2017.1302874.

Chapter 6

Anton, Michael. *The Stakes: America at the Point of No Return.* Washington, DC: Regnery Publishing, 2020.

House Investigative Committee on the Robb Elementary Shooting, Texas House of Representatives. *Interim Report 2022,* July 17, 2022. https://house.texas.gov/_media /pdf/committees/reports/87interim/Robb-Elementary-Investigative-Committee -Report.pdf.

Kirk, Russell. *The Roots of American Order.* La Salle, IL: Open Court Publishing Company, 1974.

"A New Way on Homelessness." Cicero Institute. https://ciceroinstitute.org/issues /homelessness/.

Smith, Zack, and Charles D. Stimson. *Rogue Prosecutors: How Radical Soros Lawyers Are Destroying America's Communities.* New York: Bombardier Books, 2023.

Thomas, Clarence. *My Grandfather's Son: A Memoir.* New York: Harper Perennial, 2008.

Chapter 7

Askonas, Jon. "How Tech Utopia Fostered Tyranny." *New Atlantis*, no. 57 (Winter 2019): 3–13. https://www.thenewatlantis.com/publications/how-tech-utopia-fostered -tyranny.

Clabaugh, Jeff. "Northern Virginia Still Tops Global Data Center Markets (and, What's a Gigawatt?)." WTOP News, January 17, 2022. https://wtop.com/business -finance/2022/01/n-virginia-still-tops-global-data-center-markets-and-whats-a -gigawatt/.

Cruz, Ted, and Mario Loyola. "Shield of Federalism: Interstate Compacts in Our Constitution." Texas Public Policy Foundation, December 2010. https://www .texaspolicy.com/wp-content/uploads/2018/08/2010-12-PP21-InterstateCompacts -tcruz-mloyola.pdf.

Grind, Kirsten, and Keach Hagey. "Why Did Facebook Fire a Top Executive? Hint: It Had Something to Do with Trump." *Wall Street Journal*, November 11, 2018. https:// www.wsj.com/articles/why-did-facebook-fire-a-top-executive-hint-it-had-something -to-do-with-trump-1541965245.

Lasch, Christopher. *The Revolt of the Elites and the Betrayal of Democracy.* New York: W. W. Norton, 1995.

Magill, Gord. "The De-Banking of Dissent." *Compact*, February 3, 2023. https:// www.compactmag.com/article/the-de-banking-of-dissent/.

Tocqueville, Alexis de. *Democracy in America.* Translated by Henry Reeve. New York: George Dearborn & Co., 1838.

White, Adam J. "Google.gov." *New Atlantis*, no. 55 (Spring 2018): 3–34. https:// www.thenewatlantis.com/publications/googlegov.

Chapter 8

Buckley, William F., Jr. *Gratitude: Reflections on What We Owe to Our Country.* New York: Random House, 1990.

Burtka, John A. IV, ed. *Gateway to Statesmanship: Selections from Xenophon to Churchill.* Washington, DC: Regnery Gateway, 2024.

Coates, Victoria. *David's Sling: A History of Democracy in Ten Works of Art.* New York: Encounter Books, 2016.

Copeland, Dale C. *A World Safe for Commerce: American Foreign Policy from the Revolution to the Rise of China.* Princeton, NJ: Princeton University Press, 2024.

Crawford, Neta C. "The U.S. Budgetary Costs of the Post-9/11 Wars." Watson Institute for International and Public Affairs, September 1, 2021. https://watson .brown.edu/costsofwar/files/cow/imce/papers/2021/Costs%20of%20War_U.S.%20 Budgetary%20Costs%20of%20Post-9%2011%20Wars_9.1.21.pdf.

Elbridge, Colby A. *The Strategy of Denial: American Defense in an Age of Great Power Conflict.* New Haven, CT: Yale University Press, 2021.

Freeman, Ben. "Foreign Funding of Think Tanks in America." Center for International Policy, January 2020. https://static.wixstatic.com/ugd/3ba8a1_4f06e99f35 d4485b801f8dbfe33b6a3f.pdf.

Hendrickson, David C. *Republic in Peril: American Empire and the Liberal Tradition.* New York: Oxford University Press, 2017.

Kagan, Robert. "Into Kosovo." *Weekly Standard,* March 1, 1999.

Kagan, Robert, and Bill Kristol. "Kosovo and the Republican Future." *Weekly Standard,* April 5/April 12, 1999.

Toft, Monica Duffy, and Sidita Kushi. *Dying by the Sword: The Militarization of US Foreign Policy.* New York: Oxford University Press, 2023.

Zakaria, Fareed. "Conservative Confusion on Kosovo." *Wall Street Journal,* April 14, 1999.

Chapter 9

Dudden, Arthur P. *The American Pacific: From the Old China Trade to the Present.* New York: Oxford University Press, 1994.

Green, Michael J. *By More than Providence: Grand Strategy and American Power in the Asia Pacific Since 1783.* New York: Columbia University Press, 2017.

Hammond, Samuel. "The China Shock Doctrine." *National Affairs,* Fall 2019.

Platt, Stephen R. *Imperial Twilight: The Opium War and the End of China's Last Golden Age.* New York: Alfred A. Knopf, 2018.

Schweizer, Peter. *Secret Empires: How the American Political Class Hides Corruption and Enriches Family and Friends.* New York: Harper, 2018.

Select Committee on the Chinese Communist Party. "Investigation into the Reedley Biolab," November 15, 2023. https://selectcommitteeontheccp.house.gov/sites/evo -subsites/selectcommitteeontheccp.house.gov/files/evo-media-document/scc -reedley-report-11.15.pdf.

Wang, Huning. "America Against America." Translated by Leah Holder, Aaron Hebenstreit, and Samuel George. The Center for Strategic Translation, January 1, 1991. https://www.strategictranslation.org/articles/america-against-america-2.

Ward, Jonathan D. T. *China's Vision of Victory*. Atlas Publishing and Media Company, 2019.

Chapter 10

Guinier, Lani. *The Tyranny of Meritocracy: Democratizing Higher Education in America*. Boston: Beacon Press, 2016.

Huntington, Samuel. *Who Are We?: The Challenges to America's National Identity*. New York: Simon & Schuster, 2004.

Lighthizer, Robert. "Factory to the World." *Foreign Affairs*, March/April 2024.

Lighthizer, Robert. *No Trade Is Free: Changing Course, Taking on China, and Helping America's Workers*. New York: Broadside Books, 2023.

Chapter 11

Bethel, Fr. Francis. "Let Them Be Born in Wonder." Comment, July 13, 2023. https://comment.org/let-them-be-born-in-wonder/.

Jeffers, Robinson. *The Wild God of the World*. Stanford, CA: Stanford University Press, 2003.

"Johnny Cash vs. Music Row." *Controversy*. Season 1, episode 9, 2004. https://www.imdb.com/title/tt0799048/.

ABOUT THE AUTHOR

KEVIN D. ROBERTS is the president of The Heritage Foundation—America's most influential policy organization—and Heritage Action for America. He earned his Ph.D. in American history from the University of Texas. A lifelong educator, Roberts taught history at the collegiate level before becoming president of Wyoming Catholic College. Under his leadership, the college adopted a policy of refusing to accept federal student loans and grants, lest it be forced to violate Catholic tenets. He also previously served as the CEO of the Texas Public Policy Foundation, the largest state think tank in the nation. At The Heritage Foundation, Roberts leads policy research efforts on many key national issues, including education, health care, border security, election integrity, and more. He is the host of *The Kevin Roberts Show*.